Strengthening Climate Resilience

GUIDANCE FOR GOVERNMENTS AND DEVELOPMENT CO-OPERATION

OECD

BETTER POLICIES FOR BETTER LIVES

Please cite this publication as:
OECD (2021), *Strengthening Climate Resilience: Guidance for Governments and Development Co-operation*, OECD Publishing, Paris, *https://doi.org/10.1787/4b08b7be-en*.

ISBN 978-92-64-89531-7 (print)
ISBN 978-92-64-41513-3 (pdf)

Photo credits: Cover © Artwork adapted from Shutterstock.

Corrigenda to publications may be found on line at: *www.oecd.org/about/publishing/corrigenda.htm*.

Preface

The COVID-19 pandemic had claimed well over two million lives at the time of writing. Countless millions of livelihoods have also been put on hold or permanently destroyed. For the first time since 1990, we have seen an increase in the number of people living in extreme poverty, amplifying already high levels of inequality. Despite many scientific warnings and earlier disease outbreaks, the level of preparedness for the pandemic was inadequate. This is a wake-up call to governments and others in positions of power on the urgent need to act also on the increasingly well-understood risks associated with climate change. The growing number of countries committing to net-zero emission targets by mid-century is encouraging. Even if achieved, these targets must be complemented by a focus on strengthened societal and economic resilience to the impacts of climate change that will occur, also if the global average temperature increase is limited to the goal of the Paris Agreement.

The Paris Agreement therefore encourages countries to formulate National Adaptation Plans but the share of countries that have made such submissions remains low. The Global Adaptation Summit, held at the start of the year, illustrated that climate adaptation action by state and non-state actors is both diverse and accelerating. Complemented by the increasing emphasis placed on adaptation and resilience in the context of the climate negotiations and other international processes, there is reason for optimism. But political intention must translate into action and support for that action.

Strengthening Climate Resilience aims to support governments of developing countries and providers of development co-operation in strengthening the resilience of human and natural systems to the impacts of climate change. It highlights three overall considerations to help ensure planning and implementation of actions to enhance climate resilience also support broader sustainable development objectives. It further outlines four mechanisms that can facilitate a focus on climate resilience in national, sub-national and sectoral policy processes, and three key enablers for strengthening climate resilience.

This guidance highlights actions to be considered by different stakeholders across levels of governance. It emphasises the importance of country ownership and leadership while recognising the role of development co-operation in supporting partner countries in taking climate action. To succeed and be sustainable, such support must be guided by the priorities and development pathways of partner countries.

We must learn from the COVID-19 pandemic and ensure that when it comes to climate change we will not look back and say that we failed to prepare for what was a well-known risk. As governments navigate their response and recovery from this compound health, economic and societal crisis, they must have an ambitious focus on enhancing resilience in line with the scale of the climate challenges we now face.

Jorge Moreira da Silva
Director
Development Co-operation Directorate

Rodolfo Lacy
Director
Environment Directorate

Foreword

Strengthening Climate Resilience: Guidance for Governments and Development Co-operation aims to support governments of developing countries and providers of development co-operation in strengthening the resilience of human and natural systems to the impacts of climate change. It highlights actions to be considered by different stakeholders across levels of governance, including government officials at national and sub-national levels, and providers of development co-operation. It may also provide insights to other development partners, including civil society organisations (CSOs) and private-sector actors.

The Guidance comprises four chapters:

- ***Chapter 1*** positions the Guidance within the current development and climate context and outlines the objectives, target audience and structure.
- ***Chapter 2*** presents three considerations to help ensure that planning and implementation of actions to enhance climate resilience also support broader sustainable development objectives: i) country ownership, ii) inclusiveness, and iii) environmental and social sustainability.
- ***Chapter 3*** highlights four mechanisms that can facilitate a focus on climate resilience in national and sub-national policy processes: i) governance, ii) sector-level approaches, iii) finance, and iv) monitoring, evaluation and learning.
- ***Chapter 4*** presents three enablers for strengthening climate resilience: i) data and information, ii) capacity, and iii) technologies.

This Guidance is not a planning tool. Instead, it highlights potential areas for actions through the mechanisms and enablers for strengthening climate resilience. It proposes areas for actions in the form of checklists. These checklists aim to help users navigate the Guidance. Two checklists at the end of the executive summary highlight action to be considered by i) governments and ii) providers of development co-operation. Chapters 3 and 4 contain more detailed, thematic checklists. The proposed areas for action build on the wealth of knowledge products (tools, guidelines and compilations of good practice) available. These knowledge products are summarised throughout chapters 3 and 4.

The Guidance is informed by a series of thematic studies, informed by seven case studies. The thematic studies provide nuanced analysis of approaches to strengthen climate resilience in different sectors or contexts. A digital version of the Guidance, including the thematic and case studies, is available on a dedicated online platform https://doi.org/10.1787/4b08b7be-en.

Acknowledgements

Strengthening Climate Resilience: Guidance for Governments and Development Co-operation is a joint output of the OECD Development Co-operation Directorate (DCD) and Environment Directorate (ENV). The guidance was prepared under the overall leadership of Jorge Moreira da Silva, Director of the Development Co-operation Directorate and Rodolfo Lacy, Director of the Environment Directorate. Haje Schütte, Head of Financing for Sustainable Development Division of DCD, and Simon Buckle, Head of Climate, Biodiversity and Water Division of ENV provided strategic guidance. Jens Sedemund provided overall orientation.

The guidance was drafted by Takayoshi Kato and Nicolina Lamhauge. The authors are grateful for the oversight, review, information and comments provided by the Network on Environment and Development Co-operation (ENVIRONET) of the Development Assistance Committee (DAC) and the Working Party on Climate, Investment, and Development (WPCID) of the Environment Policy Committee (EPOC).

This guidance is informed by a series of case studies. The authors thank the officials and their teams for their valuable input and support, including from Ghana (Antwi-Boasiako Amoah), Guatemala (Juan Carlos Diaz Contreras), Peru (Silvia Cristina Rodríguez Valladares and Blanca L. Aróstegui Sánchez), the Philippines (Remedios Soriano-Endencia), Senegal (Ousmane Fall Sarr) and Uttarakhand, India (R.N.Jha).

The authors are also thankful for feedback provided by experts from various organisations: African Adaptation Initiative (Kulthoum Omari-Motsumi), Food and Agriculture Organization of the United Nations (Julia Wolf), German Development Evaluation Institute (Martin Noltze, Alexandra Köngeter, Cornelia Römling, Dirk Hoffmann and Sven Harten), Inter-American Development Bank (Jennifer Doherty-Bigara), International Institute for Environment and Development (Ritu Bharadwaj and Ced Hesse), International Institute for Sustainable Development (Angie Dazé), Global Centre on Adaptation (Michael Mullan), Secretariat of the Pacific Regional Environment Programme (Espen Ronneberg), United Nations Capital Development Fund (Ludovica Amatucci and Sophie De Coninck), UNEP DTU Partnership (Jingjing Gao, Sara Lærke Meltofte Trærup and Henry Neufeldt) and World Meteorological Organization (Jochen Luther).

Finally, the authors thank OECD colleagues for their careful review and input: Catherine Anderson, Charles Baubion, Valentina Bellesi, Juan Casado Asensio, Lisa Danielson, Marc De Tollenaere, Rafael Duque Figueira, Catherine Gamper, Alejandro Guerrero-Ruiz, Anjali Karnavar, Stephanie Lyons, Carolyn Neunuebel, Mikaela Rambali, Rachel Scott, Heiwon Shin, Chantal Verger and Dawn Wells. The production benefited from the assistance of Sama Al Taher Cucci, Sabrina Bouldi, Stacey Bradbury, Sara Casadevall-Bellés, Stephanie Coic, Beth Del Bourgo, Emmanuel Deschamps, Meria Greco, Samantha Proteau, Ines Reale, Henri-Bernard Solignac-Lecomte, Shashwati Shankar Padmanabhan and Jessica Voorhees.

Table of contents

Tables

Figures

Boxes

Executive summary

The COVID-19 pandemic has exposed the vulnerabilities of human systems and the fragility of society to systemic shocks, providing a stark reminder of the importance of building resilience into development pathways. Despite continuous warnings from scientists on the risk of a global pandemic, the level of preparedness for the COVID-19 crisis was inadequate. The same can hold true for the known risks associated with climate change.

Strengthening Climate Resilience aims to support governments of developing countries and providers of development co-operation in strengthening the resilience of human and natural systems to the impacts of climate change. This guidance highlights **three overall aspirations** for consideration when planning and implementing action on climate resilience (Chapter 2). It also outlines **four mechanisms** (Chapter 3) and **three enablers** (Chapter 4) in support of climate resilience.

Proposed sets of actions are provided in the form of **two checklists** at the end of the Executive summary. The checklists are informed by the discussion and detailed actions presented in Chapters 3 and 4. They build on the wealth of knowledge products (tools, guidelines and compilations of good practice) available to governments and development co-operation when formulating and implementing climate resilience measures.

Aspire to a country-owned, inclusive, environmentally and socially sustainable approach

Emphasis on **country ownership** highlights the role of individual countries in determining their own climate resilience priorities, reflecting the nature of the climate risks they face and the broader development objectives. Development co-operation plays an important role in supporting country-owned and –led processes for climate resilience. Evidence suggests that country ownership can increase the effectiveness of development co-operation for climate resilience and broader sustainable development; failure to include this consideration can result in unintended and even adverse outcomes.

A focus on **inclusive approaches** is central to the 2030 Agenda for Sustainable Development. People marginalised due to their gender, race, age, (dis)ability or other socio-demographic factors are often more vulnerable to climate risks. They tend to have greater exposure to climate hazards and face broader socio-economic and political challenges, as well as constraints to their capacity to manage climate risks. Progress for one group on climate resilience must not compromise that of another. An inclusive approach can facilitate the participation of those most vulnerable to the impacts from climate change in decision-making processes that directly affect their climate resilience.

Consideration of **environmental sustainability** is needed to make sure that approaches to strengthening climate resilience do not further increase environmental pressures locally, nationally and internationally. The role of the natural environment in strengthening climate resilience is also increasingly recognised, as exemplified by the growing application of nature-based solutions. A focus on **social sustainability** complements environmental sustainability by emphasising that climate resilience initiatives must also consider the broader well-being of current and future generations.

Strengthen key mechanisms for action and sustainable results

An effective governance arrangement provides the foundation on which a government can co-ordinate action on climate resilience across sectors and levels of government. A governance arrangement should also facilitate inclusive decision making informed by the needs of those most vulnerable to climate risks. A governance arrangement that supports adaptive decision making in the context of climate change can help governments adjust their approaches over time by facilitating continuous learning. Adaptive governance can benefit from diverse perspectives, data and information on climate-related hazards, exposure and vulnerability, and approaches to manage the climate risks.

Climate risks are in many cases sector-specific. National climate resilience objectives must therefore be mainstreamed into sectoral development policies. Ministries responsible for climate policies and their development partners should also draw on the expertise of colleagues within respective sectors when formulating climate resilience strategies, policies and plans. Well-tested tools such as environmental assessments can also help governments and development co-operation ensure that sectoral policies, plans and projects are climate resilient.

Integration of climate risks into financial management determines how, when, to whom and by whom finance will be allocated, provided or mobilised for climate resilience. Governments and development co-operation are increasingly aware of the benefits of combining multiple types of financial mechanisms and instruments. This allows them to pursue a more comprehensive approach to strengthen the climate resilience of people, nature and the built environment.

Monitoring, evaluation and learning (MEL) can support an iterative and adaptive approach to climate resilience informed by good practices and lessons learnt. It can also inform countries' own accountability mechanisms on progress made on climate resilience. Governments and development co-operation providers need to tailor their MEL frameworks to the priorities of the climate resilience interventions, the objectives of the MEL, the data and information available, and the uncertainty surrounding the nature of climate risks, as well as the associated socio-economic contexts.

Invest in enablers for action on climate resilience

Weather, water and climate data and information, and the underlying infrastructure that supports and distributes them, are critical building blocks to guide decision making by state- and non-state actors. Governments and development co-operation play an important role in investing in institutions and infrastructure to produce accurate and legitimate data and information that can guide action, and enhancing users' capacity in accessing and using them.

Greater awareness, as well as institutional and individual capacities, drive climate action, and capacity constraints can be important barriers to implementation. Development co-operation and governments need to accelerate efforts to strengthen the capacity of people and organisations to understand the climate science and the possible impacts of climate change, and to design and implement national, sub-national and sectoral policies, plans and projects for climate resilience.

Technologies are also essential for action on climate resilience, but their characteristics should match the needs and available resources of users and their socio-economic and environmental contexts. Governments and development co-operation can further support technology-related institutions and their networks, and enhance supply- and demand-side policies. This support can foster research, development, adoption and dissemination of technology across and within countries.

Table 1. Checklist for national and sub-national governments

ACTIONS	Relevant section
Multi-level governance and policy cycles	**Section 3.1**
✓ Build and maintain an inclusive governance arrangement that facilitates effective stakeholder engagement for transparent, participatory and gender-responsive decision making on climate resilience.	
✓ Empower local action by facilitating co-ordination and collaboration across levels of governance, and ensure that climate resilience strategies at national and sub-national levels are complementary and mutually reinforcing.	
✓ Develop governance arrangements that support adaptive decision-making processes for climate resilience in the context of the uncertainties presented by climate change.	
✓ Integrate climate risks and opportunities throughout the country's policy cycle for sustainable development, making use of the National Adaptation Plan processes where relevant.	
Sector-level approaches to strengthening climate resilience	**Section 3.2**
✓ Establish clear linkages between a country's national-level climate goals and sector-level policies and plans on climate resilience.	
✓ Assess sector-specific climate hazards, analyse the exposure and vulnerability of key assets, stakeholders and natural capital within the sector, and identify actions to manage the climate risks, especially those to segments of society marginalised by e.g. their gender, race, age, (dis)ability and class identities.	
✓ Assess sector investment plans using suitable screening criteria and tools given the nature of the climate risks and broader socio-economic priorities (e.g. gender equality and social inclusion).	
✓ Use environmental impact assessments and strategic environmental assessments to systematically evaluate the environmental implications of the proposed sector-level policies, plans and projects on climate resilience.	
✓ Make the financial sector climate resilient by engaging with domestic financial institutions and regulators.	
Financial management and instruments	**Section 3.3**
✓ Identify climate resilience priorities and assess the associated financial needs.	
✓ Integrate climate resilience into public financial management (e.g. public investment, fiscal risk management, budget tagging and expenditure review, social protection, tax and subsidy reforms to generate resources for climate resilience).	
✓ Elevate the role of finance ministries in facilitating the prioritisation, provision and mobilisation of finance for climate resilience.	
✓ Maximise the benefits of risk insurance solutions as part of a comprehensive approach to manage climate risks.	
✓ Link action on financial inclusion and education with action on climate resilience.	
✓ Facilitate access of national and sub-national government entities, civil society and other domestic actors to climate finance from external sources.	
✓ Engage with the private sector to scale up investment in climate resilience (e.g. through policy reforms, knowledge exchange, capacity development, public-private partnerships and climate risk disclosure).	
Monitoring, evaluation and learning (MEL)	**Section 3.4**
✓ Invest in a national MEL system and the human and technical capacities required for it to respond to monitoring, evaluation and learning needs, including for climate resilience.	
✓ Through stakeholder consultation, identify the objectives of a MEL framework and put in place mechanisms that facilitate a transparent and iterative approach to climate resilience guided by learning.	
✓ Complement understanding of what changes are taking place with how those changes have come about, and how policy shifts can strengthen climate resilience.	
✓ Engage diverse stakeholders to determine data and information available as well as existing gaps, and develop indicators commensurate with the human and financial resources available.	
✓ Explore opportunities for aligning monitoring and reporting with existing MEL systems that may provide opportunities for aggregating data and information across sectors or levels of government.	
Data and information for implementation	**Section 4.1**
✓ Strengthen the institutional capacity of National Meteorological and Hydrological Services.	
✓ Invest in weather, water and climate observations as a basis for data and information services that can inform climate risk assessments and climate resilience decision-making processes.	
✓ Prioritise investments in forecasting and early warning systems with user friendly platforms.	
✓ Facilitate participatory approaches to understanding local climate risks, and tailor climate and weather data and information to the capacities of intended users.	
Awareness and capacity across levels of government	**Section 4.2**
✓ Strengthen individual and organisational capacity (including that of sectoral ministries, sub-national governments, universities and centres of excellence) to understand and address climate risks.	
✓ Establish the authority and mandate of the ministry, agency or unit in charge of climate resilience to convene different stakeholders	

and to co-ordinate and subsequently see through the implementation of agreed climate resilience priorities.	
✓ Support piloting of climate resilience approaches, complement these with clear exit strategies, and enhance capacities and institutions for sustained implementation, replication or scale-up.	
Technologies	**Section 4.3**
✓ Assess technology needs through consultation with different stakeholders based on multiple economic, social and environmental criteria, including gender-disaggregated needs for technologies.	
✓ Invest in institutional arrangements and networks to facilitate development, adoption and dissemination of technologies in support of climate resilience.	
✓ Harness local and Indigenous peoples' knowledge and understanding of local contexts to maximise the effectiveness of available technologies.	
✓ Strengthen supply- and demand-side policies to promote technology development and dissemination.	

Note: Actions in this list are indicative and some of them may not be relevant to all countries.

Table 2. Checklist for development co-operation

ACTIONS	Relevant section
Multi-level governance and policy cycles	**Section 3.1**
✓ Engage in dialogues across levels of governance to identify areas where development co-operation can better support partner countries in strengthening climate resilience.	
✓ Support the development of institutional arrangements for stakeholder participation to promote inclusive, transparent and gender-responsive decision making, as well as knowledge exchange on climate resilience approaches.	
✓ Support partner countries to establish or enhance adaptive decision-making processes for climate resilience in the context of the uncertainties presented by climate change.	
✓ Work with partner countries to develop or strengthen governance arrangements that enhance policy coherence between climate resilience and other development agendas, and financially support them where relevant.	
✓ Support partner countries to systematically assess climate-related hazards, exposure and vulnerability and to integrate the results through the country's policy cycles, and do the same in the development of country programmes.	
Sector-level approaches to strengthening climate resilience	**Section 3.2**
✓ Align development co-operation policies with sectoral priorities for climate resilience set by the partner country.	
✓ Assess the climate resilience of sector-specific development interventions using suitable screening criteria and tools given the nature of the climate risks and broader socio-economic priorities (e.g. gender equality and social inclusion).	
✓ Use environmental impact assessments and strategic environmental assessments to systematically evaluate the environmental implications of the development co-operation interventions (e.g. projects and policy support).	
✓ Support partner countries and their financial regulators in promoting knowledge exchange and capacity development for actors within the financial sector to better understand and manage climate risks and disclose related information.	
Financial management and instruments	**Section 3.3**
✓ Provide partner countries with technical support in assessing costs of actions to strengthen climate resilience.	
✓ Support the integration of climate resilience considerations into public financial management (e.g. budget tagging and expenditure reviews, financial protection strategies, subsidy and tax reforms).	
✓ Support partner countries in identifying, piloting and applying financial instruments and mechanisms, and where relevant, provide or catalyse finance for climate resilience initiatives.	
✓ Link development co-operation for financial inclusion with those for climate resilience.	
✓ Support capacity development initiatives to enhance access to climate finance, particularly in least developed countries and Small Island Developing States, as well as by local governments and civil society organisations.	
✓ Promote private-sector investment in climate resilience through e.g. blended finance, technical assistance for improving policy environments and capacity building in climate risk assessment and project development.	
Monitoring, evaluation and learning (MEL)	**Section 3.4**
✓ Align development co-operation MEL frameworks with national MEL systems and invest in local capacities to further develop existing systems and related capabilities.	
✓ Through stakeholder consultation, identify the key questions the MEL framework will address and support partner countries to develop a portfolio of complementary MEL tools for climate resilience.	
✓ Explore opportunities for aligning monitoring and reporting with established guidelines and standards that provide opportunities for aggregating data and information at the programme, national or international level.	

✓	Build on the data available to monitor and evaluate climate resilience and support partner countries to identify and address potential gaps consistent with the human and financial resources available.	
✓	Conduct a portfolio and qualitative content analysis to determine if the allocation of financial commitments reflects organisational priorities on climate change and supports partner countries in achieving set objectives.	
Data and information for implementation		**Section 4.1**
✓	Align development co-operation interventions with partner countries' domestic priorities for strengthening the capacity of National Meteorological and Hydrological Services, policy environments and financing models in support of weather and climate data, information and services.	
✓	Provide technical and financial support to enhance weather, water and climate observations and services including the development and operation of forecasting and early warning systems.	
✓	Support partner countries in enhancing their capacity to conduct climate risk assessments, e.g. through staff exchange, peer learning or dedicated financing schemes.	
✓	Facilitate participatory approaches to understanding local climate risks, and tailor climate and weather services to the capacities and constraints of users, including groups marginalised by e.g. their gender, race, age, (dis)ability and class identities.	
Awareness and capacity across levels of government		**Section 4.2**
✓	Support partner countries in strengthening individual and organisational capacity (e.g. sectoral ministries, sub-national governments, universities and other centres of excellence) to understand and address climate risks.	
✓	Support piloting of approaches to strengthening climate resilience with a focus on their sustained implementation, and future replication and scale-up.	
✓	Strengthen the providers' own capacity to further improve their development co-operation interventions in support of climate resilience.	
Technologies		**Section 4.3**
✓	Provide technical assistance for assessing the needs of partner countries for technologies in support of climate resilience, based on multiple economic, social and environmental criteria, including gender equality and social inclusion.	
✓	Support partner countries in establishing or strengthening domestic institutions and networks that facilitate the development, adoption and dissemination of technologies between or within countries.	
✓	Promote development and piloting of innovative technologies through dedicated interventions, e.g. in collaboration with the partner country's government, the private sector, academic institutions and financial institutions.	
✓	Support partner countries in developing or strengthening supply- and demand-side policies to promote technology development and dissemination.	

Note: Actions in this list are indicative and some of them may not be relevant to all development co-operation providers.

1. Strengthening climate resilience: Context and approach

This chapter positions the Guidance within the current development and climate context and outlines the objectives, target audience and structure. It introduces three overall aspirations for consideration when planning and implementing action on climate resilience; four mechanisms that can facilitate a focus on climate resilience in national and sub-national policy processes; and three enablers for strengthening climate resilience.

1.1. Context, objective and audience

1.1.1. Context

Global average temperature has increased by more than one degree Celsius since the pre-industrial era, and the trend is worrying. The 2011-20 decade is the warmest on record, with the warmest seven years all occurring since 2014 (NOAA, 2021[1]). The atmospheric concentrations of major greenhouse gases (GHGs) have locked-in this warming trend for generations to come. The increase of ocean temperature over the past decade has been higher than the long-term average and in 2020, the North Atlantic hurricane season had the largest number of named storms on record (WMO, 2020[2]).

Climate variability and change are altering and intensifying risk patterns with significant impacts on people, society and the environment. Changes in temperature and precipitation are leading to both extreme weather events and slow onset changes, including prolonged droughts, more frequent and extreme storms, wildfires, floods and rising sea levels (IPCC, 2018[3]). The cumulative impacts of climate change could also cause parts of the Earth system to change irreversibly, such as the loss of the Amazon rainforest or the West Antarctic ice sheet. Climate change also causes impacts that are more difficult to monetise, such as loss of life, health, territory, human mobility and cultural heritage. Both economic and non-economic impacts must be averted, minimised and addressed to strengthen climate resilience (Box 1.1).

Box 1.1. Examples of economic and non-economic impacts of climate change

Heat: Periods of extreme humidity and heat that can threaten human survival doubled between 1979 and 2017, increasing in both frequency and intensity across the world (Raymond, Matthews and Horton, 2020[4]). In a business-as-usual climate change scenario, and in the absence of migration, one-third of the global population is projected to experience a mean annual temperature of more than 29°C over the coming 50 years, currently found in only 0.8% of the Earth's land surface (Xu et al., 2020[5]).

Winds: When two cyclones made landfall in Mozambique in 2019 only a month apart, an estimated 1.85 million people were affected; around 800 000 needed assistance; and more than 111 000 households were destroyed (Hope, 2019[6]). While it is difficult to attribute individual cyclones to climate change, the more intense storm surges and associated rainfall have been linked to human-induced climate change (Hope, 2019[6]).

Biodiversity: Climate change may have already negatively impacted the distributions of almost half (47%) of threatened terrestrial flightless mammals (excluding bats) and a quarter (23%) of threatened birds. Around half of live coral cover has been lost since the 1870s, with climate change exacerbating other drivers. With a global average temperature increase of 1.5°C, coral reefs could decline to 10-30% of former cover. This would degrade important protective functions against waves, storms and floods, among others. Within the coming decades, around 1 million species on our planet may be lost, largely due to habitat loss (IPBES, 2019[7]).

Ocean warming: Intensified marine heatwaves, acidification, loss of oxygen, salinity intrusion and sea-level rise are affecting coastal ecosystems. Nearly half of coastal wetlands have been lost over the past 100 years. This loss is a result of the combined effects of ocean warming, localised pressures induced by human activities, sea-level rise and extreme climate events. The impacts of climate change on coastal ecosystems are also negatively affecting livelihoods of Indigenous peoples and local communities dependent on fisheries. At the same time, they threaten cultures, access to traditional food, opportunities for aesthetic and spiritual appreciation of the ecosystems, and marine recreational activities (IPCC, 2019[8]).

With rising impacts of climate change on lives and livelihoods – differentiated across and within countries – the urgent need for ambitious action to mitigate the emission of GHGs is evident. Changes in global average temperature have occurred and further changes are already locked-in, leading to dire consequences for the most vulnerable groups of society. These include groups marginalised by, for example, their gender, race, age, (dis)ability, class identities or geographic locations (Chaplin, Twigg and Lovell, 2019[9]; Eriksen et al., 2021[10]). Complementary efforts must therefore strengthen the resilience of people, the environment and society (Box 1.2). Risk identification and assessment, prevention, recovery and rehabilitation can break the vicious cycle that perpetuates vulnerabilities and exposures (IPCC, 2012[11]). The scale and characteristics of some changes (e.g. sea-level rise for low-lying islands or large temperature or precipitation changes in already vulnerable locations) will require transformational measures to limit far-reaching damages. Risk transfer mechanisms and social safety nets also complement these measures, and help poor households cope with devastating impacts of disasters.

The COVID-19 pandemic has highlighted the vulnerability of society to the increasing pressure of human activities on natural systems, and the need for economies to strengthen resilience to different types of risks (OECD, 2020[12]). Protecting natural systems is vital for avoiding the next pandemic. Land-use change and wildlife exploitation, for instance, can increase infectious disease risk by bringing people and domestic animals close to pathogen-carrying wildlife (OECD, 2020[13]). The COVID-19 pandemic has also demonstrated how quickly hazards can spread in an increasingly interconnected world, leading to systemic and cascading risks. Beyond the devastating health emergency affecting millions of lives, responses to contain the pandemic severely disrupted the global economy and development at every level (OECD, 2020[14]). The pandemic has also seen a spike in gender-based violence, which can worsen challenges to addressing women's disproportionate vulnerability to, among others, environmental degradation (Castañeda Carney et al., 2020[15]).

Previous crises have demonstrated that societies can take years to recover from such shocks. During that period, decisions on the recovery can determine the sustainability of development pathways for decades. As countries gradually shift their focus from the initial health emergency towards economic recovery from the crises, they will need to ensure the recovery does not build new risks into socio-economic systems. For example, they will need to avoid locking-in carbon-intensive investments or increasing vulnerabilities to climate risks, jeopardising progress on development (Buckle et al., 2020[16]). By February 2021, governments worldwide had announced investments of about USD 12.7 trillion for their responses to the crisis (Vivideconomics, 2020[17]). Most of those stimulus measures, however, only include a limited focus on climate resilience (GCA, 2021[18]).

Box 1.2. Definitions of key concepts

The term **resilience** refers to the preventive and reactive capacity of social, economic and environmental systems to resist or absorb a hazardous event, trend or disturbance, responding in ways that maintain their essential functions, identity and structure, while also maintaining the capacity to reorganise through learning, adaptation and transformation (IPCC, 2018[19]; Dornelles et al., 2020[20]). As such, it is a multifaceted term linked to governance, social, economic and environmental structures, as well as other drivers of vulnerability that all influence the resilience of a society.

Climate resilience is a component of the broader concept of resilience. It refers to the capacity of human and natural systems to learn, adapt and transform in response to risks induced or exacerbated by climate variability and change. **Climate risks** are a function of the interaction between: i) environmental hazards triggered by climate variability and change; ii) exposure of human, natural and infrastructure systems to those hazards; and iii) the systems' vulnerabilities (e.g. its sensitivity or susceptibility to hazards, and the constraints on capacity to adapt and cope) (IPCC, 2018[19]). With strengthened climate resilience, people and communities will also be more resilient to other types of risks, for instance, those that are economic or health-related in nature. Efforts to strengthen climate resilience must therefore form an integral part of national and sub-national development strategies.

A key approach to strengthening climate resilience is **climate change adaptation**. This is the process of adjustment of human and natural systems to actual and expected adverse effects of climate variability and change. Distinction can be made between incremental and transformational adaptation (IPCC, 2018[19]):

Incremental adaptation maintains the essence and integrity of a system or process at a given scale. Examples include adjustments in livelihood choices to more climate-resilient crops and the development and enforcement of land-use management regulations, as well as introduction of early warning systems.

Transformational adaptation changes the fundamental attributes of a socio-ecological system in anticipation of climate change and its impacts, when incremental adaptation is not sufficient for managing climate risks. Examples include fundamental changes in livelihood choices and the relocation of people and assets.

Approaches to strengthening climate resilience also include the management of **residual risks**. Such risks remain despite efforts to mitigate and adapt to climate change due, for instance, to economic, financial, capacity, social and cultural constraints. Residual risks can, for example, be addressed through risk transfer mechanisms or in the context of **disaster risk reduction**. This entails "preventing new and reducing existing disaster risk and managing residual risk, all of which contribute to strengthening resilience and therefore to the achievement of sustainable development" (UNDRR, n.d.[21]). Approaches to manage residual risks include: preparedness, response and recovery activities, as well as a mix of different financing instruments, including national contingency funds, contingent credit, insurance and reinsurance and social safety nets.

Source: (IPCC, 2018[19]), Annex I: Glossary, Global Warming of 1.5°, https://www.ipcc.ch/sr15/chapter/glossary/, (Dornelles et al., 2020[20]), Towards a bridging concept for undesirable resilience in social-ecological systems, https://doi.org/10.1017/sus.2020.15, (UNDRR, n.d.[21]), Disaster Risk Management | UNDRR Terminology, https://www.undrr.org/terminology/disaster-risk-reduction

1.1.2. Objective

This Guidance aims to support efforts to strengthen the resilience of developing countries to the adverse impacts of climate change and variability. The intended audience includes both government officials at national and sub-national levels, and providers of development co-operation. It may also provide insights to other development partners, including civil society organisations (CSOs) and private-sector actors. The Guidance presents the following:

- **Three high-level aspirations** recognised in practice, research and recent international agreements, including on climate change and disaster risk reduction, as key considerations for ensuring that action on climate resilience also supports broader sustainable development objectives.
- **Four mechanisms** that can facilitate a focus on climate resilience in national and sub-national policy processes. The mechanisms also aim to guide support provided by development co-operation in light of partner countries' own domestic priorities on climate change and development.
- **Three enablers** for action for strengthening climate resilience, and identifying opportunities for government officials and development co-operation to enhance these enablers.

Countries are the drivers of domestic efforts to strengthen climate resilience. The mechanisms and enablers therefore take the country perspective (including national, sub-national and community levels) as the starting point. This is complemented with a focus on the potential role of development co-operation or other actors supporting policy processes in partner countries.

This Guidance is not a planning tool. Instead, it highlights potential actions by different stakeholders across levels of governance through the proposed mechanisms and enablers to strengthen climate resilience. In each of the sections on the mechanisms and enablers, a list of tools and available guidance complements the rationale for the proposed set of actions. The aspirations are treated as cross-cutting considerations, but recommendations for action are not systematically put forward.

The Guidance builds on the *Integrating Climate Change Adaptation into Development Co-operation* report (OECD, 2009[22]). Over the past decade, however, scientists have made considerable progress in understanding climate risks.

Table 1.1 summarises recent reports by the Intergovernmental Panel on Climate Change (IPCC). In parallel, policy agendas related to climate change and sustainable development (Table 1.2), as well as effective development co-operation (Box 1.3) have also progressed. The Guidance takes account of these developments.

Table 1.1. Overview of recent IPCC reports

Name	Description	Publication
Special Report on the Ocean and Cryosphere in a Changing Climate	Highlights that with large reductions in greenhouse gas emissions, protection and restoration of ecosystems, and careful management of natural resources, preservation of the ocean and cryosphere is possible. The report also highlights the benefits of combining scientific, local and Indigenous knowledge to develop suitable options to manage climate change risks and enhance resilience.	2019
Special Report on Climate Change and Land	Provides a comprehensive overview of the entire land-climate system and addresses land itself as a critical resource that provides the principal basis for human livelihoods and well-being, including the supply of food, freshwater and multiple other ecosystem services, as well as biodiversity.	2019
Special Report on Global Warming of 1.5C	Provides an overview of research on the impact of a warming of 1.5°C on the planet, while showing evidence that limiting global warming to 1.5°C compared with 2°C would reduce challenging impacts on ecosystems, human health and well-being.	2018
Impacts, Adaptation, and Vulnerability: Working	Addresses past impacts and highlights the risks of future impacts, highlighting the way risks evolve with future climate change and investments in adaptation.	2014

Group II contribution to the Fifth Assessment Report	Provides a focus on risk, where risk is driven by hazards, exposure and vulnerability.	
Special Report on Managing the Risks of Extreme Events and Disasters to Advance Climate Change Adaptation	Focuses on the relationship between climate change, extreme weather and climate events, and their impacts; frames the challenge of dealing with extreme weather and climate events as an issue in decision making under uncertainty, analysing response in the context of risk management.	2012

Source: (IPCC, 2019[8]) IPCC Special Report on the Ocean and Cryosphere in a Changing Climate, https://www.ipcc.ch/srocc/ (IPCC, 2019[23]) Climate Change and Land, https://www.ipcc.ch/srccl/, (IPCC, 2018[3]) Global Warming of 1.5°C, https://www.ipcc.ch/sr15/ (IPCC, 2014[24]) Climate Change 2014: Synthesis Report. Contribution of Working Groups I, II and III to the Fifth Assessment Report, https://www.ipcc.ch/report/ar5/syr/ (IPCC, 2012[11]), Managing the Risks of Extreme Events and Disasters to Advance Climate Change Adaptation: Special Report of the Intergovernmental Panel on Climate Change, https://www.ipcc.ch/pdf/special-reports/srex/SREX_Full_Report.pdf.

Table 1.2. Overview of international agreements relevant to climate resilience

Name	Description	Adoption
The 2030 Agenda for Sustainable Development (United Nations)	A global commitment to eradicate poverty and achieve sustainable development by 2030, ensuring that no one is left behind. SDG 13 is dedicated to taking urgent action to combat climate change and its impacts. Action on climate resilience is nevertheless relevant to most of the 17 SDGs, including poverty eradication, economic growth, health and well-being, clean water supply and sanitation, sustainable cities, environmental protection and land use.	2015
The Paris Agreement (UNFCCC)	An agreement on the global response to climate change with a focus on adaptation, mitigation and finance. The global goal on adaptation focuses on enhancing adaptive capacity, increasing resilience and limiting vulnerability.	2015
The Sendai Framework for Disaster Risk Reduction (UNDRR)	An international framework on disaster risk reduction with four priorities for action: understanding disaster risk; strengthening disaster risk governance to manage disaster risk; investing in disaster risk reduction for resilience; enhancing disaster preparedness for effective response and to "build back better".	2015
Strategic Plan for Biodiversity 2011-2020 and the Aichi Biodiversity Targets (CBD)	Strategic Plan for Biodiversity 2011–2020 aims to halt biodiversity loss and enhance the benefits it provides to people, highlight climate change as a major pressure on biodiversity, while recognising its role in supporting adaptation to climate change. Twenty Aichi Biodiversity Targets are organised under five Strategic Goals. The Post-2020 Global Biodiversity Framework is expected to be agreed on in 2021.	2010
Addis Ababa Action Agenda (UN DESA)	A global framework that seeks to align financing flows and policies with economic, social and environmental priorities in developing countries. The Agenda recognises the role of public and private business and finance, as well as the role of international trade, debt and debt sustainability for international development. It further acknowledges the importance of addressing systemic issues, including science, technology, innovation and capacity building.	2015
New Urban Agenda (UN Habitat III)	A new global standard for sustainable urban development, whose focus includes strengthening resilience in cities to reduce the risk and the impact of disasters, as well as action to address climate change by reducing their greenhouse gas emissions.	2016

Note: CBD (Convention on Biological Diversity), SDGs (Sustainable Development Goals), UN DESA (United Nations Department of Economic and Social Affairs), UNDRR (United Nations Office for Disaster Risk Reduction), UNFCCC (United Nations Framework Convention on Climate Change).

Source: (UN, 2015[25]) Transforming our World: The 2030 Agenda for Sustainable Development, https://sustainabledevelopment.un.org/post2015/transformingourworld, (UNFCCC, 2015[26]), The Paris Agreement, https://unfccc.int/process-and-meetings/the-paris-agreement/the-paris-agreement, (UNDRR, 2015[27]) Sendai Framework for Disaster Risk Reduction 2015-2030, https://www.undrr.org/publication/sendai-framework-disaster-risk-reduction-2015-2030, (UN, 2015[28]) Addis Ababa Action Agenda of the Third International Conference on Financing for Development, https://www.un.org/esa/ffd/wp-content/uploads/2015/08/AAAA_Outcome.pdf, (UN Habitat, 2017[29]) New Urban Agenda, http://habitat3.org/the-new-urban-agenda/, (CBD, 2010[30]) Strategic Plan for Biodiversity 2011-2020, including Aichi Biodiversity Targets, https://www.cbd.int/sp/.

Box 1.3. Effective development co-operation

Created in 2011, the Global Partnership for Effective Development Co-operation aims to improve the quality of all forms of development co-operation. To that end, it promotes country-level progress in implementing the four internationally-agreed effective development co-operation principles: country ownership, a focus on results, inclusive partnerships, and transparency and mutual accountability (Busan Partnership For Effective Development Co-Operation, 2011[31]).

In the 2018 Global Partnership monitoring round, 86 partner countries and territories, in collaboration with more than 100 development partners, provided data on the effectiveness of their development co-operation. The results, included in the 2019 Global Progress report, show uneven progress. Partner country governments have made significant progress in strengthening national development planning. However, development partners' alignment to partner country priorities and country-owned results frameworks is declining. Still, stakeholders remain committed to the development effectiveness agenda as an important accelerator for sustainable development (OECD/UNDP, 2019[32]).

A growing number of countries has taken steps to identify and address climate risks through different policy processes:

- Over 130 developing countries have included adaptation components in their nationally determined contributions (NDCs) (UN Environment, 2018[33]).
- At least 120 developing countries have started to formulate their National Adaptation Plans (NAPs) (UNFCCC, 2019[34]), of which 20 had been submitted to the United Nations Framework Convention on Climate Change by January 2021 (UNFCCC, n.d.[35]).
- Nearly 50 countries have developed National or Local Disaster Risk Reduction Strategies under the Sendai Framework (UNDRR, 2019[36]).
- As of January 2021, 26 countries had adopted targets on net zero GHG emissions by the middle of the century (Climate Watch, 2021[37]). This has important implications for avoiding some of the worst consequences of climate risks.

National policies, related legislation and financing frameworks with an explicit focus on climate change can be effective in conveying a government's climate objectives and priorities to different stakeholders. These stakeholders can range from households and the private sector to development partners and CSOs, including representatives of women, Indigenous peoples and other marginalised groups. They are, however, only one vehicle through which countries pursue climate action. Sector-level decisions in the context of infrastructure, energy, agriculture, forestry, land-use changes, water supply and sanitation, and disaster risk reduction to name a few, all contribute to a country's climate resilience.

National plans and strategies inform and are informed by action at the sub-national level where a lot of implementation takes place (Matsumoto et al., 2019[38]; Dazé, Price-Kelly and Rass, 2016[39]). Sub-national authorities also oversee different sectoral policies, including on housing, land-use management, transport and natural resources management. These policies provide practical entry points for harnessing potential complementarities across sectors. The translation of planning into implementation, however, is contingent on national priorities, institutional capacities and available information, and the nature of competing demands for both human and financial resources at the local level (OECD, 2020[40]).

Other non-state actors, including the private sector and CSOs, also play an active role. Large enterprises and small firms alike continuously adjust their businesses to changes in their contexts, including climate change. In this way, they seek to maximise the profitability and long-term viability of their operations and business models. The private sector also often complements the role of the public sector in managing climate risks. Among other ways, it does this by providing technical solutions to markets, facilitating cross-border and in-country technology transfer, connecting relevant actors within a community, facilitating information exchange and developing capacity through business networks. CSOs may also play an important role in bringing to the attention of policy makers the needs of marginalised populations and advocating for their empowerment to heighten action on climate resilience (OECD, 2020[41]). Governments and development co-operation recognise the role of non-state actors and increasingly engage with them in efforts to strengthen climate resilience. This, for example, includes their roles as implementers of action, providers of finance and facilitators for networks (Casado-Asensio, Shin and Kato, forthcoming[42]).

This Guidance builds on the wealth of knowledge products already available and aims to support readers in navigating them. The shift from theory to practice has informed a diverse set of tools, guidance and compilations of good practice developed by countries, CSOs, development co-operation providers and the private sector, among others. Examples include guidance on how to conduct climate risk and vulnerability assessments; the role of climate services; public finance management; and monitoring, evaluation and learning. Some of these include a specific sector or thematic focus (e.g. agriculture, water supply and sanitation, mountain areas and biodiversity conservation).

1.2. Structure of the Guidance

Chapters 2, 3 and 4 are structured around the three components highlighted in Figure 1.1: aspirations, mechanisms and enablers. The aim of each component can be summarised as follows:

- **Aspirations for strengthening climate resilience (Chapter 2)**: This component highlights three overarching policy objectives, or aspirations, which governments and development co-operation should consider when developing and implementing climate resilience measures, recognising their context specificity: i) country ownership; ii) inclusive approaches; and iii) environmental and social sustainability. These aspirations are selected based on their documented role in supporting sustainable development and by their recognition in recent international agreements on climate change, disaster risk reduction and sustainable development.
- **Mechanisms for implementation (Chapter 3)**: This component presents approaches to developing and enhancing four mechanisms that can serve as entry points for governments and development co-operation to integrate climate resilience into sustainable development. The mechanisms discussed include i) multi-level governance and policy cycles; ii) financing; iii) sector-level approaches; and iv) monitoring, evaluation and learning.
- **Enablers for action to strengthen climate resilience (Chapter 4)**: This component highlights three enablers or building blocks for operationalising the mechanisms discussed in Chapter 3, and in the light of the aspirations outlined in Chapter 2: i) data and information; ii) capacity and awareness; and iii) technologies. This is by no means a comprehensive coverage of enablers, with an important omission being rule of law.

While all the mechanisms and enablers are arguably important for strengthening climate resilience, emphasis will depend on individual country contexts. For example, in countries where the agricultural sector is particularly hard hit by the impacts of climate change, the government may initially focus on strengthening the resilience of that sector. Thus, it will focus on the livelihoods of the people relying on agriculture before (or in parallel to) developing national resilience strategies. Similarly, priorities will depend on national circumstances. In some countries, for example, good climate data and information provide a crucial foundation to raise awareness of the risks and build capacity. Other countries with better access to quality data may prioritise training to enhance stakeholders' technical capacity. Stronger analysis, for example, could help data inform decision-making processes.

Figure 1.1. Structure of the Guidance

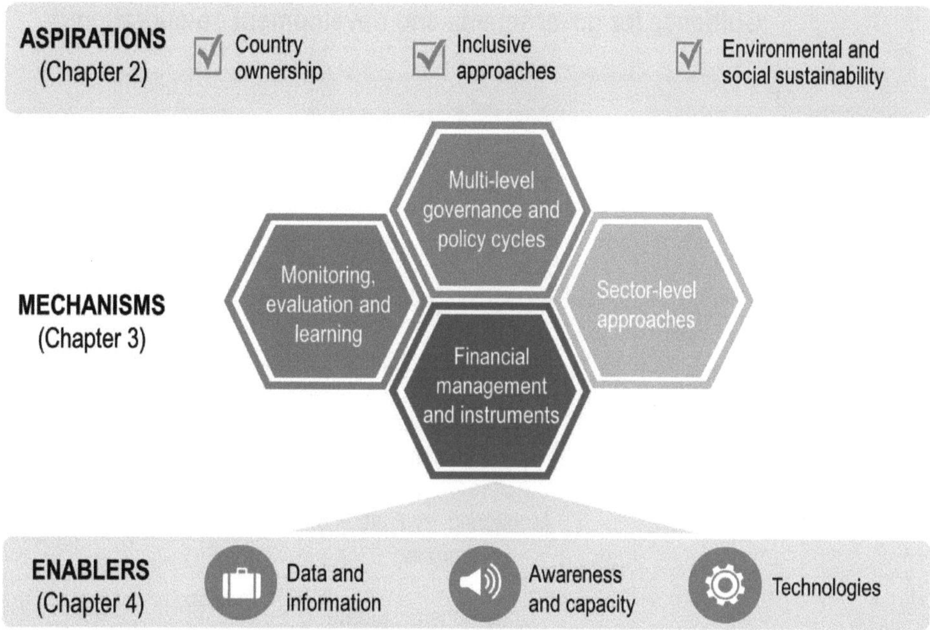

Source: Authors' own.

The discussion on mechanisms and enablers follows a standard structure that aims to make the discussion brief, action-oriented and easy to navigate:

- **A checklist for action**: A list allows readers to quickly grasp key considerations and actions required to operationalise or enhance respective approaches to increase climate resilience.
- **Rationale**: A rationale explains why and how the mechanisms and enablers can help strengthen climate resilience of people, communities and ecosystems.
- **Practical tools and guidance documents**: Short descriptions of a few specific approaches and methodologies are offered. These are accompanied by references to tools, guidance and material identified through desk-based research and in consultation with different stakeholders.

The Guidance is informed by a diverse set of inputs (see Figure 1.2). This includes a series of thematic studies that provide nuanced analysis of approaches to strengthen climate resilience in different sectors or contexts. Seven case studies informed the thematic studies, and in turn also the Guidance. The case studies aim to provide different regional perspectives and focus on countries where efforts to strengthen climate resilience are already advanced. In addition to providing learning opportunities, this approach allows for the addition of thematic or case studies over time.

Figure 1.2. Components of the Guidance

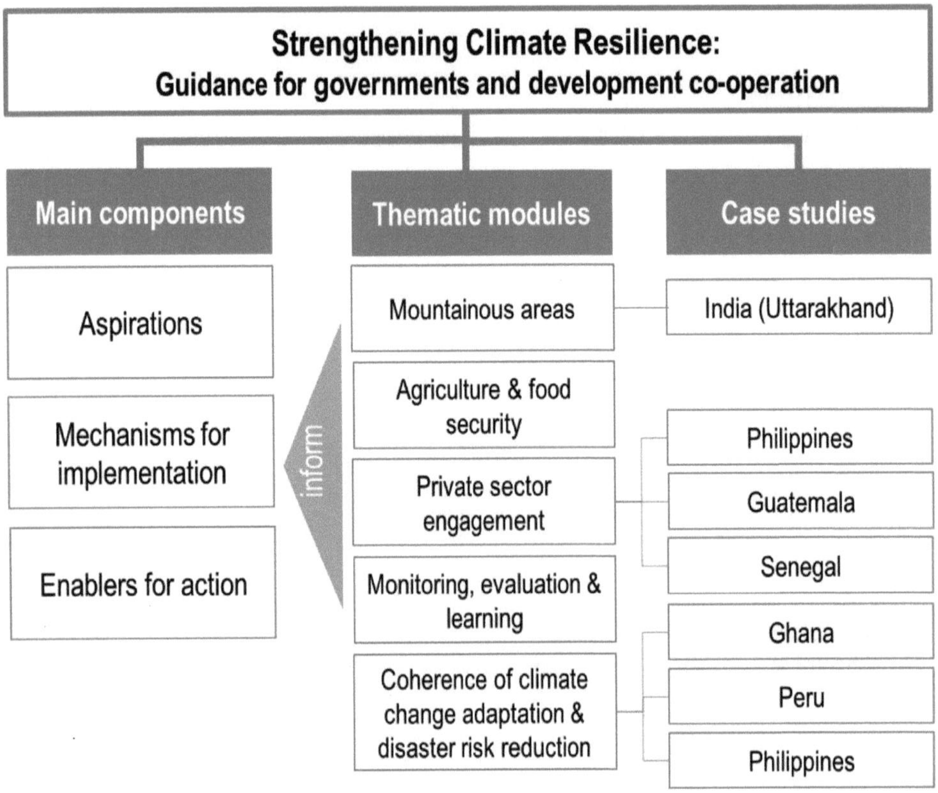

Note: Further information and publications on the different components can be found at https://doi.org/10.1787/4b08b7be-en.
Source: Authors' own

References

Buckle, S. et al. (2020), "Addressing the COVID-19 and climate crises: Potential economic recovery pathways and their implications for climate change mitigation, NDCs and broader socio-economic goals", *OECD/IEA Climate Change Expert Group Papers*, No. 2020/04, OECD Publishing, Paris, https://dx.doi.org/10.1787/50abd39c-en. [16]

Busan Partnership For Effective Development Co-Operation (2011), *The Busan Partnership agreement*, http://www.busanhlf4.org (accessed on 21 January 2020). [31]

Casado-Asensio, J., H. Shin and T. Kato (forthcoming), *Private-sector Engagement in Strengthening Climate Resilience*, OECD Publishing, Paris. [42]

Castañeda Carney, I. et al. (2020), *Gender-based Violence and Environment Linkages: The Violence of Inequality*, International Union for Conservation of Nature, Geneva, http://dx.doi.org/10.2305/iucn.ch.2020.03.en. [15]

CBD (2010), "Strategic Plan for Biodiversity 2011-2020, including Aichi Biodiversity Targets", webpage, https://www.cbd.int/sp/ (accessed on 20 January 2020). [30]

Chaplin, D., J. Twigg and E. Lovell (2019), "Intersectional approaches to vulnerability reduction and resilience-building", No. 12, BRACED Knowledge Manager, Overseas Development Institute, London, https://www.odi.org/sites/odi.org.uk/files/resource-documents/12651.pdf. [9]

Climate Watch (2021), "The Net-Zero Tracker", webpage, https://www.climatewatchdata.org/net-zero-tracker (accessed on 12 January 2021). [37]

Dazé, A., H. Price-Kelly and N. Rass (2016), "Vertical Integration in National Adaptation Plan (NAP) Processes: A Guidance Note for Linking National and Sub-national Adaptation Processes", webpage, http://www.napglobalnetwork.org (accessed on 18 February 2020). [39]

Dornelles, A. et al. (2020), "Towards a bridging concept for undesirable resilience in social-ecological systems", *Global Sustainability*, Vol. 3/e20, pp. 1-12, http://dx.doi.org/10.1017/sus.2020.15. [20]

Eriksen, S. et al. (2021), "Adaptation interventions and their effect on vulnerability in developing countries: Help, hindrance or irrelevance?", *World Development*, Vol. 141, p. 105383, http://dx.doi.org/10.1016/j.worlddev.2020.105383. [10]

GCA (2021), *State and Trends in Adaptation Report 2020*, Global Commission on Adaptation, https://gca.org/reports/state-and-trends-in-adaptation-report-2020/. [18]

Hope, M. (2019), "Cyclones in Mozambique may reveal humanitarian challenges of responding to a new climate reality", *The Lancet Planetary Health*, Vol. 3/8, pp. 338-339, http://dx.doi.org/10.1016/S2542-5196(19)30131-7. [6]

IPBES (2019), *Summary for Policymakers of the Global Assessment Report on Biodiversity and Ecosystem Services*, Intergovernmental Science-Policy Platform on Biodiversity and Ecosystem Services (IPBES), Bonn, http://dx.doi.org/10.5281/zenodo.3553579. [7]

IPCC (2019), *Climate Change and Land*, Intergovernmental Panel on Climate Change, Geneva, https://www.ipcc.ch/srccl/. [23]

IPCC (2019), *IPCC Special Report on the Ocean and Cryosphere in a Changing Climate*, Intergovernmental Panel on Climate Change, Geneva, https://www.ipcc.ch/srocc/. [8]

IPCC (2018), "Annex I: Glossary", in *Global Warming of 1.5°*, Intergovernmental Panel on Climate Change, Geneva, https://www.ipcc.ch/sr15/chapter/glossary/. [19]

IPCC (2018), *Global Warming of 1.5°C*, Intergovernmental Panel on Climate Change, Geneva, https://www.ipcc.ch/sr15/. [3]

IPCC (2014), *Climate Change 2014: Synthesis Report. Contribution of Working Groups I, II and III to the Fifth Assessment Report*, Intergovernmental Panel on Climate Change, Geneva, https://www.ipcc.ch/report/ar5/syr/. [24]

IPCC (2012), *Managing the Risks of Extreme Events and Disasters to Advance Climate Change Adaptation: Special Report of the Intergovernmental Panel on Climate Change*, Cambridge University Press, Cambridge UK, and New York, https://www.ipcc.ch/pdf/special-reports/srex/SREX_Full_Report.pdf. [11]

Matsumoto, T. et al. (2019), "An integrated approach to the Paris climate Agreement: The role of regions and cities", *OECD Regional Development Working Papers*, Vol. 2019/13, http://dx.doi.org/10.1787/96b5676d-en. [38]

NOAA (2021), *Assessing the Global Climate in 2020*, National Oceanic and Atmospheric Administration, Asheville, NC, US, https://www.ncei.noaa.gov/news/global-climate-202012 (accessed on 28 January 2021). [1]

OECD (2020), "Biodiversity and the economic response to COVID-19: Ensuring a green and resilient recovery", *Tackling Coronavirus (COVID-19): Contributing to a Global Effort*, 28 September, OECD Publishing, Paris, https://doi.org/10.1787/d98b5a09-en. [13]

OECD (2020), *Common Ground Between the Paris Agreement and the Sendai Framework: Climate Change Adaptation and Disaster Risk Reduction*, OECD Publishing, Paris, http://dx.doi.org/10.1787/3edc8d09-en. [40]

OECD (2020), *Development Assistance Committee Members and Civil Society*, The Development Dimension, OECD Publishing, Paris, https://dx.doi.org/10.1787/51eb6df1-en. [41]

OECD (2020), "Environmental health and strengthening resilience to pandemics", *OECD Policy Responses to Coronavirus (COVID-19)*, OECD Publishing, Paris, https://doi.org/10.1787/73784e04-en. [12]

OECD (2020), "What does "inclusive governance" mean?: Clarifying theory and practice", *OECD Development Policy Papers*, Vol. 27, http://dx.doi.org/10.1787/960f5a97-en. [14]

OECD (2009), *Integrating Climate Change Adaptation into Development Co-operation: Policy Guidance*, OECD Publishing, Paris, https://dx.doi.org/10.1787/9789264054950-en. [22]

OECD/UNDP (2019), "Making Development Co-operation More Effective: Headlines from the 2019 Progress Report", (flyer), OECD, Paris, United Nations Development Programme, New York, https://www.effectivecooperation.org/system/files/2020-01/GPEDC_2019-Report_Glossy_EN.pdf. [32]

Raymond, C., T. Matthews and R. Horton (2020), "The emergence of heat and humidity too severe for human tolerance", *Science Advances*, Vol. 6/19, eaaw1838, http://dx.doi.org/10.1126/sciadv.aaw1838. [4]

UN (2015), *Addis Ababa Action Agenda of the Third International Conference on Financing for Development*, United Nations, New York, https://www.un.org/esa/ffd/wp-content/uploads/2015/08/AAAA_Outcome.pdf. [28]

UN (2015), *Transforming our World: The 2030 Agenda for Sustainable Development*, United Nations, New York, https://sustainabledevelopment.un.org/post2015/transformingourworld. [25]

UN Environment (2018), *Adaptation Gap Report 2018*, United Nations Environment Programme, Nairobi, https://www.unenvironment.org/resources/adaptation-gap-report. [33]

UN Habitat (2017), *New Urban Agenda*, United Nations Human Settlements Programme, Nairobi, http://habitat3.org/the-new-urban-agenda/. [29]

UNDRR (2019), *Global Assessment Report on Disaster Risk Reduction 2019*, United Nations Office for Disaster Risk Reduction, Geneva, https://gar.unisdr.org. [36]

UNDRR (2015), *Sendai Framework for Disaster Risk Reduction 2015-2030*, United Nations Office for Disaster Risk Reduction, Geneva, https://www.undrr.org/publication/sendai-framework-disaster-risk-reduction-2015-2030. [27]

UNDRR (n.d.), *Disaster Risk Management | UNDRR Terminology*, webpage, https://www.undrr.org/terminology/disaster-risk-reduction (accessed on 23 January 2020). [21]

UNFCCC (2019), *Progress in the Process to Formulate and Implement National Adaptation Plans: Note by Secretariat*, United Nations Framework Convention on Climate Change, Bonn, https://unfccc.int/sites/default/files/resource/sbi2019_INF.15.pdf. [34]

UNFCCC (2015), *Paris Agreement*, United Nations Framework Convention on Climate Change, Bonn, https://unfccc.int/process-and-meetings/the-paris-agreement/the-paris-agreement. [26]

UNFCCC (n.d.), *National Adaptation Plans: NAPs from Developing Countries*, United Nations Framework Convention on Climate Change, Bonn, https://www4.unfccc.int/sites/NAPC/Pages/national-adaptation-plans.aspx (accessed on 13 February 2021). [35]

Vivideconomics (2020), "Greenness of Stimulus Index", webpage, https://www.vivideconomics.com/casestudy/greenness-for-stimulus-index/ (accessed on 30 July 2020). [17]

WMO (2020), *WMO Provisional Report on the State of the Global Climate 2020*, World Meteorological Organization, Geneva, https://library.wmo.int/index.php?lvl=notice_display&id=21804#.X_wb9Nj0mUl. [2]

Xu, C. et al. (2020), "Future of the human climate niche", *Proceedings of the National Academy of Sciences*, Vol. May/201910114, http://dx.doi.org/10.1073/pnas.1910114117. [5]

2. Aspirations for strengthening climate resilience

This chapter first situates the discussion on climate resilience within broader sustainable development. It then positions the discussion within the broader notion of resilience of systems to cope with hazardous events, trends or disturbances. It identifies global commitments including the Paris Agreement and the Sendai Framework for Disaster Risk Reduction, that recognise the importance of enhanced resilience across sectors and scales. Finally, it highlights three aspirations that governments and providers of development co-operation should consider when developing and implementing climate resilience measures: i) country ownership; ii) inclusive approaches; and iii) environmental and social sustainability.

2.1. Strengthened climate resilience for sustainable development

Poverty eradication and economic development are key priorities for most governments, especially in developing countries. This has become an even more pressing concern as governments around the world are responding to the COVID-19 pandemic. By February 2021, over 2 million lives had been lost and billons more affected by the economic impacts of responses to the pandemic. The UN World Food Programme estimated that over 270 million people were acutely food insecure in 2020, an 82% increase compared to the pre-COVID estimate (WFP, 2020[1]). The socio-economic crises further threaten to push around 100 million people into poverty and 70 million into extreme poverty, contributing to an increase in global poverty levels for the first time since 1990 (Mahler et al., 2020[2]).

COVID-19 policy responses and recovery packages initially focused on saving lives and health. This was in most cases followed by a focus on preserving and creating jobs, sustaining livelihoods and maintaining income to limit the adverse impact on the economy (OECD, 2020[3]). The environmental sustainability of the response and recovery measures has been questioned. Some analysts contend the measures risk further exacerbating the looming emergencies associated with climate change and biodiversity loss (Vivideconomics, 2020[4]; CarbonBrief, 2020[5]; OECD, 2020[6]; Buckle et al., 2020[7]).

Climate change, compounded by other stressors such as poverty and inequality, threatens the ability of countries to achieve sustainable development objectives (Kharas and Hamel, 2020[8]; Hallegatte et al., 2016[9]). The international community has collectively agreed to limit global average temperature increase and to strengthen resilience (UNFCCC, 2015[10]). Climate-resilient development pathways consist of strategies and actions to mitigate greenhouse gas (GHG) emissions and to strengthen climate resilience to achieve the Sustainable Development Goals (SDGs) (IPCC, 2014[11]) (Box 2.1). Such development pathways are shaped by iterative processes for managing change within complex systems to reduce disruption and enhance capacities to manage risks (IPCC, 2018[12]).

Box 2.1. Climate-resilient development pathways

The Intergovernmental Panel on Climate Change's Special Report: Global Warming of 1.5°C presents climate-resilient development pathways (represented by green arrows in Figure 2.1). A climate-resilient development pathway spans from a current world where countries and communities exist at different levels of development (section A) to future scenarios, referred to as "Future Worlds" (section D) that range from climate-resilient (bottom) to unsustainable (top).

Section B illustrates that climate-resilient development pathways involve societal and systems transformations, as well as adaptation and mitigation choices and trade-offs. Pathways are best positioned to achieve climate-resilient futures if they achieve the SDGs by 2030, strive for net-zero emissions around the middle of the 21st century and stay within the 1.5°C target of global warming by the end of the 21st century, while ensuring equity and well-being for all (sections C and D).

Figure 2.1. Climate-resilient development pathways

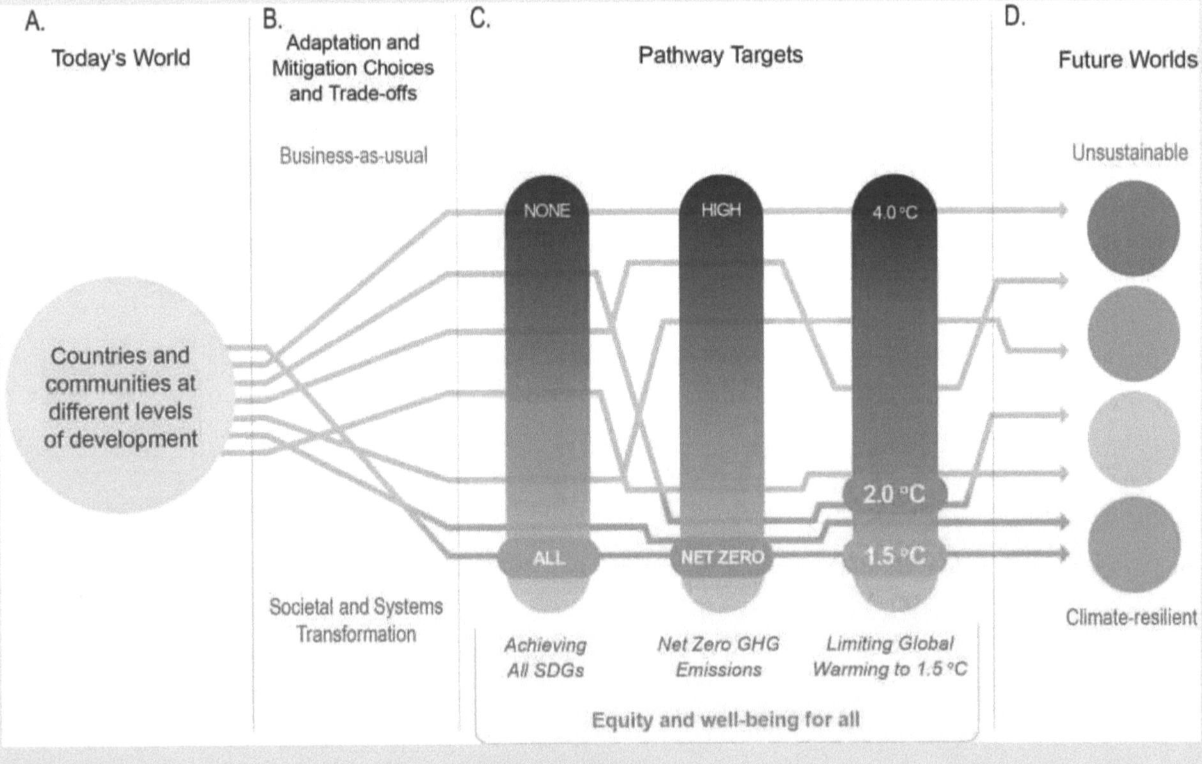

Source: (IPCC, 2018[12]), Global warming of 1.5°C, https://www.ipcc.ch/sr15/.

Efforts to strengthen climate resilience will be needed under any climate scenario. However, the scale, extent and nature of these efforts will substantially differ if, say, global average temperatures were to increase by 1.5°C compared to 4°C (IPCC, 2018[12]). Uncertainties of the response of the climate system to GHG emissions are compounded by uncertainties in how those responses may translate into impacts on the ground (IPCC, 2014[13]). These uncertainties also limit the applicability of historical data to understand future climate risks and even the appropriateness of predicting impacts in a probabilistic manner (Adger, Brown and Surminski, 2018[14]; Buurman and Babovic, 2016[15]; Cavallo and Ireland, 2014[16]; IPCC, 2019[17]). Instead, an overview of the envelope of possible impacts, including extremes, is needed rather than just the most likely outcome (Weaver et al., 2017[18]). Uncertainty in socio-economic and technological contexts also greatly affects the decision making on climate action. Scientific information based on climate models and weather data needs to be complemented with information on other ecological, economic and social factors that drive risks.

The intrinsic uncertainty, however, must not prevent efforts to both mitigate risks and to strengthen resilience, given the costs of inaction or delayed action (Ayeb-Karlsson, Fox and Kniveton, 2019[19]). Decision-making processes can be effective in taking the agenda forward, if they address the inherent uncertainty of the understanding of climate change and can be adjusted as future changes unfold, or are sufficiently robust to perform well under a wide range of conditions (Ayeb-Karlsson, Fox and Kniveton, 2019[19]; UCS, 2016[20]). Such flexible and robust decision-making processes rely on institutional structures that encourage and facilitate learning, either through innovation and peer learning or the monitoring and evaluation of actions.

A range of approaches exist for decision making under uncertainty. Storyline approaches, for example, combine climate information with other ecological, economic and social factors. Rather than asking what will happen, storyline approaches focus on the impact of particular actions in a context where future changes in the climate are uncertain (Shepherd, 2019[21]). Dynamic Adaptive Policy Pathways instead call on planners to establish a framework for action. This framework would be informed by a strategic vision of the future and guided by short-term actions that can be adjusted to reflect changing circumstances (Haasnoot et al., 2013[22]). Alternative approaches to support decision making under uncertainty also include Multi-criteria Analysis, Robust Decision Making, Real Options Analysis and Portfolio Analysis (see (OECD, 2015[23]) and Chapter 3.1). Common to all these approaches is the explicit recognition of the interconnectedness, non-linearity, feedbacks and thresholds across different systems and impacts, and the need to take a broader systems approach.

2.2. A focus on climate resilience

The focus of this Guidance on climate resilience refers to the capacity of human and natural systems to learn, adapt and transform in response to risks that are induced or exacerbated by climate variability and change. Climate risks result from the interaction of the following (IPCC, 2018[12]):

- climate-related hazards and the likelihood of their occurrence
- exposure of human and natural systems to those hazards
- vulnerability (i.e. sensitivity or susceptibility) of affected systems to climate-related hazards.

Climate resilience is embedded within the broader notion of resilience of systems to cope with hazardous events, trends or disturbances. This implies links to various governance, social, economic and environmental factors, and the interaction among them (see also Box 1.2 on definitions of key concepts).

Global commitments on development, including the Paris Agreement and the Sendai Framework for Disaster Risk Reduction, recognise the importance of enhanced resilience across sectors and scales. The Paris Agreement establishes "the global goal on adaptation of enhancing adaptive capacity, strengthening resilience and reducing vulnerability to climate change, with a view to contributing to sustainable development" (Article 7.1) (UNFCCC, 2015[10]). A priority of the Sendai Framework is "investing in disaster risk reduction for resilience", highlighting the importance of public and private investment in disaster risk prevention and reduction to strengthen the economic, social, health and cultural resilience of people, communities and countries (UNDRR, 2015[24]). Two other considerations are increasingly recognised as crucial in the pursuit of the SDGs: risk-informed development (a decision-making process to enable development that takes account of complex risks) (Opitz-Stapleton et al., 2019[25]) and comprehensive risk management (to assess, reduce, transfer and retain risks) (UNFCCC, 2019[26]; BMZ, 2019[27]).

The COVID-19 pandemic has raised people's awareness about the importance of strengthening the resilience of society to different types of shocks. The urgent need to respond to the health emergency and to recover from the economic crisis can, however, overshadow other risks linked to environmental sustainability, including climate change and biodiversity loss. If left unchecked, the direct impacts of climate change on lives and livelihoods, as well as the indirect economic, social and political impacts, will lead to further and in some cases irreversible damages. The populations already living in poverty, or otherwise marginalised or facing discrimination, with limited capacity to address their vulnerabilities or exposure to hazards, are most at risks in terms of their livelihoods.

Different actors have different needs and capacities to manage climate risks, whether financial, environmental, human or social. A focus on climate resilience therefore begs the question of resilience for whom, for what, and over what timeframe. Lessons from fragile contexts provide a reminder of potential disagreements on the nature of risks and how to address them (see Box 2.2). In some cases, decisions by people in power may even put segments of the population at greater risk.

Box 2.2. Resilience Systems Analysis

Guiding questions developed for Resilience Systems Analysis for fragile contexts can provide a useful starting point when exploring approaches to strengthening climate resilience:

- **Resilience of what system?** A system can consist of physical, human, social, political, natural and financial capitals. For practical purposes, a boundary of the system to be analysed may need to be drawn. Inclusions and exclusions of people for a resilience-related issue may also need to be justified.
- **Resilience of whom?** This depends on the target layer of society for whom resilience should be strengthened (e.g. individuals, communities, specific groups, state and its institutions), and how their resilience relies on that of others.
- **Resilience to what risk?** Risks can be geo-political, socio-economic, natural and environmental. They may include both systemic risks that affect all assets or actors within the system and idiosyncratic risks that affect specific individuals. This may result in compound risks (e.g. climate hazards during the COVID-19 pandemic).
- **Resilience over what timeframe?** The longer the timeframe, the more likely that shocks will occur. Yet the understanding of how the system can cope with those shocks will be more uncertain. Thus, it will not be clear how to support these capacities.

Source: Adjusted from (OECD, 2014[28]) Guidelines for Resilience Systems Analysis: Facilitation Guide, https://dx.doi.org/10.1787/a0714975-en.

Policy makers have different tools that can make climate risks tangible and manageable. These range from engineering design standards and environmental labelling to economic incentives that can also steer decisions in directions that help reduce risk (GCA, 2019[29]). The availability of such policy tools, however, does not guarantee their enforcement (OECD, 2020[30]). Further, they may not sufficiently address issues associated with feedbacks in the systems and relationships between elements of a human or natural system in question. Application of these policy tools must therefore be guided by a good understanding of the synergies, trade-offs and feedbacks between different approaches, the interaction of climate-related impacts with social, environmental and economic drivers across spatial and temporal scales. Close collaboration between science, policy and practice can support this process (Zscheischler et al., 2020[31]). Several knowledge products are also available to support policy makers, development co-operation providers and other non-state actors in developing and implementing approaches to strengthening climate resilience. Some documents and platforms provide strategic direction and guidance (see examples in

Box 2.3). Others are thematic and sector-specific tools, methodologies and compilations of good practice, discussed in Chapters 3 and 4.

Box 2.3. Examples of overarching guidance for climate resilience

National Adaptation Plans: Technical guidelines for the national adaptation plan process (The Least Developed Countries Expert Group [LEG] of the UNFCCC)

These technical guidelines, developed and adopted under the United Nations Framework Convention on Climate Change (UNFCCC), aim to support developing countries in building their adaptive capacity and climate resilience. To that end, they facilitate the integration of climate change adaptation into development planning. The guidelines are framed around the four elements of the National Adaptation Plan (NAP) process: laying the groundwork and addressing gaps; preparatory elements; implementation strategies; and reporting, monitoring and review (LEG, 2012[32]). Thematic guides that supplement these LEG guidelines are also available on the UNFCCC website (UNFCCC, 2019[33]).

The NAP Global Network

Established by 11 countries during in the margins of the 20th Conference of the Parties (COP20), the NAP Global Network aims to enhance national adaptation planning and action in developing countries. It facilitates sustained peer learning on NAP development and implementation, supports national-level action and enhances effectiveness of bilateral support for adaptation and climate-sensitive sectors. The Network and its website provide a comprehensive set of knowledge products to support NAP processes (NAP Global Network, n.d.[34]).

Adapt Now: A global call for leadership on climate resilience (The Global Commission for Adaptation)

The report explores how to transform key economic systems, making them more resilient and productive. The report considers five areas of climate adaptation: early warning systems, climate-resilient infrastructure, improved dryland agriculture, mangrove protection and investments to make water resources more resilient. These represent just a portion of the total investments needed and total benefits available (GCA, 2019[29]).

Adaptation Principles: A guide for designing strategies for climate change adaptation and resilience (World Bank Group)

The Adaptation Principles offer a guide to effective climate change adaptation, containing hands-on guidance to the design, implementation and monitoring of national adaptation strategies. Six guiding principles, which correspond to common policy domains, offer concrete and practical tools. These include screening questions to identify the priority actions; toolboxes that illustrate common datasets and methodologies to support decisions; and indicators to monitor and evaluate progress (Hallegatte, Rentschler and Rozenberg, 2020[35]).

Words into Action guidelines: Developing national disaster risk reduction strategies (UNDRR)

The United Nations Office for Disaster Risk Reduction (UNDRR) has a Words into Action series that presents guidelines designed to support country progress towards the achievement of the Sendai Framework. This includes guidelines that focus on the development of national disaster risk reduction strategies (UNDRR, 2019[36]) and the implementation of local disaster risk reduction and resilience strategies (UNDRR, 2019[37]). Additional guidance outlines particular considerations for UN Resident Coordinator Offices and UN Country Teams on "Integrating Disaster Risk Reduction and Climate Change Adaptation in the UN Sustainable Development Cooperation Framework" (UNDRR, 2020[38]).

2.3. Aspirations for strengthening climate resilience

Approaches to strengthening climate resilience will be context-specific, informed by the climate risks and the underlying hazards, exposures and vulnerabilities, as well as the broader development context. The 2030 Agenda for Sustainable Development is centred on economic, social and environmental sustainability. It recognises the prerequisites of ending poverty and hunger; combating inequalities; leaving no one behind; and protecting the rights and dignity of all segments of society, the most vulnerable in particular (UN, 2015[39]). Many of these high-level objectives or aspirations are also reflected in the Paris Agreement that highlights the importance of inclusive processes, the rights of all people, the particular needs of Least Developed Countries (LDCs) and the need to preserve the environment, to name just a few (UNFCCC, 2015[10]). These aspirations are also highlighted in other international agreements that contribute to the broader development agenda such as the Sendai Framework for Disaster Risk Reduction and the New Urban Agenda.

Taking note of these high-level objectives, the rest of this chapter focuses on three aspirations that governments and development co-operation should consider when developing and implementing climate resilience measures:

- country ownership
- inclusive approaches
- environmental and social sustainability.

These aspirations highlight the importance of ensuring that measures in support of climate action do not exacerbate current vulnerabilities or create new ones. Instead, they should support broader sustainable development. They present measures for consideration rather than a prescription for action.

2.3.1. Country ownership

A focus on country ownership highlights the role of individual countries in determining their own development pathways, and within that, their response to global challenges including climate change. In this Guidance, country ownership encompasses the role of both national and sub-national governments, as well as that of non-state actors. In the context of development co-operation, country ownership is defined by the Global Partnership for Effective Development Co-operation as "the aspiration by which countries determine their own development priorities and based on these, define, lead and implement their preferred model of development" (OECD/UNDP, 2016[40]). For climate resilience, this entails a focus on countries' specific climate risks and their experience of known and tested approaches. The ease of securing country ownership to strengthen climate resilience will also depend on the extent to which climate resilience is prioritised in national development objectives, and reflected in governance arrangements and policy cycles (OECD, 2009[41]).

Country ownership was central to the successful adoption of the Paris Agreement in 2015. This is illustrated by the submission of over 180 Intended Nationally Determined Contributions (INDCs) by Parties to the United Nations Framework Convention on Climate Change (UNFCCC). With the ratification of the Paris Agreement, the INDCs became Nationally Determined Contributions outlining domestic contributions to the objectives of the Agreement. The Paris Agreement requests Parties to engage with sub-national actors to build their capacity in a way that fosters their ownership of activities and responds to countries' needs for climate action effectively (UNFCCC, 2015[10]). National Adaptation Plans (NAPs), established under the UNFCCC, are also a country-driven process to identify priority actions to strengthen climate resilience and integrate them into national and sectoral development plans and budgets.

Many countries have made considerable progress in establishing multi-level, and cross-sectoral co-ordination mechanisms. However, fragile contexts or countries with weak institutions may not have a central body to co-ordinate and oversee the process. In these cases, the capacity of governance systems to manage risks may be weak as well. Further, they may not consider all members of society equally. In other contexts, such as states in conflict, the government will intrinsically be divided, limiting the notion of country ownership and what it represents to only a segment of the population. In such contexts, decision-making processes can be characterised by pervasive mistrust among different stakeholders rather than inclusive considerations of climate resilience priorities (Chambote and Shankland, 2011[42]). A national co-ordination mechanism will also have limited ability to advance climate resilience objectives if it lacks legitimacy, capacity and accountability measures (Watson-Grant, Xiong and Thomas, 2016[43]; Peterson Carvalho, 19 July 2013[44]; OECD/UNDP, 2019[45]; Peters et al., 2020[46]; Crawford et al., 2015[47]).

Experience suggests that approaches to climate resilience led by sub-national and non-state actors can be well suited to address climate vulnerabilities (Carothers, 2015[48]; Keijzer et al., 2018[49]; LIFE-AR, 2019[50]) (see examples in Box 2.4). Sub-national and non-state actors can also play an important role in piloting and testing climate resilience measures at the local level. Lessons learnt from the pilots should, in turn, inform the development of national-level policies and plans to enable the scale-up of successful approaches over time.

This Guidance recognises the importance of a whole-of-society approach. In practice, non-state actors often have limited access to decision-making processes, including those related to domestic finance allocation and access to international climate finance. This is partly because they are usually not a united entity but rather a complex web of actors with diverse objectives, interests or ability to engage in national processes (RC&D, 2017[51]). In some countries, most businesses operate in the informal sector, making it harder to engage in decision-making processes on policies, plans and projects for climate resilience (Casado Asensio, Kato and Shin, forthcoming[52]).

Box 2.4. Examples of ownership at different levels

The Least Developed Countries (LDCs) Initiative for Effective Adaptation and Resilience (LIFE-AR)

LIFE-AR is an LDC-led and -owned initiative established in 2019 with a vision to: i) enable all LDCs to be on climate-resilient development pathways by 2030; and ii) deliver net-zero emissions by 2050 to ensure that societies and ecosystems thrive (LIFE-AR, 2019[50]). It emerged from three beliefs: business-as-usual approaches to climate change are not working; the adaptation financing gap in developing countries is wide; and short-term, project-based and sectoral-specific climate responses have limited impact. LIFE-AR is guided by the principles of inclusion, participation, justice, equity and leaving no one behind. As such, it seeks to deepen climate knowledge and access to predictable and reliable finance – domestic, international, public and private – to develop technology and capabilities to support the emergence of the following (LIFE-AR, 2019[50]):

- climate-resilient people living in just, inclusive, happy and poverty-free societies
- climate-resilient economies that are net-zero and prosperous, with vibrant and sustainable growth within ecological limits
- climate-resilient landscapes and ecosystems that are sustainably managed, less vulnerable to climate shocks and stresses, and used through nature-based solutions.

Africa Adaptation Initiative (AAI)

AAI is an initiative of the African Union. It was launched by African Heads of State at COP21 to ensure the African continent urgently adapts to the adverse impacts of climate change, to strengthen collaboration on adaptation across the continent and to galvanise support needed to significantly scale up adaptation efforts (AAI, 2016[53]). AAI takes a strategic view of adaptation across Africa by identifying gaps and connecting regional partners – public and private. In this way, it aims to identify, refine and prioritise activities aligned with four agreed AAI focus areas or pillars:

- enhancing climate information services
- strengthening policies and institutions
- enhancing on the ground action
- climate finance and investments.

It identifies nine guiding principles: i) be stakeholder-driven; ii) be relevant to Africa; iii) build and strengthen new partnerships; iv) support African countries to engage with processes under the UNFCCC; v) promote regional and trans-boundary co-operation; vi) develop work packages in line with immediate, short, medium and long-term adaptation needs; vii) enhance communication; viii) employ a phased-approach; and ix) promote transparency (AAI, 2016[53]).

C40 Cities

C40 connects 96 cities around the world (representing over 700 million people and one-quarter of the global economy) that are committed to delivering on the goals of the Paris Agreement (C40, n.a.[54]). C40 Participation Standards encourage all cities to develop and start implementing a climate action plan by the end of 2020. These plans would be compatible with the goals of the Paris Agreement of limiting global average temperature increase, while improving resilience and inclusivity. The C40 Finance Facility aims to strengthen the capacity of public entities in accessing public and private finance, developing bankable projects and scaling up their investment on climate (C40, n.a.[54]).

Development co-operation plays a role in supporting country-owned and -led processes for climate resilience. Evaluation of development assistance, including for climate finance, suggests that country ownership facilitates more effective development and climate-related results (UNSD, 2018[55]; GCF IEU, 2019[56]; Sherman and Ford, 2014[57]). A greater level of ownership will also likely enhance the continuity of policy interventions supported by governments and development co-operation. Yet this notion of ownership is often ambiguous (e.g. what to be owned and by whom) and varies across contexts. The approach of development co-operation to country-owned processes will also be influenced by the values of individual providers and the associated policy standards and commitments. Governments of developing countries have improved the overall quality of national development planning over recent years. However, alignment of approaches by development co-operation to priorities of developing countries and country-owned results frameworks, as well as in-country planning and budget preparation systems, is declining (GCF IEU, 2019[56]; Ye Zou and Ockenden, 2016[58]; OECD/UNDP, 2019[45]) (see Box 2.5).

Box 2.5. Country ownership for sustainable development results

The 2019 Progress Report by the Global Partnership for Effective Development Co-operation emphasises the importance of country ownership for long-lasting development results, calling for a whole-of-society approach by both state and non-state actors. Developing country governments are making continued progress in strengthening the policies and institutional arrangements required to lead development efforts. This is especially the case for planning national development policies and public financial management systems. Implementation mechanisms and capacities for those policies and systems, however, remain a major challenge. Development co-operation plays an important role in continued and enhanced support to build strong national systems that can establish and oversee the policy and institutional arrangements for progress towards the SDGs, including climate resilience.

Source: (OECD/UNDP, 2019[45]), Making Development Co-operation More Effective: 2019 Progress Report, https://dx.doi.org/10.1787/26f2638f-en.

Country ownership is also recognised in the guiding principles for international climate funds such as the Green Climate Fund (GCF), the Global Environment Facility and the Adaptation Fund. The GCF, for instance, pursues country ownership through the establishment of National Designated Authorities, collaboration with Accredited Entities for direct access, engagement with various stakeholders including civil society organisations (CSOs) and the private sector, and the country programming processes (GCF, 2017[59]). On broader development co-operation agendas, the Busan Partnership Agreement for Effective Development Co-operation also recognises country ownership as one of four principles of effective development co-operation. Other international agreements highlight country ownership as a guiding principle as well (see Table 2.1).

Table 2.1. Ownership in key international agreements related to sustainable development

Agreement	Description of country ownership
2030 Agenda for Sustainable Development	Nationally owned sustainable development strategies (supported by integrated national financing frameworks) is key to achieve the Sustainable Development Goals. Public policies and the mobilisation and effective use of domestic resources are central to pursuing sustainable development.
Paris Agreement	Action on adaptation to "follow a country-driven, gender-responsive, participatory and fully transparent approach". Provision of finance and development of capacity should consider country-driven strategies, priorities and needs.
Sendai Framework for Disaster Risk Reduction	Managing and reducing disaster risk requires all-of-society and all-of-state institutions engagement. It also requires strong commitment and involvement of political leadership in every country at all levels.
New Urban Agenda	Cities and human settlements are to be participatory; promote civic engagement; engender a sense of belonging and ownership among all their inhabitants; and prioritise safe, inclusive, accessible, green and quality public spaces.

Source: (UN, 2015[39]), Transforming our world: The 2030 Agenda for Sustainable Development, https://sustainabledevelopment.un.org/post2015/transformingourworld, (UNFCCC, 2015[10]), The Paris Agreemen, https://unfccc.int/process-and-meetings/the-paris-agreement/the-paris-agreement, (UNDRR, 2015[24]), Sendai Framework for Disaster Risk Reduction 2015-2030, https://www.undrr.org/publication/sendai-framework-disaster-risk-reduction-2015-2030, (UN, 2017[60]), The New Urban Agenda, http://habitat3.org/wp-content/uploads/NUA-English.pdf.

2.3.2. Inclusive approaches

Central to the 2030 Agenda for Sustainable Development is making both development processes and their outcomes inclusive so that no one is left behind. This also applies to the context of climate resilience. LDCs and poorer segments of the population are often especially vulnerable to the impacts of climate change. The same is true for those marginalised or discriminated against on the basis of, for example, their gender, ethnicity, and sexual or political orientation. These factors intersect with each other to shape individual identities (e.g. women in a marginalised Indigenous community) that influence exposure and vulnerability to climate hazards (Chaplin, Twigg and Lovell, 2019[61]; Djoudi et al., 2016[62]).

Efforts to strengthen climate resilience must embrace three principles. First, they must ensure that progress for one group or country does not compromise that of another. Second, they must target the needs of the most vulnerable. Finally, associated benefits must be equitably shared across stakeholder groups. Unless carefully managed, efforts to strengthen climate resilience can also imply trade-offs with other development objectives (IPCC, 2014[63]; UNEP, 2019[64]). For instance, increased fertiliser and pesticide use may increase economic resilience of the agriculture sector but it can also cause loss of ecosystem services and increased water scarcity (IPCC, 2018[12]).

Approaches to climate resilience that prioritise the most vulnerable require a good understanding of underlying factors that drive their specific vulnerabilities and explicit consideration of existing wealth and power dynamics (Dazé, 2019[65]). Inclusive approaches facilitate and value the contribution of both state and non-state actors, such as community-based organisations, the private sector, CSOs and academia to identify, prioritise, finance and implement climate resilience measures (see Chapter 3 for further discussion). Indigenous and natural resource-dependent communities, for example, have established traditions of responding to changes in the climate by drawing on local knowledge, social systems, cultural values and norms. These can also provide valuable input to national processes (UNESCO, 2017[66]).

Inclusive stakeholder processes are time- and resource-intensive. Even when prioritised, it can be difficult to incentivise stakeholder participation due to competing demands for their time, limited awareness of the climate risks and insufficient capacity to actively engage (Sherman and Ford, 2014[57]). In some cases, administrative procedures for non-state actors to participate in policy dialogues are cumbersome, discouraging their engagement in decision-making processes on policies (Casado Asensio, Kato and Shin, forthcoming[52]). At the same time, representation and participation in decision-making processes on their own do not result in inclusive development outcomes (OECD, 2020[6]).

The three sub-sections below briefly highlight the role of gender equality and engagement by the private sector and CSOs in pursuing an inclusive approach to climate resilience. However, there are also other important considerations to keep in mind. These include the risks to different segments of society that are marginalised by e.g. their age, (dis)ability, race, class or beliefs [see e.g. (HelpAge International, 2019[67]; GFDRR, 2018[68]; Handicap International, 2017[69])], or the circumstances of minority and Indigenous groups' vulnerability to climate change and their role in climate action [see e.g. (ILO, 2017[70]; Minority Rights Group International, 2019[71])].

Focus on gender

A focus on gender is an important means of addressing vulnerability of society to climate change. Social norms, gender division of labour, disadvantaged access to resources and information, and the prevalence of gender-based violence may increase women's exposure and vulnerability to climate hazards. Women at the same time play an active role in negotiating and adapting to changes brought upon their lives and those of their family members by climate change (Huyer and Partey, 2020[72]). However, prevailing norms can limit their potential as agents of change. International commitments and initiatives have recognised the importance of gender equality and the ability of both women and men to access resources for and benefits of climate resilience. Different tools have been developed to guide the integration of gender considerations into climate-related policies, programmes and institutions (see section 3.1).

Private-sector engagement

Private-sector engagement in climate resilience is deepening and broadening. It ranges from large corporations and small businesses to groups that represent the interests of the private sector such as industry associations, chambers of commerce and co-operatives (UNEP DTU Partnership, 2018[73]; UNDP, 2018[74]; Casado Asensio, Kato and Shin, forthcoming[52]). The private sector continuously adjusts its operations to the changing context of the business environment. Climate change, however, is making such adjustments increasingly difficult by adding new challenges. These include the financial viability of climate resilience projects, uncertainty of the predicted impacts of climate change on individual businesses, and lack of awareness and knowledge about potential solutions to manage climate risks (UNEP DTU Partnership, 2018[73]; Crawford and Church, 2019[75]; Casado Asensio, Kato and Shin, forthcoming[52]).

Engagement with CSOs

CSOs can reach people on the frontlines of poverty, inequality and vulnerability, and complement – or in some cases – assume the roles of the public sector. This makes them an integral part to fulfilling the 2030 Agenda, including on climate resilience (OECD, 2020[76]; Casado Asensio, Kato and Shin, forthcoming[52]). Through dialogue and advocacy, CSOs can bring into public policy processes the perspectives of marginalised members of society who may not be able to participate due to the perceptions of their identities by society (OECD, 2020[76]). CSOs in remote communities can also help bring attention to local climate risks and vulnerabilities, including in national policy processes (Mascarinas, 2016[77]). CSOs also play an important role in supporting the implementation of climate resilience measures by governments or development co-operation providers (Mascarinas, 2016[77]). In some cases, CSOs can also support local communities in accessing climate data and information by connecting them with, for instance, research institutions and National Meteorological and Hydrological Services (Canales, 2011[78]). Despite these important roles, gaps remain in the effectiveness and accountability of CSOs' development activities. These gaps have led to concerns among development co-operation providers about CSOs' legitimacy, their results and the challenges of co-ordination between CSOs and government agencies (OECD,

2020[76]). Overcoming these challenges will require commitment and resources by all actors involved, including governments and providers of development co-operation.

2.3.3. Environmental and social sustainability

Action on climate resilience is closely linked with that on protecting and sustainably managing the natural environment. Healthy wetlands, forests and coastal systems, for example, provide ecosystem services that can help mitigate the impacts of weather- and climate-related hazards. **At the same time, c**limate change is among the key drivers of the unprecedented loss of biodiversity (IPBES, 2019[79]). This interacts with non-climatic drivers of environmental degradation, such as population growth and lifestyle choices that increase demand for natural resources. Approaches to strengthening climate resilience must avoid generating further pressures on local and global biodiversity. Efforts for climate resilience should instead be aligned with regulatory measures to protect the environment and restore, manage and conserve ecosystems.

The COVID-19 pandemic has further highlighted the importance of healthy natural systems for human health, well-being and the economy. The exploitation of wildlife and the degradation of ecosystems have increased the risk of zoonotic diseases (that jump from animals to humans) (OECD, 2020[80]). At the same time, the COVID-19 crisis has revealed the potentially catastrophic risk of not building resilience to well-known risks. The risks of pandemics were clear following the SARS, MERS and Ebola outbreaks, but the experiences did not adequately prepare most countries for future pandemics or spur action to reduce risks.

The environment has for decades been positioned within the development paradigm as one pillar alongside economic and social objectives. In practice, however, many governments and practitioners often assume trade-offs between the environment and economic growth (Elder and Olsen, 2019[81]). The 2030 Agenda calls for a more integrated approach, as illustrated by the SDGs that explicitly focus on the environment (SDG 6 Clean Water and Sanitation; SDG 13 Climate Action; SDG 14 Life Below Water; SDG 15 Life on Land) and the environment-related targets included in the other SDGs (see Table 2.2). This integrated approach to development represents an important milestone for the environment agenda. However, the focus has largely remained on achieving both economic growth and environmental management rather than on questioning the sustainability of development models (Elder and Olsen, 2019[81]). There may also be a range of trade-offs between different environment-related targets in implementing such integrated approaches.

Table 2.2. SDG targets related to the environment

Target No.	Content related to environment	Target No.	Content related to environment
1.5	Resilience to climate and environmental, shocks and disasters	7.b	**Infrastructure and technology**
2.4	**Sustainable food production systems**	8.4	**Resource efficiency and decoupling economic growth from environmental degradation**
2.5	Genetic diversity	8.8	Labour rights and safe working environment
3.3	Death and illness from pollution	8.9	**Sustainable tourism**
3.9	Water-borne diseases	9.1	**Sustainable and resilient infrastructure**
4.7	**Education for sustainable development**	9.2	**Sustainable industrialisation**
5.a	**Women's equal rights to economic resources, property, natural resources**	9.4	**Sustainability upgrading and resource efficiency**
6.1	Access, safe water	9.a	**Financial, technical and technological support for sustainable and resilient infrastructure**
6.2	**Sanitation**	11.1	Adequate, safe, affordable housing
6.3	**Water quality**	11.2	**Sustainable transport**
6.4	**Use-efficiency, scarcity**	11.3	**Inclusive and sustainable urbanisation**
6.5	**Integrated water management**	11.4	Protect and safeguard cultural and natural heritage
6.6	Ecosystems	11.6	Environmental impact, air quality, **waste management**
6.a	**Capacity building**	11.7	Green and public spaces
6.b	**Local participation**	11.a	**National and regional development planning**
7.2	**Renewable energy**	11.b	**Integrated policies on inclusion, resource efficiency, climate mitigation and adaptation, resilience, disaster risk management**
7.3	**Energy efficiency**	11.c	**Support for sustainable and resilient building**
7.a	**Related investment**	12-15	**All except 14.a**

Notes:

- Grey box: environmental condition to be improved.
- Bold text: means to improve the environment.
- Grey box and bold text: the target combines the environmental condition to be improved with means to improve it.
- Normal text: ends which benefit from an improved environment.

Source: (Elder and Olsen, 2019[81]), The design of environmental priorities in the SDGs, https://doi.org/10.1111/1758-5899.12596.

The role of the natural environment in strengthening climate resilience is increasingly recognised. Nature-based solutions are "measures that protect, sustainably manage or restore natural capital, with the goal of maintaining or enhancing ecosystem services to address a variety of social, environmental and economic challenges" (OECD, 2020[82]). The use of nature-based solutions has been increasing in developing and developed countries, with evidence emerging of the value and multiple benefits of such approaches (University of Oxford, n.d.[83]; UNEP, 2019[84]). Examples include forest conservation in Chile to reduce landslides and avalanches while enhancing carbon sequestration; wetland restoration in Nepal to secure water supplies; and improved mangrove management in El Salvador to restore water flows and reduce downstream flooding (Jones and Reid, 2019[85]).

Despite the documented benefits of nature-based solutions, their uptake continues to be limited. This can be partly explained by their characteristics, such as the time lag between implementation and the materialisation of the benefits; the spatial scales; and the dynamic nature of ecosystems that increase uncertainty in planning. Additionally, gaps in governance arrangements, policies, regulatory requirements, capacity and funding and financing mechanisms can all prevent nature-based solutions from being considered on equal footing with other options (OECD, 2020[82]).

A focus on social sustainability and well-being benefits, complementary to environmental sustainability, is also a crucial consideration for seizing opportunities to pursue climate-resilient development pathways

(IPCC, 2018[12]). Achieving social sustainability includes meeting physical, emotional and social needs of current and future generations (Rogers et al., 2012[86]). An essential element of social sustainability is equity and broader well-being considerations, such as income and gender equality, health, housing, jobs and labour rights, cultural identity, social stability and public participation (Mensah, 2017[87]; Saith, 2006[88]; Munzel, Meyer-Waarden and Galan, 2018[89]).

The OECD well-being framework measures societal progress through the improvement of people's current and future well-being (Figure 2.2). When applied to the context of climate action, people's well-being must be placed at the centre of decision-making processes to increase the political and social support for more ambitious mitigation action and to overcome barriers for change (OECD, 2019[90]). A similar people-centred approach, focused on well-being, is also essential for addressing the vulnerability and exposure of people to the looming emergencies associated with climate change and biodiversity loss (OECD, 2019[90]).

Figure 2.2. OECD well-being framework

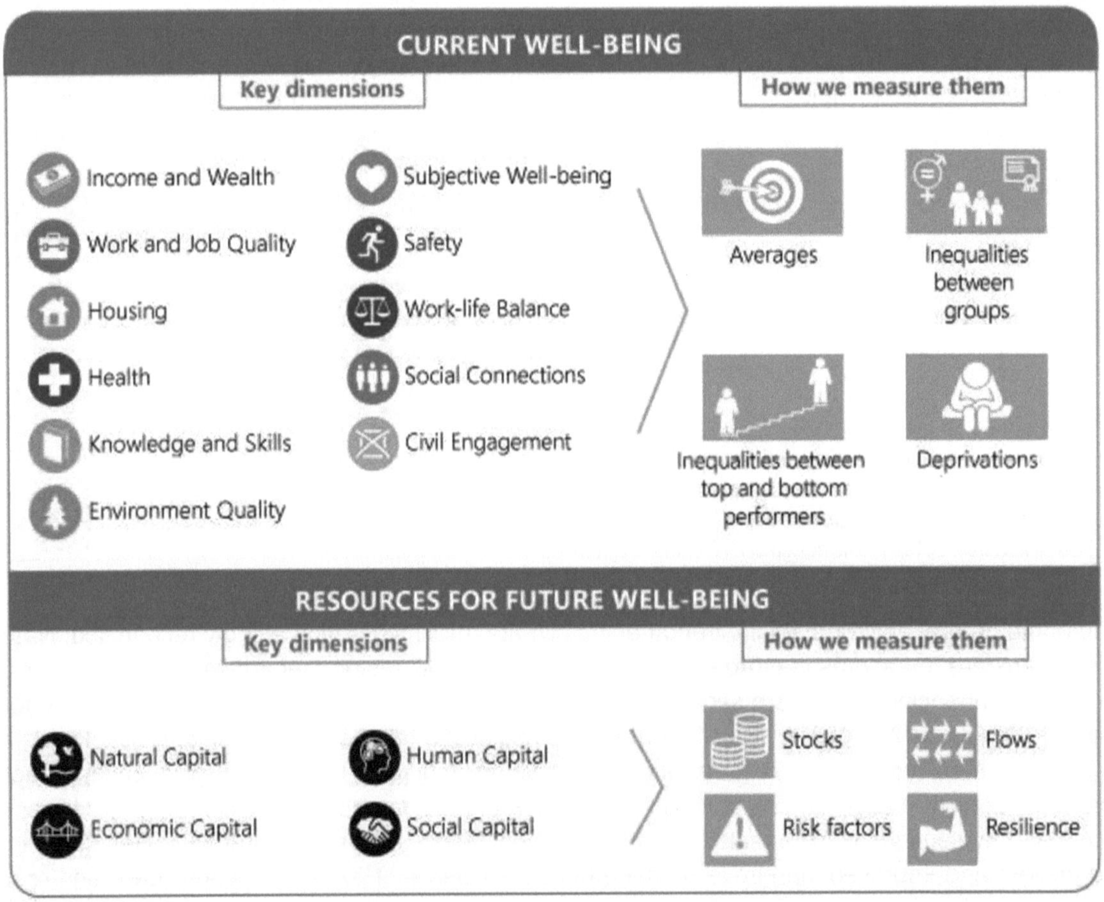

Source: (OECD, 2013[91]), How's Life? 2013: Measuring Well-being, https://doi.org/10.1787/9789264201392-en.

References

AAI (2016), *Enhancing Action on Adaptation and Addressing Loss and Damage in Africa*, Africa Adaptation Initiative, https://www.africaadaptationinitiative.org/assets/aai_framework_en_2016.pdf. [53]

Adger, W., I. Brown and S. Surminski (2018), "Advances in risk assessment for climate change adaptation policy", *Philosophical Transactions of the Royal Society A*, Vol. 376/2121, http://dx.doi.org/10.1098/rsta.2018.0106. [14]

Ayeb-Karlsson, S., G. Fox and D. Kniveton (2019), "Embracing uncertainty: A discursive approach to understanding pathways for climate adaptation in Senegal", *Regional Environmental Change*, Vol. 19/6, pp. 1585-1596, http://dx.doi.org/10.1007/s10113-019-01495-7. [19]

BMZ (2019), *Comprehensive Risk Management: The Approach of German Development Cooperation for Dealing with Disaster and Climate Risks*, Federal Ministry of Economic Cooperation and Development, Bonn, https://www.bmz.de/en/publications/type_of_publication/information_flyer/information_brochures/Materilie400_risk_management.pdf. [27]

Buckle, S. et al. (2020), "Addressing the COVID-19 and climate crises: Potential economic recovery pathways and their implications for climate change mitigation, NDCs and broader socio-economic goals", *OECD/IEA Climate Change Expert Group Papers*, No. 2020/04, OECD Publishing, Paris, https://dx.doi.org/10.1787/50abd39c-en. [7]

Buurman, J. and V. Babovic (2016), "Adaptation Pathways and Real Options Analysis: An approach to deep uncertainty in climate change adaptation policies", *Policy and Society*, Vol. 35/2, pp. 137-150, http://dx.doi.org/10.1016/j.polsoc.2016.05.002. [15]

C40 (n.a.), *C40 Cities*, website, https://www.c40.org/ (accessed on 20 January 2020). [54]

Canales, N. (2011), "Civil Society and the Integration of Climate Change Risks into Planning and Policy-making", webpage, https://www.wri.org/our-work/project/world-resources-report/civil-society-and-integration-climate-change-risks-planning (accessed on 27 July 2020). [78]

CarbonBrief (2020), "Coronavirus: Tracking how the world's 'green recovery' plans aim to cut emissions", 16 June, International Policy, CarbonBrief, https://www.carbonbrief.org/coronavirus-tracking-how-the-worlds-green-recovery-plans-aim-to-cut-emissions (accessed on 30 July 2020). [5]

Carothers, T. (2015), "The deeper struggle over country ownership", in *A Governance Practitioner's Notebook: Alternative Ideas and Approaches*, OECD Publishing, Paris, https://www.oecd.org/dac/accountable-effective-institutions/governance-practitioners-notebook.htm. [48]

Casado Asensio, J., T. Kato and H. Shin (forthcoming), *Private-sector Engagement in Strengthening Climate Resilience*, OECD Publishing, Paris, https://doi.org/10.1787/22220518. [52]

Cavallo, A. and V. Ireland (2014), "Preparing for complex interdependent risks: A System of Systems approach to building disaster resilience", *International Journal of Disaster Risk Reduction*, Vol. 9, pp. 181-193, http://dx.doi.org/10.1016/j.ijdrr.2014.05.001. [16]

Chambote, R. and A. Shankland (2011), *Mozambique Case Study Report: Country Ownership, Stakeholder Participation and the Political Economy of Priority-Setting in the Mozambique Pilot Program for Climate Resiliece*, Institute of Development Studies, University of Sussex, UK, https://www.ids.ac.uk/projects/understanding-the-political-economy-of-low-carbon-and-climate-resilient-development/. [42]

Chaplin, D., J. Twigg and E. Lovell (2019), “Intersectional approaches to vulnerability reduction and resilience-building”, No. 12, BRACED Knowledge Manager, Overseas Development Institute, London, https://www.odi.org/sites/odi.org.uk/files/resource-documents/12651.pdf. [61]

Crawford, A. and C. Church (2019), “Advancing National Adaptation Planning: Engaging the Private Sector in the Process”, webinar, 7 November, NAP Global Network, https://www.napglobalnetwork.org/resource/webinar-advancing-national-adaptation-planning-engaging-the-private-sector-in-the-process/ (accessed on 30 January 2020). [75]

Crawford, A. et al. (2015), *Promoting Climate-Resilient Peacebuilding in Fragile States*, International Institute for Sustainable Development, Winnipeg, Canada, https://www.iisd.org/library/promoting-climate-resilient-peacebuilding-fragile-states. [47]

Dazé, A. (2019), “Why gender matters in climate change adaptation”, IISD blog, https://www.iisd.org/library/gender-climate-change. [65]

Djoudi, H. et al. (2016), “Beyond dichotomies: Gender and intersecting inequalities in climate change studies”, *Ambio*, Vol. 45/S3, pp. 248-262, http://dx.doi.org/10.1007/s13280-016-0825-2. [62]

Elder, M. and S. Olsen (2019), “The design of environmental priorities in the SDGs”, *Global Policy*, Vol. 10/S1, pp. 70-82, http://dx.doi.org/10.1111/1758-5899.12596. [81]

GCA (2019), *Adapt Now: A Global Call for Leadership on Climate Resilience*, Global Commission on Adaptation, https://cdn.gca.org/assets/2019-09/GlobalCommission_Report_FINAL.pdf. [29]

GCF (2017), *GCF/B.17/14: Guidelines for Enhanced Country Ownership and Country Drivenness*, Green Climate Fund, Songdo, https://www.greenclimate.fund/document/gcf-b17-14. [59]

GCF IEU (2019), *Independent Evaluation of the GCF’s Country Ownership Approach: Inception Report*, Green Climate Fund Independent Evaluation Unit, Songdo, Republic of Korea, https://ieu.greenclimate.fund/sites/default/files/evaluation/coa-inception-report.pdf. [56]

GFDRR (2018), *Disability Inclusion in Disaster Risk Management: Promising Practices and Opportunities for Enhanced Engagement*, Global Facility for Disaster Reduction and Recovery, Washington, DC, https://www.gfdrr.org/sites/default/files/publication/GFDRR%20Disability%20inclusion%20in%20DRM%20Report_F.pdf. [68]

Haasnoot, M. et al. (2013), “Dynamic adaptive policy pathways: A method for crafting robust decisions for a deeply uncertain world”, *Global Environmental Change*, Vol. 23/2, pp. 485-498, http://dx.doi.org/10.1016/j.gloenvcha.2012.12.006. [22]

Hallegatte, S., J. Rentschler and J. Rozenberg (2020), *The Adaptation Principles A Guide for Designing Strategies for Climate Change Adaptation and Resilience*, World Bank, Washington, DC, http://hdl.handle.net/10986/34780. [35]

Hallegatte, S. et al. (2016), *Unbreakable: Building the Resilience of the Poor in the Face of Natural Disasters*, Climate Change and Development series, World Bank Group, Washington, D.C., http://dx.doi.org/10.1596/978-1-4648-1003-9. [9]

Handicap International (2017), *Inclusive Disaster Risk Reduction Post 2015*, Handicap International, Geneva, https://handicap-international.ch/sites/ch/files/documents/files/inclusive_disaster_risk_reduction_post201_hi_expertise.pdf. [69]

HelpAge International (2019), *Age Inclusive Disaster Risk Reduction – A Toolkit*, HelpAge International, London, https://www.preventionweb.net/files/68082_ageinclusivedisasterriskreductionat.pdf. [67]

Huyer, S. and S. Partey (2020), "Weathering the storm or storming the norms? Moving gender equality forward in climate-resilient agriculture", *Climatic Change*, Vol. 158, pp. 1-12, http://dx.doi.org/10.1007/s10584-019-02612-5. [72]

ILO (2017), *Indigenous Peoples and Climate Change: From Victims to Change Agents through Decent Work*, International Labour Organization, Geneva, https://www.ilo.org/wcmsp5/groups/public/---dgreports/---gender/documents/publication/wcms_551189.pdf. [70]

IPBES (2019), *Summary for Policymakers of the Global Assessment Report on Biodiversity and Ecosystem Services of the IPBES*, Intergovernmental Science-Policy Platform on Biodiversity and Ecosystem Services Secretariat, Bonn, https://ipbes.net/global-assessment. [79]

IPCC (2019), *Climate Change and Land*, Intergovernmental Panel on Climate Change, Geneva, https://www.ipcc.ch/srccl/. [17]

IPCC (2018), *Global warming of 1.5°C*, Intergovernmental Panel on Climate Change, Geneva, https://www.ipcc.ch/sr15/. [12]

IPCC (2014), *Climate Change 2014: Synthesis Report. Contribution of Working Groups I, II and III to the Fifth Assessment Report*, Intergovernmental Panel on Climate Change, Geneva, http://www.ipcc.ch/report/ar5/syr/. [63]

IPCC (2014), "Climate-resilient pathways: Adaptation, mitigation, and sustainable development", in *Climate Change 2014: Impacts, Adaptation, and Vulnerability. Part A: Global and Sectoral Aspects. Contribution of Working Group II to the Fifth Assessment Report of the Intergovernmental Panel on Climate Change*, Cambridge University Press, Cambridge and New York, https://www.ipcc.ch/site/assets/uploads/2018/02/WGIIAR5-Chap20_FINAL.pdf. [11]

IPCC (2014), "Integrated risk and uncertainty assessment of climate change response policies", in *Climate Change 2014: Mitigation of Climate Change. Contribution of Working Group III to the Fifth Assessment Report of the Intergovernmental Panel on Climate Change*, Cambridge University Press, Cambridge, UK and New York, https://www.ipcc.ch/site/assets/uploads/2018/02/ipcc_wg3_ar5_chapter2.pdf (accessed on 3 December 2020). [13]

Jones, X. and H. Reid (2019), "Time to team up with nature to adapt to climate change", Climate Change blog, https://www.iied.org/time-team-nature-adapt-climate-change. [85]

Keijzer, N. et al. (2018), *Seeking Balanced Ownership in Changing Development Cooperation Relationships*, Expert Group for Aid Studies, Stockholm, http://www.eba.se/. [49]

Kharas, H. and K. Hamel (2020), "Turning back the poverty clock: How will COVID-19 impact the world's poorest people?", Brookings blog, https://www.brookings.edu/blog/future-development/2020/05/06/turning-back-the-poverty-clock-how-will-covid-19-impact-the-worlds-poorest-people/. [8]

LEG (2012), "Guidelines for national adaptation plans", https://unfccc.int/topics/adaptation-and-resilience/workstreams/national-adaptation-plans-naps/guidelines-for-national-adaptation-plans-naps (accessed on 25 July 2020). [32]

LIFE-AR (2019), *LDC 2050 Vision: Towards a Climate-resilient Future*, LDC Initiative for Effective Adaptation and Resilience, http://www.ldc-climate.org/wp-content/uploads/2019/09/2050-Vision.pdf. [50]

Mahler, D. et al. (2020), "Updated estimates of the impact of COVID-19 on global poverty", Data blog, https://blogs.worldbank.org/opendata/updated-estimates-impact-covid-19-global-poverty. [2]

Mascarinas, R. (2016), "What CSOs can do for climate change accountability", Asian Development blog, https://blogs.adb.org/blog/what-csos-can-do-climate-change-accountability. [77]

Mensah, J. (2017), "Sustainable development: Meaning, history, principles, pillars, and implications for human action: Literature review", *Cogent Social Sciences*, Vol. 5/1, http://dx.doi.org/10.1080/23311886.2019.1653531. [87]

Minority Rights Group International (2019), *Minority and Indigenous Trends 2019: Focus on Climate Justice*, Minority Rights Group International, London, http://www.minorityrights.org. [71]

Munzel, A., L. Meyer-Waarden and J. Galan (2018), "The social side of sustainability: Well-being as a driver and an outcome of social relationships and interactions on social networking sites", *Technological Forecasting and Social Change*, Vol. 130/May, pp. 14-27, https://doi.org/10.1016/j.techfore.2017.06.031. [89]

NAP Global Network (n.d.), "The NAP Global Network", webpage, https://napglobalnetwork.org/ (accessed on 20 January 2020). [34]

OECD (2020), "Building back better: A Sustainable, resilient recovery after COVID-19", *OECD Policy Responses to Coronavirus (COVID-19)*, OECD Publishing, Paris, https://doi.org/10.1787/52b869f5-en. [3]

OECD (2020), *Common Ground between the Paris Agreement and the Sendai Framework: Climate Change Adaptation and Disaster Risk Reduction*, OECD Publishing, Paris, http://dx.doi.org/10.1787/3edc8d09-en. [30]

OECD (2020), *Development Assistance Committee Members and Civil Society*, The Development Dimension, OECD Publishing, Paris, https://dx.doi.org/10.1787/51eb6df1-en. [76]

OECD (2020), "Environmental health and strengthening resilience to pandemics", *OECD Policy Responses to Coronavirus (COVID-19)*, OECD Publishing, Paris, https://doi.org/10.1787/73784e04-en. [80]

OECD (2020), "Nature-based solutions for adapting to water-related climate risks", *OECD Environment Policy Papers*, No. 21, OECD Publishing, Paris, https://dx.doi.org/10.1787/2257873d-en. [82]

OECD (2020), "What does "inclusive governance" mean?: Clarifying theory and practice", *OECD Development Policy Papers*, Vol. 27, http://dx.doi.org/10.1787/960f5a97-en. [6]

OECD (2019), *Accelerating Climate Action: Refocusing Policies through a Well-being Lens*, OECD Publishing, Paris, https://dx.doi.org/10.1787/2f4c8c9a-en. [90]

OECD (2015), *Climate Change Risks and Adaptation: Linking Policy and Economics*, OECD Publishing, Paris, https://doi.org/10.1787/9789264234611-en. [23]

OECD (2014), *Guidelines for Resilience Systems Analysis: Facilitation Guide*, Best Practices in Development Co-operation, OECD Publishing, Paris, https://dx.doi.org/10.1787/a0714975-en. [28]

OECD (2013), *How's Life? 2013: Measuring Well-being*, OECD Publishing, Paris, http://dx.doi.org/10.1787/9789264201392-en. [91]

OECD (2009), *Integrating Climate Change Adaptation into Development Co-operation: Policy Guidance*, OECD Publishing, Paris, https://dx.doi.org/10.1787/9789264054950-en. [41]

OECD/UNDP (2019), *Making Development Co-operation More Effective: 2019 Progress Report*, OECD Publishing, Paris, https://dx.doi.org/10.1787/26f2638f-en. [45]

OECD/UNDP (2016), *Making Development Co-operation More Effective: 2016 Progress Report*, OECD Publishing, Paris, https://dx.doi.org/10.1787/9789264266261-en. [40]

Opitz-Stapleton, S. et al. (2019), *Risk-informed Development: From Crises to Resilience*, United Nations Development Programme, New York. [25]

Peters, K. et al. (2020), *Climate Change, Conflict and Fragility: An Evidence Review and Recommendations for Research and Action*, Overseas Development Institute, London, https://www.odi.org/sites/odi.org.uk/files/resource-documents/odi_climate_change_conflict_and_fragility.pdf. [46]

Peterson Carvalho, A. (19 July 2013), "3 ways country ownership is being put to the test with climate change funding", Politics of Poverty blog, https://politicsofpoverty.oxfamamerica.org/2013/07/3-ways-country-ownership-is-being-put-to-test-with-climate-change-funding/. [44]

RC&D (2017), *Non-state Actors: Towards a Leading Role in the Implementation of the Paris Agreement*, Réseau Climat & Développement, Montreuil, https://www.climate-chance.org/en/library/rcd-non-state-actors/. [51]

Rogers et al. (2012), "A vision for human well-being: Transition to social sustainability", *Current Opinion in Environmental Sustainability*, Vol. 4, pp. 61-73, http://dx.doi.org/10.1016/j.cosust.2012.01.013. [86]

Saith, A. (2006), "From universal values to Millennium Development Goals: Lost in translation", *Development and Change*, Vol. 37/6, pp. 1167-1199, http://dx.doi.org/10.1111/j.1467-7660.2006.00518.x. [88]

Shepherd, T. (2019), "Storyline approach to the construction of regional climate change information", *Proceedings of the Royal Society A*, Vol. 475/20190013, http://dx.doi.org/10.1098/rspa.2019.0013. [21]

Sherman, M. and J. Ford (2014), "Stakeholder engagement in adaptation interventions: An evaluation of projects in developing nations", *Climate Policy*, Vol. 14/3, pp. 417-441, http://dx.doi.org/10.1080/14693062.2014.859501. [57]

UCS (2016), *Toward Climate Resilience A Framework and Principles for Science-Based Adaptation*, Union of Concerned Scientists, Cambridge, MA, US, https://www.ucsusa.org/resources/toward-climate-resilience#ucs-report-downloads. [20]

UN (2017), *The New Urban Agenda*, United Nations Human Settlements Programme Secretariat, Nairobi, http://habitat3.org/wp-content/uploads/NUA-English.pdf. [60]

UN (2015), *Transforming our world: The 2030 Agenda for Sustainable Development*, United Nations, New York, https://sustainabledevelopment.un.org/post2015/transformingourworld (accessed on 24 January 2020). [39]

UNDP (2018), *UNDP Climate Change Adaptation: Engaging Private Sector*, United Nations Development Programme, New York, https://www.adaptation-undp.org/privatesector/. [74]

UNDRR (2020), *Integrating Disaster Risk Reduction and Climate Change Adaptation in the UN Sustainable Development Cooperation Framework*, UNDRR, https://unsdg.un.org/resources/integrating-disaster-risk-reduction-and-climate-change-adaptation-un-sustainable. [38]

UNDRR (2019), *Words into Action guidelines: Implementation guide for local disaster risk reduction and resilience strategies*, UNDRR, https://www.undrr.org/publication/words-action-guidelines-implementation-guide-local-disaster-risk-reduction-and. [37]

UNDRR (2019), *Words into Action-guidelines: Developing national disaster risk reduction strategies*, UNDRR, https://www.undrr.org/publication/words-action-guidelines-developing-national-disaster-risk-reduction-strategies. [36]

UNDRR (2015), *Sendai Framework for Disaster Risk Reduction 2015-2030*, United Nations Office for Disaster Risk Reduction, Geneva, https://www.undrr.org/publication/sendai-framework-disaster-risk-reduction-2015-2030 (accessed on 24 January 2020). [24]

UNEP (2019), "Maladaptation to climate change", in *UNEP Frontiers 2018/19 Emerging Issues of Environmental Concern*, United Nations Environment Programme, Nairobi, http://www.unenvironment.org. [64]

UNEP (2019), "NBS Contributions Platform", webpage, https://www.unenvironment.org/fr/node/25257 (accessed on 12 February 2020). [84]

UNEP DTU Partnership (2018), *Private-sector Action in Adaptation: Perspectives on the Role of Micro, Small and Medium-size Enterprises*, UNEP DTU Partnership, Copenhagen, https://unepdtu.org/publications/private-sector-action-in-adaptation-perspectives-on-the-role-of-micro-small-and-medium-size-enterprises/. [73]

UNESCO (2017), *Local Knowledge, Global Goals*, United Nations Educational, Scientific and Cultural Organization, Paris, http://www.unesco.org/new/fileadmin/MULTIMEDIA/HQ/SC/pdf/ILK_ex_publication_E.pdf. [66]

UNFCCC (2019), *Compendium on Comprehensive Risk Management Approaches*, United Nations Framework Convention on Climate Change, Bonn, https://unfccc.int/sites/default/files/resource/FINAL_AA3_Compendium_September_2019%28revised%29.pdf. [26]

UNFCCC (2019), "Supplementary Materials to the NAP Technical Guidelines", webpage, https://www4.unfccc.int/sites/NAPC/Guidelines/Pages/Supplements.aspx (accessed on 17 November 2020). [33]

UNFCCC (2015), "The Paris Agreement", webpage, https://unfccc.int/process-and-meetings/the-paris-agreement/the-paris-agreement (accessed on 20 January 2020). [10]

University of Oxford (n.d.), "Nature-based Solutions Evidence Platform", webpage, https://www.naturebasedsolutionsevidence.info/evidence-tool/ (accessed on 12 February 2020). [83]

UNSD (2018), *Indicator 17.15.1: Extent of use of country-owned results frameworks and planning tools by providers of development cooperation*, (database), https://unstats.un.org/sdgs/metadata/?Text=&Goal=17&Target=17.15 (accessed on 30 January 2020). [55]

Vivideconomics (2020), "Greenness of Stimulus Index", webpage, https://www.vivideconomics.com/casestudy/greenness-for-stimulus-index/ (accessed on 30 July 2020). [4]

Watson-Grant, S., K. Xiong and J. Thomas (2016), *Country Ownership in International Development: Toward a Working Definition*, Measure Evaluation, University of North Carolina, https://www.measureevaluation.org/resources/publications/wp-16-164. [43]

Weaver, C. et al. (2017), "Reframing climate change assessments around risk: Recommendations for the US National Climate Assessment", *Environmental Research Letters*, Vol. 12/9, http://dx.doi.org/10.1088/1748-9326/aa846a. [18]

WFP (2020), *WFP Global Update on COVID-19: November 2020. Growing Needs, Response to Date and What's to Come in 2021*, World Food Programme, Rome, https://docs.wfp.org/api/documents/8162681183bd492ab8e1cfc66435c956/download/. [1]

Ye Zou, S. and S. Ockenden (2016), "What Enables Effective International Climate Finance in the Context of Development Co-operation?", *OECD Development Co-operation Working Papers*, No. 28, OECD Publishing, Paris, https://dx.doi.org/10.1787/5jlwjg92n48x-en. [58]

Zscheischler, J. et al. (2020), "Multivariate extremes and compound events", in Sillmann, J., S. Sippel and S. Russo (eds.), *Climate Extremes and their Implications for Impact and Risk Assessment*, Elsevier, http://dx.doi.org/10.1016/B978-0-12-814895-2.00004-5. [31]

3. Mechanisms for strengthening climate resilience

This chapter presents four mechanisms that provide opportunities for governments and development co-operation providers to integrate climate resilience considerations into their decision making and implementation of actions. These mechanisms are: i) multi-level governance and policy cycles; ii) sector-level approaches; iii) financial management and instruments; and iv) monitoring, evaluation and learning. Each mechanism provides a checklist for action, rationale for the importance of the mechanism, recommended actions and references to tools and guides.

3.1. Multi-level governance and policy cycles

3.1.1. Checklist for action

Actions	Actor(s)[1]
Build inclusive governance arrangements for climate resilience	
✓ Identify groups of society in particularly vulnerable social, cultural, economic or environmental circumstances (e.g. women, the elderly, people with disabilities, Indigenous peoples, religious minorities and other marginalised populations).	Governments with support from dev-co2
✓ Analyse the needs of those vulnerable groups of society and identify underlying factors for their vulnerability.	Governments with support from dev-co
✓ Build mechanisms for stakeholder participation into the local governance arrangements (e.g. formal and informal consultation processes for policy making, multi-stakeholder advisory committees, organised forums for discussion).	Governments with support from dev-co
✓ Engage with non-state actors, such as CSOs and the private sector, for assessing climate risks and associated development challenges, and discussing policy options to address them in a transparent manner.	Governments and dev-co
Empower local action by facilitating collaboration across levels of governance	
✓ Facilitate dialogues among actors across levels of government to ensure that strategies to build climate resilience at national and sub-national levels are complementary and mutually reinforcing.	Governments
✓ Identify existing good practices by local actors, and build upon, replicate and expand such practices for different communities and regions through training and information exchange.	Governments and dev-co
✓ Build on existing local governance arrangements to link climate resilience with the policy processes for local socio-economic development.	Governments with support from dev-co
✓ Build, where relevant, on the government's initiatives in decentralisation to promote local-level action on climate resilience.	Governments with support from dev-co
Develop governance mechanisms for adaptive decision making	
✓ Establish and enhance governance arrangements that support adaptive decision making for climate resilience in the context of the uncertainty presented by climate change.	Governments with support from dev-co
✓ Explore and apply methodological tools to support adaptive decision making (e.g. the vertical and horizontal exchange of information, robust decision making, dynamic adaptive policy pathways, storyline approaches).	Governments and dev-co
✓ Support continuous learning about the evolving climate risks, and adjust ongoing or planned measures for climate resilience where possible.	Governments and dev-co
Enhance governance for greater coherence across different development agendas	
✓ Gain high-level political support for cross-sectoral policy co-ordination, while keeping the co-ordination process transparent.	Governments
✓ Ensure that sector ministries and agencies have information and incentives to integrate climate resilience across their portfolios, and that they are aligned and consistent with objectives of NDCs, NAPs and other policies on climate change and disaster risk reduction.	Governments with support from dev-co
✓ Make use of sector ministries and agencies with a local presence to integrate national-level climate policies into local development plans on different policy agendas and vice-versa.	Governments with support from dev-co
✓ Strengthen the mandate of the sector ministries and agencies to enforce existing regulatory measures, provide them with incentives to support climate resilience, and hold them accountable.	Governments
Integrate climate risks and opportunities throughout a policy cycle	
✓ Explicitly recognise climate-related risks and opportunities in the long-term goals on the country's sustainable development, and in its mid-term national, local and/or sectoral development plans.	Governments with support from dev-co
✓ Enhance the understanding of socio-economic, cultural and political factors that affect the planning and implementation of climate resilience policies (e.g. gender and social norms and laws, interests and incentives among different actors, roles of formal and informal institutions, social, political and cultural values).	Governments and dev-co
✓ Make full use of NAP processes and the revision of NDCs to address underlying causes of vulnerability and develop implementable actions, monitor progress and adjust approaches over time.	Governments with support from dev-co
✓ Put in place a Monitoring, Evaluation and Learning system to pursue mutual accountability of actions taken, and shared learning for improvement of the policy cycle (see also section 3.1.7).	Governments and dev-co

Note 1: Key actors (i.e. governments or development co-operation, or both) who play the primary role in promoting individual actions can greatly vary among countries and sectors. This column nevertheless indicates the likely leader in each of the actions. Some actions are led by governments but in many cases also supported by development co-operation (indicated as "Governments with support from dev-co").
Note 2: Dev-co: providers of development co-operation.
Note 3: Actions in this list are indicative and some may not be relevant to all countries or development co-operation providers.
Other: CSOs: civil society organisations; NAP: National Adaptation Plans; NDCs: Nationally Determined Contributions.

3.1.2. Rationale

Governance is a comprehensive concept of the full range of means for deciding, managing, implementing and monitoring policies and measures with accountability and transparency (IPCC, 2019[1]). An effective governance arrangement also provides an important basis for a government to co-ordinate actions on climate resilience by different ministries and agencies, sub-national governments, non-state actors and development co-operation providers.

Measures to strengthen climate resilience, whether initiated by domestic or external actors, need to consider wealth and power structures, and must not exacerbate economic and social inequality (UNFCCC, 2015[2]; Dazé, 2019[3]; LIFE-AR, 2019[4]; OECD, 2020[5]). A governance arrangement for action on climate resilience must therefore be inclusive to ensure its approaches are informed by the needs of the most vulnerable people. Women and people in marginalised and Indigenous groups often face barriers to participating in decision making, from the household level to national policy-making processes (Dazé and Church, 2019[6]). Developing inclusive governance should thus pay attention to equitable engagement of vulnerable stakeholders in decision making for climate resilience. This includes, for instance, improving their access to information and considering the domestic responsibilities of women (Chingarande et al., 2020[7]).

Inclusive governance arrangements also facilitate the generation of context-specific information about climate risks and possible solutions to address them (IPCC, 2014[8]). Governance arrangements that foster coherence between climate policies and other policy agendas can also help governments pursue broader sustainable development goals. Such policy coherence may contribute to improving efficiency in the use of financial and human resources, and minimising misalignment between different policy objectives (e.g. climate mitigation, health and well-being, agriculture sector development, disaster risk reduction, water resource management and conservation of biodiversity) (Worker and Northrup, 2018[9]; UCS, 2016[10]; OECD, 2020[11]).

Governance in the context of climate resilience is an established area of research. This section draws on the definitions put forward by the Intergovernmental Panel on Climate Change (IPCC) of multi-level governance, participatory governance, and adaptive and flexible governance (see Box 3.1). The Guidance also recognises political economy aspects, such as the underlying incentives or interests of different stakeholders. These aspects greatly influence the way in which levels of governance relate, public participation is organised, and adaptive and flexible governance processes are designed and operated (OECD, 2020[5]). All these aspects must be explicitly integrated into different steps of a country's policy cycle. This ranges from formulation, planning, resource allocation and implementation to monitoring, evaluation and learning (MEL) (OECD, 2009[12]; IPCC, 2019[11]) (see also Figure 3.1 in section 3.1.7).

This section provides governments and development co-operation with guidance on developing governance arrangements that facilitate decision making, co-ordination, local-level actions, participatory processes and policy coherence in support of climate resilience. The section also discusses approaches to integrating climate resilience consideration throughout policy cycles as an integral part of governance. Based on good practices and lessons learnt, this section proposes several approaches around the following action areas:

- Build inclusive governance arrangements for climate resilience.
- Empower local action by facilitating collaboration across levels of governance.
- Develop governance mechanisms for adaptive decision making.
- Enhance governance for greater coherence across different development agendas.
- Integrate climate risks and opportunities throughout a policy cycle

Box 3.1. Definitions of different types of governance

IPCC defines **governance** as a "comprehensive and inclusive concept of the full range of means for deciding, managing, implementing and monitoring policies and measures". Associated concepts include the following:

- **Multi-level governance** identifies relationships among governance processes of different institutions at international, national, regional and local levels. Institutional relationships may take place directly between the transnational, regional and local levels and thus may bypass the national level. Multi-level governance also includes a vertical "layering" of governance processes at different levels.
- **Participatory governance** is a process that enables direct public engagement in decision making. It may use a variety of techniques, such as direct votes, community deliberation and participatory budgeting, among others. The approach can be applied in formal and informal institutional contexts from national to local levels but is usually associated with devolved decision making.
- **Adaptive governance** refers to the evolution of formal and informal institutions of governance for planning, implementation and evaluation of policies through iterative social learning. Similarly, **flexible governance** is introduced as a form of governance at various levels, which prioritises the use of social learning and rapid feedback mechanisms in planning and policy making, often through incremental, experimental and iterative management processes.

Source: (IPCC, 2019[1]) Annex I: Glossary, IPCC Special Report on Climate Change and Land, https://www.ipcc.ch/srccl/.

3.1.3. Build inclusive governance arrangements for climate resilience

Inclusive governance for climate resilience strives for equity in both processes and outcomes of climate resilience measures. It embraces the right of stakeholders to participate in making decisions that affect them. Building inclusive governance therefore calls for explicit efforts to engage with public/private and formal/informal stakeholders, each with their own needs, priorities, political interests and decision-making processes (OECD, 2020[5]; IPCC, 2014[8]; Casado Asensio, Kato and Shin, forthcoming[13]; Woor, 2017[14]) (see also Box 3.2). Inclusive governance should strive to create spaces where stakeholders can interact to identify unintended consequences of certain climate resilience measures (e.g. forestation that reduces pasture areas in highlands, or controlled periodic flooding that limits agricultural crop options). This sub-section highlights a few types of stakeholders whose participation is particularly important but challenging: women, the elderly and people with disabilities, and Indigenous and marginalised groups. It also highlights various roles of civil society organisations (CSOs) and the private sector in inclusive approaches to strengthening climate resilience.

Box 3.2. Political economy factors that influence and inform a policy cycle for climate resilience

Political economy factors often drive and influence decision-making processes for climate resilience (Gogoi, Bahadur and Rumbaitis del Rio, 2017[15]). These factors tend to be highly context-specific and interact in a complex manner. Different members of a community will have varying levels of power and influence, as well as interest in climate resilience. Such power, influence and interest may depend on their socio-economic status, gender, political affiliation, age or ethnicity to name a few factors (Worker, 2017[16]).

A greater understanding of such political economy factors will benefit efforts towards inclusive governance for action on climate resilience. Action on Climate Today, a multi-year programme funded by the United Kingdom to build climate resilience in South Asia, provides some insight on how such political economy factors influence climate action on the ground (Worker, 2017[16]).

Table 3.1. Examples of political economy factors and their potential impact on vulnerability

Political economy factors	Examples of potential impact on vulnerability
Interests and incentives	In a coastal town, more well-off residents, or more organised groups, may build sea walls around their neighbourhood for flood protection, but the wall may lead to increased flood risks to poorer communities.
Role of formal institutions and informal social, political and cultural norms	The policy-making process on climate resilience can be affected by institutional players with "veto" power and whose agreement is necessary to make a decision.
Values and ideas, including political ideologies, religion and culture	Within certain ethnic groups, forests play a particularly important cultural role, which influences how they view forestry programmes. Any external influence may be opposed even if it supports strengthened climate resilience of the groups or forests.

Source: Authors' elaboration based on (Worker, 2017[16]) National Climate Change Governance: Topic Guide, https://gsdrc.org/topic-guides/national-climate-change-governance/.

To better consider these factors, development co-operation providers are increasingly aware of political economy analysis (PEA). PEA is a structured approach to examining power dynamics and economic and social factors that influence development. These factors include key actors, incentives, relationships and resources, and examine the interests and incentives operating in the sector that an initiative is targeting (USAID, 2018[17]; Rocha Menocal et al., 2018[18]). Results of PEA can help facilitate the development of networks or coalitions among different stakeholders around common goals, including those on climate resilience (e.g. public and private actors, community-based groups) (OECD, 2020[5]).

Some groups of people are particularly vulnerable to climate risks due to factors such as their gender, age and disability (Handicap International, 2017[19]). Gender-, disability- and age-responsive climate action is therefore a key consideration for inclusive governance that seeks to strengthen climate resilience (Handicap International, 2017[19]; Dazé, 2019[3]; HelpAge International, 2019[20]). For instance, gender analysis can help governments and development co-operation providers identify differences among women, men, girls and boys in terms of their roles and responsibilities, as well as access to and control over resources for strengthening climate resilience [see Box 3.3 for an example from Côte d'Ivoire, and also (Dekens and Dazé, 2019[21]; Government of Canada, 2017[22])]. An increasing number of international commitments and initiatives have established targets and contributed to tools to integrate gender considerations into climate-related policies, programmes and institutions (Dekens and Dazé, 2019[21]). A similar focus on the role of age or disability in vulnerability to climate hazards is also important [see (Handicap International, 2017[19]; HelpAge International, 2019[20])].

Including Indigenous groups in policy-making processes on climate resilience is also crucial (ILO, 2017[23]). In many cases, Indigenous groups depend for their livelihoods on natural resources that are at significant climate risk. Thus, decision making on climate resilience must consider needs and priorities of Indigenous groups as users of natural resources within the community. Such groups also tend to live in geographical areas that are highly exposed to climate-related hazards, including the polar regions, tropical forests, high mountains, coastal areas, and arid and semi-arid lands (ILO, 2017[23]; Baird, 2008[24]). Inclusive governance therefore should enhance the recognition of these challenges facing Indigenous groups, their rights and institutions. Furthermore, it should facilitate their participation in policy-making processes that can directly affect their climate resilience (Minority Rights Group International, 2019[25]; ILO, 2017[23]).

Box 3.3. Gender analysis for Côte d'Ivoire's National Adaptation Plan

Côte d'Ivoire conducted a gender analysis to inform development of its gender and climate change strategy. The analysis sought to examine how climate change affects women and men differently, and to identify the factors that drive these differences and actions to address them (MINEDD, 2018[26]). The result of the gender analysis provides several recommended actions on gender-specific issues in Côte d'Ivoire's National Adaptation Plan (NAP), including the following:

- Ensure appointment of a gender specialist as Head of the Communication and Gender Unit.
- Clearly define the mandate and role of the specialist so that she or he has responsibility to verify effective integration of gender issues into the whole NAP process.
- Organise training workshops for both gender and climate focal points, focusing on assessment of climate risks and vulnerabilities, and capacities that are also related to gender issues.
- Integrate a gender analysis into assessments of the climate risks and vulnerability, as well as the socio-economic impacts within the priority sectors.
- Identify and include gender-disaggregated indicators to monitor progress on efforts to reduce gender inequality.
- Create gender-sensitive financing mechanisms to better monitor the benefits of interventions for climate resilience.

The roles of non-state actors, such as CSOs and the private sector, are crucial for inclusive governance of climate resilience measures. For instance, given their ability to reach people on the frontlines of poverty, inequality and climate risks, CSOs often bring the vulnerabilities of marginalised populations into public debates and policy processes (OECD, 2020[27]). Similarly, CSOs can play a critical role in monitoring climate risks and vulnerabilities in the long term – after public administrations change or development projects end. CSOs often provide many services (e.g. humanitarian aids after disasters) that some governments do not have the capacity, resources or will to provide. The participation of CSOs in monitoring and evaluation also promotes accountability by providing enhanced scrutiny and transparency (Canales, 2011[28]). Further, CSOs can help local populations obtain climate data and information by facilitating their access to, for instance, research institutions and national meteorological and hydrological service providers (Canales, 2011[28]).

Despite those important roles, gaps remain in effectiveness and accountability of CSOs' development activities. The gaps have also led to concerns among development co-operation providers about CSOs' legitimacy, their results and the challenges of co-ordination among them and with government agencies (OECD, 2020[27]). Box 3.4 provides some examples of approaches to enhanced engagement between governments and CSOs in Latin America and the Caribbean, and the Philippines.

Box 3.4. Partnerships between governments and CSOs: Lessons from Latin America and the Caribbean and the Philippines

While governments are increasingly engaging civil society organisations (CSOs) in climate action, there remains scope to broaden and deepen this engagement. A study by the Inter-American Development Bank examined how it could provide effective support for climate action and sustainable development to the governments of Latin America and the Caribbean through greater engagement with CSOs. Recommendations put forward by the study include: establishing methodologies and indicators to measure the impact of co-operation between the government and CSOs; facilitating access to engagement spaces considering gender and socio-cultural norms and barriers; and institutionalising protocols to promote inclusive dialogues between government institutions and CSOs, among others (IDB, 2019[29]).

In the Philippines, Cadiz City started a participatory planning process for a five-year plan on climate resilience and disaster risk management while recovering from the impact of typhoon Haiyan in 2013. CSOs collaborated with local government agencies and other technical specialists. This facilitated their access to government-established, local and national funds for disaster risk reduction and management. The collaborative relationships between CSOs and the local government facilitated participation of various actors from the private and public sectors in the city. Local governance structures were developed to oversee and steer the plan's activities. These structures have become key to ensure the plan's effective implementation and sustainability and to facilitate communication between local government units, CSOs and other stakeholders (GNDR, 2019[30]).

The roles of the private sector in building climate resilience are also increasingly recognised. The nature of the roles varies significantly among actors ranging from large corporations and small businesses to interest groups such as industry associations, chambers of commerce and co-operatives (see Table 3.2). Examples of their roles include: implementation of activities in support of climate resilience; production of information, goods and services for climate risk management; direct or indirect financing and provision of risk transfer solutions (e.g. insurance) (Schaer and Kuruppu, 2018[31]; UNDP, 2018[32]; Crawford, Church and Ledwell, 2020[33]; Casado Asensio, Kato and Shin, forthcoming[13]). In countries[1] that have participated in the Private Markets for Climate Resilience programme, for instance, the private sector has contributed to weather forecasting, agro-climatic simulations, flood control, soil management, resistant construction materials and infrastructure design, among others (IDB and NDF, 2020[34]).

Strong relationships with key private-sector actors can also help government bodies integrate the voices and views of the private sector into policy making on climate resilience. While appropriate environmental and social safeguards must be applied to private-sector activities, they could better reflect the interest of the private sector. This might allow such climate resilience policies to incentivise businesses to act on climate resilience (Crawford, Church and Ledwell, 2020[33]; Casado Asensio, Kato and Shin, forthcoming[13]). The private sector often creates and facilitates networks that focus on resilience of businesses. For instance, to develop the resilience of micro, small and medium-sized entities (MSMEs) in the Philippines, the National MSME Resilience Core Group lays out strategies such as the National Roadmap for MSME Disaster Resilience. This group enables the government to collaborate with various private-sector actors, including the Philippines Chamber of Commerce and Industry. The priorities of the group include promoting business continuity planning for MSMEs so they can cope with a shock and continue to operate in the aftermath of a disaster (Casado Asensio, Kato and Shin, forthcoming[13]).

Table 3.2. Private sector typology and examples on climate resilience building

Sectors and groups	Type of private-sector actors	Implementation	Facilitator	Data & Info	Financier	Further descriptions based on the case studies
Non-financial institutions	Large-scale enterprises	√	√	√	√	Implement own climate resilience initiatives, form networks to collaborate with other public and private entities, provide technical and financial support to MSMEs through supply chains, provide climate-related information complementing the role of National Meteorological and Hydrological Services. Set up quality standards, including climate resilience.
	Micro, medium and small-sized enterprises (MSMEs)	√	√			Implement own initiatives, form coalitions with other MSMEs and large companies around common interests (e.g. participation in policy-making processes), provide input to local-level climate risk and vulnerability assessments.
Financial institutions	Commercial banks and other non-bank financial institutions	√			√	Design and provide loan and other financial products to be used for measures by MSMEs on climate resilience.
	Insurance companies	√	√		√	Develop and provide insurance solutions against climate and other risks to MSMEs.
Business associations and their networks	Chambers of commerce, business associations, employers' associations, associations of banks/insurance companies/microfinance organisations, etc.	√	√	√		Implement trainings and organise workshops for their members, facilitate collaboration between the government and other public and private stakeholders to help MSMEs build resilience. Develop sectoral norms, codes, labels and certification to increase climate resilience of their business.
Business support service	Start-up incubators	√		√		Support social enterprises that provides innovative products and services that can contribute to MSMEs' resilience.

Source: (Casado Asensio, Kato and Shin, forthcoming[13]). Private-sector Engagement in Strengthening Climate Resilience.

Participation by diverse stakeholders, including those mentioned above, is paramount for inclusive governance. There are, however, still a number of challenges that may undermine the effectiveness of the participatory approaches. For example, some stakeholders may be reluctant to participate in organised dialogues due to time constraints. Different stakeholders may have varying views on the underlying drivers of climate-related vulnerability; involving diverse stakeholders may make it challenging for them to reach a meaningful agreement. Asymmetries of political power can also discourage minority groups to express their perspectives. Participatory approaches can also be manipulated by the organisations promoting them, which may undermine trust between participating stakeholders (Munaretto, Siciliano and Turvani, 2014[35]; Tonmoy, Rissik and Palutikof, 2019[36]). Government actors also often lack capacity and resources for participatory approaches. Inclusive participation tends to be time consuming, and pressures on government officials to move policy development and implementation forward may discourage extensive engagement with stakeholders. These are all common challenges to building effective governance for sustainable development, and relevant to climate resilience as well.

Several governments and development co-operation providers have been working to address such challenges and build inclusive governance arrangements for climate resilience measures. Such approaches can include formal and informal consultation processes, multi-stakeholder advisory committees, social audits and organised discussion forums. The engagement processes should also ensure that participatory processes are transparent, for instance, by making information about the consultations publicly available and outlining opportunities for engagement. Table 3.3 summarises examples of many tools and guides that support such inclusive approaches.

Table 3.3. Build inclusive governance arrangements for climate resilience: Guidance and tools

Guidance and tools	Focus	Audience
Assessing and Addressing Climate Governance Challenges in Low- and Middle-Income Countries (AFD)	This guide aims to help interested stakeholders to identify and address potential domestic governance barriers to implementing and enhancing climate policies and actions.	✓ Staff in governments and development co-operation working on governance for climate resilience
Stakeholder Participation in Climate Change Adaptation (USAID)	This document presents practical steps for encouraging stakeholder participation and tools to disseminate information or gather information from stakeholders.	✓ Staff in governments in charge of stakeholder engagement for climate resilience
"Participate!" (SEI)	These online classes are designed to help readers create and conduct more effective interactive engagements on climate change adaptation and/or disaster risk reduction.	✓ Staff in governments and development co-operation interested in tools to facilitate interactive engagement with stakeholders
Quick Reference Guide Gender & Climate (Netherlands)	This guide aims to foster understanding and commitment to the integration of gender equality into climate activities.	✓ Staff in governments and development co-operation
Toolkit for a Gender-Responsive Process to Formulate and Implement National Adaptation Plans (IISD)	This toolkit is designed to support country efforts to pursue a gender-responsive NAP process, while also complementing the UNFCCC Technical Guidelines for the NAP Process.	✓ Staff in governments and development co-operation whose work includes NAP process
Gender Analysis (Canada)	This website provides key objectives, steps and useful resources for gender analysis in development co-operation.	✓ Development co-operation
Mainstreaming Gender in Green Climate Fund Projects (GCF)	This toolkit guides stakeholders on how to include women, girls, men and boys from socially excluded and vulnerable communities in all aspects of finance for climate action.	✓ Staff in governments and development co-operation whose work includes NAP process
Age-Inclusive Disaster Risk Reduction Toolkit (HelpAge International)	This toolkit adopts a practical approach to age-inclusive disaster risk reduction, using tools and methods that strengthen inclusion.	✓ Governments and development co-operation
Disability Inclusion in Disaster Risk Management (GFDRR)	This document illustrates promising practices related to disability-inclusive disaster risk management and identifies key gaps in knowledge and practice.	✓ Development co-operation
Indigenous Peoples and Climate Change (ILO)	This report outlines various factors that make Indigenous peoples particularly vulnerable to climate change, and what could be done to support them in their role as agents of change to promote action on climate resilience.	✓ Governments and development co-operation
Toolkit for Engaging the Private Sector in National Adaptation Plans (IISD)	This toolkit aims to help governments develop strategies for effective engagement of private-sector actors in the NAP process.	✓ Staff in governments responsible for private sector engagement in climate resilience
Governments and Civil Society Advancing Climate Agendas (IDB)	This document describes, among others, good practices in CSO engagement in the climate change and environmental sustainability agendas.	✓ Staff in governments, CSOs and development co-operation with a focus on climate resilience

Note: CSO: civil society organisation; NAP: National Adaptation Plan; UNFCCC: United Nations Framework Convention on Climate Change.

3.1.4. Empower local action by facilitating collaboration across levels of governance

A focus on climate resilience requires a good understanding of the impact of climate change on local livelihoods and development, as well as on local ecosystems (Vermeulen et al., 2013[37]; LIFE-AR, 2019[4]). In most countries, national governments oversee development of climate-related policy objectives and frameworks. However, local actors – such as sub-national governments, communities, local businesses and their networks, and CSOs – are at the forefront of planning and implementing individual measures (Dazé, Price-Kelly and Rass, 2016[38]; OECD, 2020[11]; Casado Asensio, Kato and Shin, forthcoming[13]).

Local actors, including Indigenous groups, often have detailed knowledge on the specific climate hazards and causes of the underlying vulnerabilities in their communities, as well as local experiences of past weather- or climate-related events and local responses to them (ILO, 2017[23]). Such actors are also often in a good position to resolve tensions among different actors within the community (LIFE-AR, 2019[39]; OECD, 2020[5]). Local action for climate resilience can also better deal with issues of gender inequality and social exclusion through local women's organisations or networks (Dazé and Church, 2019[6]). Some development co-operation providers support such organisations. Resilient, Inclusive, and Sustainable Environments (RISE) Challenge, for example, provides grants to environmental and gender organisations. RISE Challenge supports interventions to address gender equality through a range of environmental programmes around the world, including in Colombia, the Democratic Republic of Congo, Fiji, Guatemala, Kenya, Peru, Uganda and Viet Nam (USAID, 2019[40]).

Experience of developing countries, including Least Developed Countries (LDCs), suggests that locally planned actions for climate resilience tend to address local specificities in climate risks more effectively than top-down approaches (Ensora et al., 2016[41]; Dunford, 2018[42]; LIFE-AR, 2019[39]). Locally-led approaches are increasing (OECD, 2020[11]; LIFE-AR, 2019[39]; UNCDF, 2019[43]). For example, local climate change adaptation plans are being developed in countries such as Benin, Bhutan, Lao People's Democratic Republic, Nepal, Mozambique, the Philippines and Tuvalu. In addition, local-level early warning systems are emerging in, for instance, the Pacific states and Viet Nam. Meanwhile, other countries such as South Africa, the Philippines, Fiji and Tanzania are embarking on urban climate change actions.

Despite the recognised role of local actors in managing climate risks, they often face significant financial, technical and human resource constraints to plan and implement locally-led actions effectively (Dazé, Price-Kelly and Rass, 2016[38]; OECD, 2020[11]). Multi-level co-ordination aims to help address such challenges by ensuring that annual, medium-term and long-term plans at the local level factor in climate risks and opportunities. Such processes should also have opportunities to access necessary funding (UNCDF, 2019[43]) (see examples in Box 3.5). Locally-led actions should also be connected to the national level actions, and multi-level co-ordination can, in turn, facilitate the inclusion of local realities into national policies on climate resilience [e.g. National Adaptation Plans (NAPs)] (Dazé, Price-Kelly and Rass, 2016[38]). In many countries, this top-down and bottom-up interaction is complemented by horizontal co-ordination across different stakeholders and sectors, including the private sector, CSOs and academia.

To operationalise multi-level co-ordination for climate resilience, lessons can be learnt from the ongoing development of NAPs and sector-specific development plans that focus on climate resilience These could include policies on climate-smart agriculture, sustainable forestry and resilient urban development (Ziervogel et al., 2019[44]; Dazé, Price-Kelly and Rass, 2016[38]; UNCDF, 2019[43]; Aytur, Hecht and Kirshen, 2015[45]).

Lessons can also be drawn from countries such as Ghana, Peru and the Philippines that already have governance arrangements to link climate resilience with national and local development planning (OECD, 2020[11]). Examples of such lessons are summarised below, while Table 3.4 outlines guidance and tools that may support local action by enhancing co-ordination across levels of governance:

- Facilitate dialogue among actors across levels of government to ensure that policies and plans for climate resilience at the national and local levels are complementary and mutually reinforcing.
- Build on existing local governance arrangements to link climate resilience with local policy processes.

- Identify local institutional arrangements that are already functioning well, and design technical assistance programmes on climate resilience accordingly to build upon or replicate such arrangements.
- Build on the government's initiatives in decentralisation where relevant, revising any guidelines on decentralisation to incorporate issues related to climate resilience.
- Develop knowledge management systems (e.g. hosted by local research institutes or universities) that draw on both local knowledge and top-down scientific data and information.

Table 3.4. Empower local action by facilitating collaboration across levels of governance: Guidance and tools

Guidance and tools	Focus	Audience
Vertical Integration in National Adaptation Plan Processes (NAP Global Network)	This document provides background on the rationale for linking national and sub-national adaptation efforts, drawing on the policy framework and guidance for the process. It focuses on institutional arrangements, information, capacity building, planning, implementation, and monitoring and evaluation as key points for vertical integration into NAP processes.	✓ Staff in national and sub-national governments (those working on NAP and other stakeholders interested in strengthening vertical integration)
Urban Adaptation Support Tool (EEA)	This tool was developed as a practical guide to assist cities, towns and other local authorities in developing, implementing and monitoring climate change adaptation plans in urban areas.	✓ National and sub-national government officials and development co-operation practitioners working on urban climate change adaptation
Financing Local Adaptation to Climate Change (UNDCF)	As a synthesis of performance-based climate resilience grants by UN Capital Development Fund (UNCDF), this document provides key lessons on how to enhance local government capacities to handle climate finance and draws attention to the role of local authorities in addressing climate change challenges.	✓ Sub-national governments and their local and national stakeholders
The 8 Steps: Practical Method for Developing Local DRR Strategies/Plans (JICA)	This guide provides a practical method to develop local disaster risk reduction (DRR) strategies and plans with concrete measures for investment.	✓ Officials in planning ministries and/or sub-national governments
Climate Vulnerability and Capacity Analysis (CVCA) Handbook: Informing Community-Based Adaptation, Resilience and Gender Equality (CARE International)	This handbook guides a participatory process of gathering and analysing information on community-level vulnerability to climate change and the capacity to adapt, applying a gender lens to the process.	✓ Staff in national and sub-national governments
Adaptation Planning and Local Early Action Plan: A Guide for Indigenous Communities (Lynes and Byod)	This guide aims to support communities in weaving local knowledge into scientific data that will help them prepare and implement practical strategies for community-led adaptation.	✓ Local Indigenous communities and those who support them
Words into Action guidelines: Implementation guide for local disaster risk reduction and resilience strategies (UNDRR)	This guide aims to support local governments (authorities, planners and managers at city or other sub-national levels) in developing and implementing a holistic and integrated local DRR strategy.	✓ Local officials ✓ Other stakeholders with a focus on disaster risk reduction
Flood Resilience Portal (Zurich Flood Resilience Alliance)	The portal provides practitioners who live and work in flood-affected communities with easy access to the resources they need to build resilience to floods.	✓ Local officials ✓ Other stakeholders with a focus on flood resilience

Box 3.5. Examples of mechanisms for local-level resource mobilisation for climate resilience

The Local Climate Adaptive Living (LoCAL) Facility of the UN Capital Development Fund is a mechanism to integrate climate change adaptation into local governments' planning and budgeting systems (with financial support from the European Union and Sweden). LoCAL combines its capacity building support with performance-based climate resilience grants to ensure programming and verification of climate change expenditures at the local level (UNCDF, 2020[46]). To date, LoCAL is active in more than 20 countries across Africa and Asia, improving community resilience for some 11 million people through the realisation of more than 1 200 local interventions in support of climate resilience. LoCAL's publication *Financing Local Adaptation to Climate Change: Experience with Performance-Based Climate Resilience Grants Mechanism* was endorsed by the Least Developed Countries Expert Group to the United Nations Framework Convention on Climate Change. It was a supplement to its National Adaptation Plan Technical Guidelines (see also Table 3.4).

The governments of Mali, Senegal, Tanzania, Kenya and the Philippines have also piloted devolved climate finance approaches to fund measures for climate change resilience. These approaches establish nationally owned mechanisms to channel climate-related finance to sub-national governments. This includes the creation of local climate adaptation funds that operate under the discretionary authority of elected local authorities with transparent fiduciary mechanisms and high levels of accountability to local communities (LIFE-AR, 2019[39]). The funds can be capitalised from various sources, including local government budgets and national funds dedicated to, for instance, climate change as well as disaster risk reduction and management. Bilateral and multilateral providers of development finance may also provide finance to these funds (LIFE-AR, 2019[39]; OECD, 2020[11]).

3.1.5. Develop governance mechanisms for adaptive decision making

Most decisions related to climate resilience are made under the uncertainties presented by climate change and various other factors. They include the projections of climate change and its associated impacts; external shocks unrelated to climate change; and the evolution of socio-economic, as well as technological contexts. Governments and other stakeholders, including development co-operation, therefore need to adapt their ongoing or planned activities to evolving circumstances (Haasnoot et al., 2013[47]).

Governments and development co-operation may make their decisions adaptive based on multiple considerations. For instance, "flexibility" enables actions to change, evolve or be adjusted as new information or circumstances emerge. This could include nature-based solutions, business continuity management in disasters and beach nourishment against coastal erosion. "Robustness" makes actions and their functionality work over a range of climate scenarios to accommodate the increasing frequency and intensity of extreme events. One example of robustness would be building infrastructure to a higher standard. Another is having excess capacity and back-up systems for the infrastructure to help maintain core function in the event of a disaster (Hardoy et al., 2018[48]; WEF, 2012[49]; Vallejo and Mullan, 2017[50]).

A governance arrangement that enables such adaptive decision making can benefit from the perspectives of diverse national and local stakeholders, their shared objectives on climate resilience, and experimentation and learning (Fünfgeld, 2012[51]; Munaretto, Siciliano and Turvani, 2014[35]; IPCC, 2019[1]; Tonmoy, Rissik and Palutikof, 2019[36]). An adaptive governance arrangement should therefore facilitate vertical and horizontal exchange of information for consensus building among different stakeholders. These could include government agencies, local communities, development co-operation, the private sector, civil society and academia (Worker and Northrup, 2018[9]; Roelich and Giesekam, 2019[52]). To promote such exchange, scientific information on climate risks and their impacts should be in a form that is accessible and relevant to local stakeholders (Dazé, Price-Kelly and Rass, 2016[38]; Worker and Northrup, 2018[9]) (see also section 4.1).

The experimental nature of adaptive governance for climate resilience implies the continuous modification of measures as new information becomes available (Munaretto, Siciliano and Turvani, 2014[35]). For instance, coastal protection or water storage infrastructure could allow for mid-term adjustments as severity of storms increases and floods occur more often with climate change (Porthin et al., 2013[53]). This experimental aspect of adaptive governance is closely linked with learning about the evolving climate risks and the adaptive capacities of stakeholders and ecosystems in question. See section 3.4 for further discussion on MEL for strengthening climate resilience.

There has been a range of proposed approaches to support decision making as part of adaptive governance for climate resilience. Challenges remain to apply these approaches in practice. However, they explicitly recognise deep uncertainty in, and the interconnectedness among, various climatic and non-climate factors, as well as non-linearity between climate change and its impacts (McDermott and Surminski, 2018[54]; OECD, 2015[55]). Some examples are listed below and in Box 3.6, while Table 3.5 outlines tools and guidance documents to support adaptive governance for climate resilience.

- **Dynamic Adaptive Policy Pathways** approach aims to establish a framework for action that is informed by a strategic vision of the future and guided by short-term actions that can be adjusted to reflect changing circumstances (e.g. National Adaptive Flood Risk Management in Thailand) (Haasnoot et al., 2013[47]).
- **Robust Decision Making** supports processes to make robust – rather than optimal – decisions under deep uncertainty by testing large numbers of scenarios and identifying low- and no-regret options in different possible scenarios (e.g. an assessment of options for climate-resilient irrigation systems in Nigeria) (Mereu et al., 2018[56]; OECD, 2015[55]).
- **Real Options Analysis** allows economic analysis of future option values and economic benefits of different measures. This approach can be useful especially for infrastructure investments to identify options that are both robust and flexible. On the one hand, these options would be strong enough to withstand downside changes of circumstances. On the other, they would be flexible enough to capture upside benefits if favourable climate conditions arise (e.g. large water storage projects in Ethiopia along the Blue Nile) (Jeuland and Whittington, 2013[57]; OECD, 2015[58]).
- **Storyline approaches** combine climate information with other ecological, economic and social factors, and focus on the impact of actions in a context where changes in the climate are uncertain (Shepherd, 2019[59]).

Box 3.6. An example of adaptive governance from State of Odisha, India

Institutional arrangements for adaptive governance can build on existing local networks, or create new ones where relevant stakeholders can discuss different perspectives and agree on common goals (Aytur, Hecht and Kirshen, 2015[45]). For instance, Odisha state in India developed an adaptive governance arrangement with a strong political commitment after a cyclone caused heavy casualties in 1999 (Walch, 2017[60]). Odisha's adaptive governance arrangement focuses on flexibility and learning for better response to climate risks and disasters through collaboration across different stakeholder groups operating across social and ecological scales within the state. This adaptive approach contributed to fewer causalities in a similarly large-scale cyclone in 2013 (Walch, 2017[60]).

Table 3.5. Develop governance mechanisms for adaptive decision making: Guidance and tools

Guidance and tools	Focus	Audience
Local Climate Change Adaptation Planning (Fünfgeld)	This guide highlights the importance of adaptive governance of climate adaptation and provides, among others, concrete recommendations on using collaboration for better adaptation outcomes.	✓ Government officials, particularly at local level
Tandem Guidance (SEI)	This website provides a framework that aims to facilitate co-design, transdisciplinary knowledge and integration processes for climate services and climate resilience.	✓ Government officials and other national stakeholders (e.g. providers of climate information, intermediaries, knowledge brokers, planners, advisers, decision makers, researchers and practitioners)
Participatory Monitoring, Evaluation, Reflection and Learning for Community-based Adaptation (CARE)	This manual provides concepts and practical tools on how to develop a participatory process that supports monitoring and evaluation, reflection and learning in community-based adaptation projects.	✓ Project practitioners in governments and development co-operation working on community-based adaptation
The Global Learning for Adaptive Management (GLAM)	While focusing on broader topics than climate change, this online platform provides various tools and studies on adaptive management to help identify, operationalise and promote rigorous evidence-based approaches to adaptive governance.	✓ Staff in governments and development co-operation in charge of governance issues

3.1.6. Enhance governance for greater coherence across different development agendas

Climate resilience is closely linked to other development objectives such as poverty eradication, good health and well-being, gender equality and education, as well as water, energy and food security (GWP-Med, 2019[61]). The need for policy coherence is not unique to climate resilience. Implementing the Sustainable Development Goals (SDGs) requires strengthened governance arrangements to address policy interactions across sectors (OECD, 2019[62]). National and local administrations normally consist of different professional functions and institutions with their own internal interests and priorities. The institutional rigidity of these structures can often contribute to fragmentation of responsibilities, information and tasks (IPCC, 2014[8]; OECD, 2020[11]).

A fragmented approach to climate resilience without sufficient consideration for other development objectives may be sub-optimal in terms of efficacy. Moreover, it may also undermine efforts for the entire sustainable development agenda of the country. For instance, exploiting distant groundwater to address water scarcity might discourage investments in long-term solutions such as rainwater harvesting and water treatment and reuse. Some insurance policies may discourage insured farmers to allocate funding for risk reduction measures before disasters hit [see (UNEP, 2019[63]) for more examples]. A government body in charge of environmental issues and climate change (e.g. environment ministries, agencies, committees, co-ordination councils) typically develops climate policies and co-ordinates related government bodies. Planning and implementation of these policies, however, requires commitments and capacity of all implicated sectors. This is not always the case, and especially at local levels (Worker and Northrup, 2018[9]; GCA, 2019[64]). In addition, planning and finance ministries allocate public financial resources to climate resilience initiatives across different economic sectors. This role is important in the light of the impact of these resources on sustainable development. Integration of climate resilience into sectoral investment plans is discussed in section 3.2.5, while section 3.3.5 examines the role of finance ministries.

Governments and development co-operation are already taking steps to enhance the coherence between action on climate resilience and that for other development objectives (OECD, 2020[11]; UNFCCC, 2017[65]). The potential benefits of more coherent approaches are multidimensional, including:

- economic (e.g. increased long-term viability of economic activities, reduced costs of project implementation, greater value-added in the agriculture and tourism sectors)
- social and environmental (e.g. improved public health, increased employment, conservation of ecosystems)
- geopolitical (e.g. enhanced regional co-operation in the management of shared resources) (OECD, 2020[11]; GWP-Med, 2019[61]; UNFCCC, 2017[65]).

Box 3.7 provides some examples of approaches to promote policy coherence. Box 3.8 shows how development co-operation providers can support partner countries in prompting policy coherence for sustainable development at the strategic, operational and technical levels.

Based on experience in development co-operation, the list below outlines key considerations for enhancing governance between climate resilience and development in various areas, while Table 3.6 shows some tools and guides that could support such policy coherence (Worker and Northrup, 2018[9]; LIFE-AR, 2019[39]; OECD, 2020[11]):

- Gain high-level political support for policy co-ordination.
- Ensure that ministries and agencies at the national level have information and incentives to integrate climate resilience across their portfolios, and report back on progress centrally for evaluation.
- Make use of ministries and agencies with a presence at the local level to ensure that national-level directives on climate resilience are integrated into local development plans on different policy agendas (and vice-versa).
- Reinforce the mandate of relevant ministries and agencies to enforce regulations and provide incentives in support of climate resilience and other related policy objectives (e.g. land-use management and environmental protection).
- Enhance transparency of the co-ordination body to ensure its accountability.

Box 3.7. Examples of governance approaches for greater policy coherence between climate resilience and sustainable development

The nature of governance for policy coherence varies by country and thematic focus. Examples of governance approaches to pursuing policy coherence include the following:

- Initiatives that promote climate resilience in the agriculture sector often create linkages between the provision of sub-national extension services by the Ministry of Agriculture and other government bodies in charge of local economic development, climate change and environment, irrigation, animal husbandry, forest management and meteorological services (LIFE-AR, 2019[39]).
- Nature-based solutions for the management of stormwater drainage across watersheds, for instance, requires joint decision making by different local, regional or even national governments and among multiple ministries (agriculture, forestry, and environment, finance, development, transport). This requires active co-operation and co-ordinated action between stakeholders whose priorities, interest, or values may not align or may even conflict (Seddon et al., 2020[66]).
- Integrated landscape management requires co-ordination between different stakeholders to achieve the multiple objectives of managing the shared landscape, such as forests, watersheds, rangelands and coastal zones (Scherr, Shames and Rachel, 2013[67]). Examples of effective horizontal collaboration for integrated landscape management include (LIFE-AR, 2019[39]):

- transboundary management of water resources in the Niger Basin
- catchment-based integrated water resource management in Uganda
- linkages between actors across the value chain for forestry in Gambia
- collaboration between local government, CSOs and communities for city-level landscape management in Fiji.

- Land-use and urban planning can be a powerful tool for building climate resilience across different sectors and households within a given area by using hazard maps that consider climate risks. The quality of construction norms and building regulations are also key to supporting climate resilience. When governments have little capacity to develop and enforce measures for land-use and urban planning, alternative approaches could include allocating the riskiest land such as flood zones to non-residential use (e.g. urban parks to minimise the risk of encroachment) (Hallegatte, Rentschler and Rozenberg, 2020[68]).

Table 3.6. Enhance governance for greater coherence across different development agendas: Guidance and tools

Guidance and tools	Focus	Audience
Water, Energy & Food Security Resource Platform: Tools and Databases (EU)	This online platform on the water, energy and food security nexus provides an extensive list of tools and guides on nexus approaches.	✓ Governments
Ecosystem-based Adaptation Handbook (IUCN)	This document provides a step-by-step guide for setting up an Ecosystem-based Adaptation (EbA) intervention. It promotes an integrated approach to EbA with the ultimate goal of building resilient socio-ecological systems.	✓ Governments and development co-operation
Climate Smart Agriculture Sourcebook (FAO)	This sourcebook consists of 18 modules covering every aspect of planning and implementing climate-smart agriculture policies and projects.	✓ Governments
Coherence Cookbook for Building Resilience in an Integrated Way (GNDR)	This book, with particular focus on civil society organisations, includes recommendations for coherent action in disaster risk reduction, climate change adaptation and sustainable development.	✓ Civil society organisations
Policy Coherence for Disaster Risk Reduction and Resilience: A Toolkit for Practitioners (ESCAP)	This toolkit aims to help practitioners pursue policy coherence for disaster risk reduction, focusing on strategies and plans, mainstreaming, budget and financing, monitoring and reporting systems, institutions, among others.	✓ Governments and development co-operation
KLIMOS – Generating Capacity for the Sustainability Transition	This toolkit is focused on environmental mainstreaming in development co-operation. It consists of i) a database of environmental information, organised by country, theme, sector and publication type; and ii) two screening forms – a quick scan for a first environmental assessment and a more in-depth and robust environmental assessments.	✓ Development co-operation
Achieving Climate Change Adaptation through Integrated Landscape Management (Shames and Sherr)	This report provides a conceptual framework of integrated landscape management for climate adaptation and a concise list of farm, field, household and community adaptation actions in key land-use sectors.	✓ Governments and development co-operation
Disaster and Climate Change Risk Assessment Methodology for Inter-American Development Bank (IDB) Projects: A Technical Reference Document for IDB Project Teams	This reference document aims to provide guidance for IDB project teams to conduct disaster and climate change risk assessments. While intended for IDB projects, the content can apply to activities by other institutions as well.	✓ Development co-operation

Box 3.8. Role of development co-operation in supporting coherent approaches

Development co-operation plays an important role in supporting partner countries in prompting policy coherence for sustainable development. Coherence in approaches to climate change adaptation (CCA) and disaster risk reduction (DRR) is one example. Development co-operation provides technical and financial support for different levels of coherence but is particularly crucial for supporting operational and technical coherence.

- **Strategic coherence**: Support partner countries in aligning their visions, goals and priorities with those agreed upon as part of global commitments on CCA and DRR. At the same time, it can reflect needs of vulnerable groups through facilitating inclusive dialogue among stakeholders at various levels. Development co-operation can also raise awareness and foster incentives across institutions on the benefits and limitations of enhanced coherence. In this way, it can support the mainstreaming of CCA and DRR visions into broader national development strategies.
- **Operational coherence**: Support partner countries in identifying opportunities for coherence in implementation through strengthened policy frameworks and institutional arrangements that support local implementation. Development co-operation is also well-placed to fund and pilot initiatives that support coherence and are aligned with countries' domestic CCA and DRR priorities. There is also value in continuing, replicating or scaling up pilots that have demonstrated potential but that require time and continued support to fully mature.
- **Technical coherence**: Support initiatives to strengthen technical capacities to assess climate and disaster risks and opportunities, and to identify and prioritise CCA and DRR measures. Adequate time must be factored into the support provided to ensure that stakeholders can assimilate new skills and knowledge. Development co-operation can also facilitate learning and exchange.

Source: (OECD, 2020[11]), Common Ground Between the Paris Agreement and the Sendai Framework: Climate Change Adaptation and Disaster Risk Reduction, https://doi.org/10.1787/3edc8d09-en.

3.1.7. Integrate climate risks and opportunities throughout a policy cycle

As an integral part of governance, a policy cycle entails different steps: from formulation, planning, resource allocation and implementation to MEL (OECD, 2009[12]; IPCC, 2019[1]). Efforts to strengthen climate resilience require explicit consideration of challenges caused and opportunities created by climate change. Different factors such as the political structure of a country, socio-economic conditions, values and development priorities will influence decisions at each step (IPCC, 2014[8]).

While recognising that policy making is rarely linear, Figure 3.1 aims to illustrate how different stages of developing and implementing policies (policy cycle) can consider climate resilience. The figure also distinguishes between national and sub-national processes, depicting the sequence and interaction between them. This involves centralised decision making at the national level; policy planning and implementation at the national and local levels; transfer of resources and information; and project implementation, monitoring and evaluation. The bullet points following the figure offer further examples of these steps.

Figure 3.1. Integration of climate resilience into a policy cycle (a stylised model)

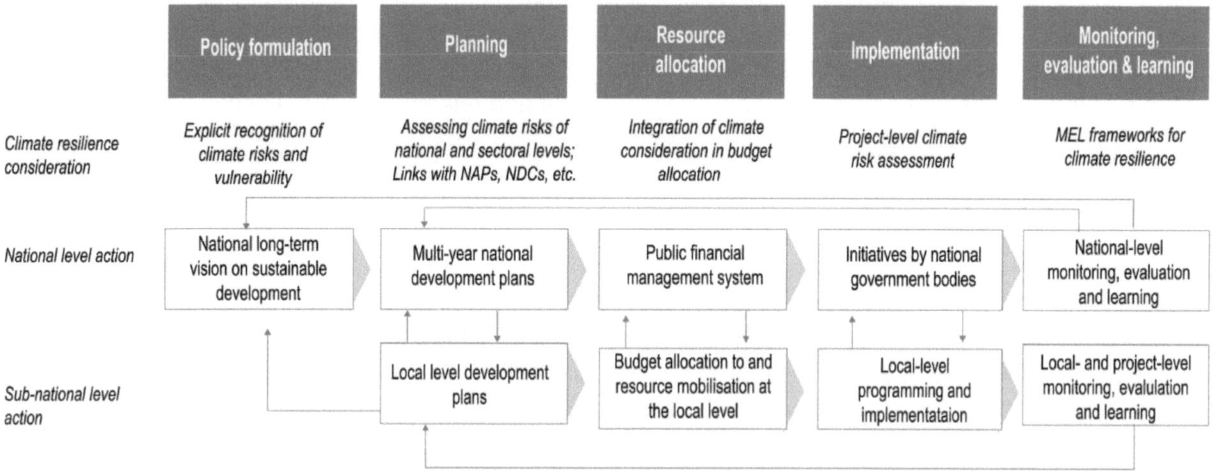

Note 1: Arrows represent flows of resources, information or feedback across different governance levels and stages.
Note 2: NAPs: National Adaptation Plans; NDCs: Nationally Determined Contributions; MEL: Monitoring, evaluation and learning.
Source: Authors' elaboration based on (OECD, 2009[12]) Integrating Climate Change Adaptation into Development Co-operation: Policy Guidance, https://doi.org/10.1787/9789264054950-en, (Dazé, Price-Kelly and Rass, 2016[38]) Vertical Integration in National Adaptation Plan (NAP) Processes: A Guidance Note, https://www4.unfccc.int/sites/NAPC/Documents%20NAP/Supplements/Vertical-Integration-in-NAP-Processes-Guidance-Note.pdf, (LDC Expert Group, 2012[69]) National Adaptation Plans: Technical Guidelines for the National Adaptation Plan Process, https://unfccc.int/topics/adaptation-and-resilience/workstreams/national-adaptation-plans-naps/guidelines-for-national-adaptation-plans-naps.

- **Policy formulation**: Identification of climate risks and vulnerabilities, as well as policy priorities to address them, and explicit recognition of these risks and vulnerabilities in the country's long-term development plan (e.g. a long-term social and economic development vision that highlights climate resilience as a priority policy area).
- **Planning**: Development of multi-year national, local and sectoral development plans that include priority activities and timeframes. These include national and local climate adaptation plans (e.g. NAPs) and sector-specific climate action plans, or sector development plans that integrate climate resilience (e.g. a climate-smart agriculture strategy).
- **Resource allocation**: Translating national and sectoral plans into budget allocations and broader public financial management (PFM) systems on an annual or multi-annual basis (e.g. integration of resilience-related criteria into public investment plans, tracking of development finance flows, and tagging national and sub-national budgets and expenditures, facilitating private-sector investment) (see also section 3.3.4).
- **Implementation**: Implementation of specific actions to manage climate risks and programming of individual investments. Approaches include development and implementation by national and sub-national governments in light of objectives set by national, sectoral and local plans.
- **Monitoring, evaluation and learning**: Pursuing mutual accountability and responsibility for actions taken, and to extract and share learning for further improvements of policy formulation and planning processes in the future.

Countries develop climate-specific strategies or plans such as Nationally Determined Contributions (NDCs) and NAPs. They also develop sector-specific action plans (e.g. climate-smart agriculture strategies, sustainable forest management plans and national disaster reduction strategies). A NAP presents the overarching national vision on climate resilience. However, it may still leave room for local-level interpretation to enable effective implementation that is tailored to the local context. Yet the actions needed to strengthen climate resilience may also go beyond those covered in NAPs. This necessitates coherence between a NAP, sectoral, thematic and transboundary policies within a country. The NAP process aims to achieve this coherence by iteratively integrating climate change adaptation into other plans and policies over time. The UNFCCC website provides a list of supplementary technical guidelines for the NAP process published by the Least Developed Countries Expert Group in 2012 (see Box 3.9). Box 3.10 provides an example of India's National Action Plan on Climate Change and related state-level action plans.

Box 3.9. Technical guidelines and supplementary material for National Adaptation Plan (NAP) processes

National Adaptation Plan (NAP) processes aim to reduce vulnerability to the impacts of climate change by building adaptive capacity and resilience. They also aim to help integrate climate change adaptation into relevant new and existing policies, programmes and activities. This occurs within relevant sectors and at different levels, as appropriate (LDC Expert Group, 2012[69]).

The technical guidelines for the NAP process prepared by the LDC Expert Group (2012[69]) is complemented by a range of supplementary material on specific thematic issues. This material catalogued on the UNFCCC website details different steps related to components of the NAP formulation and implementation. Examples relevant to issues covered in this Guidance include:

- Toolkit for a gender-responsive process to formulate and implement NAPs
- Addressing water in NAPs
- Financing local adaptation to climate change
- Addressing urban and human settlements issues in NAPs
- Financing NAP processes
- Addressing agriculture, forestry and fisheries in NAPs
- Vertical Integration in NAP processes
- Climate services for supporting climate change adaptation: Supplement to the technical guidelines for the NAP process

More materials can be found on the UNFCCC webpage: (UNFCCC, 2019[70]).

Table 3.7. Integrate climate resilience consideration throughout policy cycles: Guidance and tools

Guidance and tools	Focus	Audience
Supplementary Materials to the NAP Technical Guidelines (UNFCCC and various partner organisations)	This website provides a list of supplementary guides and tools that offer in-depth coverage of selected steps of the process to formulate and implement NAPs (biodiversity, civil society engagement, health, climate services, etc.).	✓ Staff in government agencies and development co-operation providers who work on relevant thematic areas to the materials presented on the website
A Framework for Mainstreaming Climate Resilience into Development Planning (IIED) (2013)	This document provides concepts of climate resilience mainstreaming and a practical instrument for government planners to think through the integration of climate-resilient responses into policy.	✓ Government officials in charge of inter-ministerial co-ordination and integration of climate resilience consideration
National Climate Change Governance: Topic Guide (GSDRC)	This guide aims to signpost policy makers and practitioners to the key debates and evidence on the topic of focus, to support decision making.	✓ Staff in government agencies and development co-operation providers
Mainstreaming Climate Change Adaptation in the Pacific (SPREP)	This guide aims to provide a practical step-by-step framework on how to mainstream climate change into development planning and decision-making processes in Pacific Island Countries and Territories (PICTs).	✓ Primarily staff in PICT government agencies and development co-operation providers

Box 3.10. National and state-level action plans on climate change in India

India adopted the National Action Plan on Climate Change (NAPCC) in 2008, which provides a policy framework for adaptation and mitigation to climate change. To achieve its missions, NAPCC called for a State Action Plan on Climate Change (SAPCC) from each state. Most of the Indian states have prepared their SAPCC based on their climate risks and priorities. Figure 3.2 depicts linkages between NAPCC and SAPCC in India and their objectives and relevant stakeholders, based on (Aryal et al., 2015[71]; Government of India, 2008[72]).

Figure 3.2. Linkages between the national and state action plans on climate change

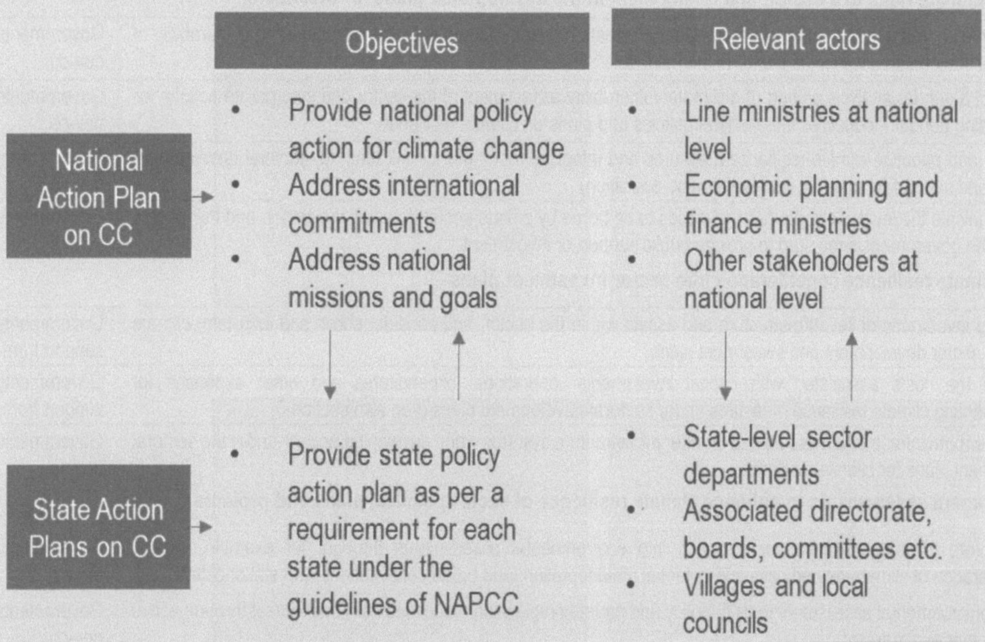

Note: CC: climate change.
Source: Authors' elaboration based on (Aryal et al., 2015[71]) Framework Guidelines and Governance for Designing Local Adaptation Plans of Action to Mainstream Climate Smart Villages in India, https://cgspace.cgiar.org/bitstream/handle/10568/68326/LAPA.pdf?sequence=1&isAllowed=y.

3.2. Sector-level approaches

3.2.1. Checklist for action

Actions	Actor(s)[1]
Establish linkages between national climate goals and sector-specific policies on climate resilience	
✓ Establish clear linkages between national policy frameworks on climate resilience and sectoral climate resilience policies, and align their objectives.	Governments with support from dev-co[2]
✓ Engage sectoral government entities and relevant non-state actors in determining policy objectives and priority actions for climate resilience, and in assigning the responsibilities for overseeing and implementing the actions.	Governments with support from dev-co
✓ Use budget processes to encourage sectoral government entities to ensure their budget proposals consider climate resilience (see also section 3.3.4).	Governments
Assess the climate risks to a sector, and reflect them in the development plans for that sector	
✓ Develop a shared understanding of sector-specific climate hazards, and analyse the exposure and vulnerability of different stakeholders within the sector to the hazards.	Governments and dev-co
✓ Conduct a gender analysis as part of a climate vulnerability assessment of the sector and incorporate actions for addressing gender inequalities into sectoral policies and plans on climate resilience.	Governments and dev-co
✓ Identify and prioritise climate resilience measures and integrate them into, or link them to, sectoral development plans (and support for them by development co-operation).	Governments and dev-co
✓ Communicate the level of climate risk that needs to be borne by private-sector actors in the sector, and the level at which the government is required to provide public support or investment.	Governments
Integrate climate resilience consideration into sector investment plans	
✓ Develop inventories of key infrastructure and assets within the sector, and consider short- and long-term climate risks in sector development and investment plans.	Governments with support from dev-co
✓ Assess the costs associated with capital investments, operational expenditures and other expenses for implementing climate resilience measures under sectoral development plans (see also section 0).	Governments with support from dev-co
✓ Consider both infrastructure assets and broader infrastructure systems when developing actions under the sectoral investment plans for climate resilience.	Governments and dev-co
Use environment assessments to enhance climate resilience of sector policies, plans and projects	
✓ Incorporate climate resilience consideration into environmental assessments through, for example, explicit consideration of climate-related risks and potential maladaptation, and broad consultations with stakeholders.	Governments and dev-co
✓ Apply environmental assessment tools to policy and project preparation processes from their outset through active stakeholder engagement.	Governments and dev-co
✓ Use strategic environmental assessment to systematically evaluate the environmental implications of the proposed sectoral policy or plan.	Governments and dev-co
Enhance climate resilience of the financial sector	
✓ Support financial institutions in developing internal technical and financial expertise to conduct analysis of climate risks to their financial operations and assets, and of opportunities arising from policy reforms in support of climate resilience.	Financial regulators with support of dev-co
✓ Integrate climate resilience considerations, informed by physical and transitional climate risk analyses, into relevant areas of financial sector governance, including regulations, standard setting, incentives and monetary policy.	Financial regulators with support of dev-co
✓ Encourage or require domestic financial institutions to disclose information on climate-related risks to their assets (and where possible their portfolios).	Financial regulators with support of dev-co
✓ Support development of a domestic capital market in a way that also considers climate risks.	Financial regulators with support of dev-co

Note 1: Key actors (i.e. governments or development co-operation, or both) that play the primary role in promoting individual actions can greatly vary among countries and sectors. This column nevertheless indicates the likely leader in each of the actions. Some actions are led by governments but in many cases also supported by development co-operation (indicated as "Governments with support from dev-co").
Note 2: Dev-co: providers of development co-operation.
Note 3: Actions in this list are indicative and may not be relevant to all countries or development co-operation providers.

3.2.2. Rationale

The nature of climate risks and vulnerabilities varies across sectors. Certain sectors are particularly sensitive to the impacts of climate change and variability. Hence, they have greater need to factor climate risks into their policies and plans as a priority. Examples of such sectors include agriculture, energy, health, insurance, tourism, transport and water. A review of 19 NAP documents available on the UNFCCC's website as of the end of December 2020 found all included some reference to priority sectors (Dazé, forthcoming[73]).

The exposure and vulnerability to impacts of climate change can greatly differ between different groups of society within a given sector. Thus, in analysing sector-level climate risks, gender equality and social inclusion are a critical factor for identifying plans and policies to address the risks. For example, large-scale agricultural and extractive industries can be linked to increased human rights violations that disproportionately affect women, children or Indigenous peoples. Consequently, they require specific approaches to protect their rights and build their resilience (Bebbington et al., 2018[74]; ACHPR, 2018[75]).

The climate resilience goals and policies of individual sectors can directly affect their investment activities. Policies with a sector-wide reach include, for example, building codes, design standards, regulations on the price of crops and water tariffs, fiscal support for use of agricultural technologies, and standards for facilities and equipment in health sector. At the same time, development of new policies with a focus on climate resilience, or adjustment of existing ones, may lead to potentially conflicting priorities or interests between different sectors or among stakeholders within a sector (Clar and Steurer, 2019[76]). For instance, promotion of hydropower development for a better energy access might decrease availability of water for small-scale irrigation systems, riparian-corridor ecosystem services and other natural resource-based livelihoods in downstream areas (Buechler et al., 2016[77]).

There can be various entry points to address climate risks through specific sectoral policies, plans and projects. This section discusses how governments and development co-operation can better integrate climate resilience into sectoral policies, plans and projects in light of national commitments on sustainable development and climate change. In this section, the "sector level" includes bodies with policy and planning authority and functions within a given sector in a country (or, in a decentralised system, within a given sector in a state or province) (OECD, 2009[12]). The section uses the terms "policies", "plans" and "projects" as follows based on EC (2005[78]), while recognising that there are many other definitions of these terms:

- A **policy** means guidance that rationalises the course of action of a government for a certain development agenda or agendas, including that on objectives on climate resilience.
- A **plan** means a set of proposed actions linked to objectives set out in the policy, possibly with a timeframe and associated costs and investment plans.
- A **project** means an individual activity that aims to contribute to, or is in line with, the objectives of the policy and plan.

A sectoral focus on climate resilience by individual ministries or development co-operation must build on the knowledge and expertise of those institutions and sector experts. In the agriculture sector, for example, several questions can be asked. How will changes in maximum temperature affect arable lands? Will crop changes or diversification of farming practices be needed? How will these adaptation measures affect the livelihood strategies of women and men? How will such changes be made, and by whom? In the energy sector, the risk of changes in precipitation due to climate change could lead to a significant change in a country's long-term potential for hydropower development options. How might the relevant infrastructure be resilient to slow and rapid onset events?

Actors that play an important role in strengthening climate resilience at the sector level include line ministries and agencies, sector-specific commissions and parliamentary committees focused on sectoral issues (OECD, 2009[12]). They may also include local offices of sectoral ministries and sectoral departments of sub-national governments (see also section 3.1.4). In many developing countries, development co-operation and CSOs with a sectoral focus also support such efforts. The selection of priority sectors may be influenced by their perceived economic importance, the relative power of different ministries and entities, or the availability of information about climate risks on particular sectors (i.e. sectors whose climate risks are better understood might have a higher priority) (Dazé, forthcoming[73]). Nevertheless, sectoral approaches can present important and practical entry points for integrating climate resilience aspects into development of individual sectors.

Focusing on such sectoral processes, this section outlines approaches for governments and development co-operation to integrate climate resilience into policies, plans and projects. It focuses on individual sectors and issues listed below, and reflects national-level goals on climate resilience. Some of these approaches can also be closely linked to governance arrangements for policy coherence across policy agendas, integration of climate resilience into different steps of the policy cycle, and inclusive and multi-level engagement processes as highlighted in section 3.1:

- Establish linkages between national climate goals and sector-specific policies on climate resilience.
- Assess the climate risks to a sector, and reflect them in the development plans for that sector.
- Integrate climate resilience consideration into sector investment plans.
- Use environment assessments to enhance climate resilience of sector policies, plans and projects.
- Enhance climate resilience of the financial sector.

3.2.3. Establish linkages between national climate goals and sector-specific policies on climate resilience

A focus on climate resilience at the sector level needs to be aligned with the country's development goals and complementary policies and plans, particularly those on climate resilience. These goals, policies and plans set out the strategic direction on different development agendas, including on economic growth, poverty eradication, well-being, gender equality and climate change. These, in turn, guide the development of sectoral policies, including their approach to climate resilience.

The development of sectoral policies on climate resilience often begins with a review of national-level policy documents. These could include national development visions and strategies, national-level climate change policies (e.g. NAPs, NDCs and national climate change strategies). The review could also examine sector-specific development plans (e.g. a national agriculture and food security strategy, an energy-sector development plan and a water sector development plan). This review process can provide an overview of commitments on climate action. It can also outline the broader national contexts that guide development of more detailed measures on climate resilience at the sector level, where most implementation takes place. The process also helps the government align sectoral and national-level objectives on climate resilience (see Box 3.11 for an example from Ghana's National Climate-Smart Agriculture and Food Security Action Plan).

Translating national policy goals into sectoral policies, and establishing clear linkages between the two, benefits the government's effort to strengthen climate resilience in different ways:

- Ensuring that sectoral approaches to climate resilience are consistent with national development frameworks [e.g. India's National Action Plan on Climate Change established eight "National Missions" that guide sectoral and thematic actions (Government of India, 2008[72])].
- Improving understanding of sector-specific climate risks and vulnerabilities, complementing results of national climate risk and vulnerability assessments [e.g. Senegal has been developing its NAP through a sectoral approach, such as agriculture, fisheries, health and tourism, and other cross-cutting thematic components (Casado Asensio, Kato and Shin, forthcoming[13])].

- Informing future discussion on national policy development (e.g. national development strategies, NAPs and NDCs), based on experience in implementing sectoral action plans on climate resilience). See also section 3.4 on monitoring, evaluation and learning).

Coherence between national development goals and sectoral policies involves careful co-ordination across different ministries and agencies. Through budget processes, for instance, an economic or finance ministry, together with a ministry in charge of climate policies, may request sector ministries to identify and articulate the climate risks to their sectors. In this case, sector ministries may need to articulate how measures in their budget proposals consider such climate risks. In Peru, the Presidency of the Council of Ministers and the Ministry of Economy and Finance operate a multi-sectoral budget programme with a budget line for "Vulnerability Reduction and Disaster Response". The budget programme aims to finance disaster risk reduction measures across sectors and levels of governments with objectives aligned to the country's national disaster risk management plan (OECD, 2020[11]).

Table 3.8 provides examples of tools and guidance documents. It focuses on incorporating climate-related risks and opportunities into the formulation and implementation of sectoral policies, programmes and plans. These are considered in light of national goals on climate resilience and broader sustainable development.

Box 3.11. Ghana: National Climate-Smart Agriculture and Food Security Action Plan

The government of Ghana launched the National Climate Change Policy (NCCP) in 2014 as the primary national-level strategy on climate change. To address climate risks to, and vulnerability of the agriculture sector and food systems in Ghana, the Ministry of Food and Agriculture, with its development co-operation partners, also developed the National Climate-Smart Agriculture and Food Security Action Plan of Ghana.

The overall goal of the action plan is to facilitate and operationalise the NCCP for effective integration of climate change considerations into food and agriculture sector development policies and programmes. Consistent with the policy objectives of the agriculture-related focus areas in the NCCP, this action plan aims to:

- develop climate-resilient agriculture and food systems for all agro-ecological zones
- develop human resource capacity for climate-resilient agriculture
- elaborate on the implementation framework and the specific climate-smart agriculture activities to be carried out at the respective levels of governance.

As a first step, the project team that developed the action plan reviewed the various policy documents that guide stakeholders on measures related to climate change and other development agendas in Ghana. This review highlighted the main strands in the policy documents that form the basis for further action on agricultural practice in ways also resilient to climate change. The documents reviewed in the action plan include Ghana's Shared Growth and Development Agenda 2014–2017, the National Environment Policy 2014, the NCCP and the Food and Agriculture Sector Development Policy 2009-2015, among other documents.

Source: (Ministry of Food and Agriculture, 2015[79]) National Climate-Smart Agriculture and Food Security Action Plan, https://ccafs.cgiar.org/publications/national-climate-smart-agriculture-and-food-security-action-plan-ghana-2016-2020#.X6r3lGj0mUl.

Table 3.8. Establish linkages between national climate goals and sector-specific policies on climate resilience: Guidance and tools

Guidance and tools	Focus	Audience
Climate-Smart Agriculture (CSA) Sourcebook (FAO)	This guide aims to promote CSA, consisting of modules on climate change adaptation and mitigation; integrated production systems; support for rural producers with knowledge of CSA; gender in CSA; the theory of change for CSA approach: and a guide to evidence-based implementation at the country level.	✓ Governments and development co-operation working on agriculture sector (e.g. programme managers, sectoral experts, academics, staff at agriculture extension services)
Climate-Smart Agriculture 101 (CGIAR)	This guidance provides various tools and guides on promoting CSA, including the entry points, development of CSA plans and finance solutions, as well as a practical resource library.	✓ Governments and development co-operation working on agriculture sector
Addressing Agriculture, Forestry And Fisheries In National Adaptation Plans (FAO)	These guidelines aim to support developing countries in the formulation and implementation of NAPs in the context of agriculture, forestry and fisheries sectors; and enhancing the integration of adaptation into these sectors' policies, programmes and plans.	✓ Government bodies in charge of climate policies and/or agriculture forestry and fisheries sectors and their development co-operation partners
Promoting Gender-Responsive Adaptation in the Agriculture Sectors: Entry Points Within National Adaptation Plans (FAO)	This document provides an overview of the key issues to consider and main entry points for gender mainstreaming in the development of NAPs for the agriculture sectors.	✓ Governments and development co-operation working on agriculture sector
Addressing Water in National Adaptation Plans: Water Supplement to the UNFCCC NAP Technical Guidelines (GWP)	This document aims to help governments incorporate water-related adaptation needs and opportunities in the formulation and implementation of NAPs, NDCs and national communications. It also aims to enhance the integration of water-related adaptation into broader development policies, programmes and plans.	✓ Governments and development co-operation working on water sector
Climate Change and Water Tools (US EPA)	This website provides a compendium of tools and guides that can be useful for building climate resilience in water and wastewater management sectors.	✓ Government bodies in charge of water and wastewater management
Guidance to Protect Health from Climate Change through Health Adaptation Planning (WHO)	This guidance outlines the process for identifying national strategic goals for building health resilience to climate change, and developing a national plan with prioritised activities to achieve these goals, within a specific time period and given available resources.	✓ Government bodies in charge of climate policies and/or health sector
Operational Framework for Building Climate-resilient Health Systems (WHO)	This framework provides guidance for health systems and public health programmes to increase their capacity in protecting people's health from impacts of climate change.	✓ Government bodies and development co-operation working on health sector
Guidance for Climate-Resilient and Environmentally Sustainable Health Care Facilities (WHO)	This guidance aims to enhance the capacity of health care facilities to protect and improve the health of their target communities in a changing climate; and to empower them to be environmentally sustainable.	✓ Professionals working in health care settings
Climate Change Adaptation in the Transport Sector: Guidance Manual (The Solomon Islands and Australian Aid)	This document provides step-by-step guidance on how to integrate a focus on climate change into transport infrastructure design and management to reduce the economic and social costs to the Solomon Islands.	✓ Practitioners in transport sector

3.2.4. Assess the climate risks to a sector, and reflect them in the development plans for that sector

A sectoral policy on climate resilience needs to be complemented by concrete plans that outline specific measures, responsible actors and relevant timeframes to be implemented effectively. Identifying and prioritising those measures require reliable climate and weather data and information. It also demands good understanding of the socio-economic, technological and market contexts that influence the nature of the climate risks faced by the sector. Finally, it requires knowledge of underlying factors that affect its vulnerability (see also section 4.1). Examples of such factors include the sector's sensitivity or susceptibility to climate hazards, and its lack of capacity to adapt and cope. Assessment of these factors should also consider the social and gender dimensions within the sector.

A gender analysis as part of a climate vulnerability assessment of the sector, as well as incorporating actions for addressing gender inequalities into sectoral policies on climate resilience, can help promote gender-responsive measures for climate resilience. These actions include promoting equitable access to resources, information and support between women and men; involving gender experts in the planning processes of sectoral policies; training sector experts to better understand the gender dimensions of policy priorities for climate resilience; and articulating gender consideration in sectoral funding proposals for climate finance (Dazé and Church, 2019[6]).

Based on information on climate risks and other sectoral contexts, a ministry in charge of climate policies, or a sectoral ministry/agency, should communicate the level of climate risk that private-sector actors need to bear (Hallegatte, Rentschler and Rozenberg, 2020[68]). For instance, governments can set and communicate the level of flood protection which the government is required to provide. This could allow firms to decide where to operate their businesses. It could also help them plan for investment in any additional flood protection measures (Hallegatte, Rentschler and Rozenberg, 2020[68]).

Table 3.9 provides an example of steps to consider during a climate risk and vulnerability assessment at the sectoral level. It suggests how results of the assessment can inform the development or adjustments of sectoral climate resilience plans. Such an approach was used, for instance, in Afghanistan to facilitate multi-stakeholder consultation to promote drought- and disease-resistant wheat seeds in the agriculture sector in hilly mountain areas. The consultation also led to an agreement that farmers would take an active role in co-ordinating and implementing rainwater harvesting with support from Oxfam (Morchain and Kelsey, 2016[80]). Box 3.12 provides other examples from the Former Yugoslav Republic of Macedonia and Fiji on their sectoral plans on climate resilience that have been informed by a climate risk assessment.

Table 3.9. An example of application of climate risk and vulnerability assessment to sectoral plans on climate resilience

Steps	Expected action
Initial climate hazards and vulnerability assessment	Develop a common understanding of climate hazards affecting the sector and of the exposure and sensitivity of different stakeholders to those hazards.
Impact chain analysis	Map and assess potential impacts of hazards and their implications throughout the sector in the short- and long-term. Generate initial ideas on possible actions that can be taken based on the assessment.
Capacity assessment	Assess the capacity needed to implement identified actions, including that of sectoral institutions, their assets, entitlements and governance, knowledge, data and information technologies, etc. Based on the assessed capacity, elaborate and prioritise possible measures for climate resilience.
Alignment of findings with opportunities	Consider which measures identified above could be inserted into existing or new plans, either of the sector itself or of related sectors with which it interacts.

Source: Authors' elaboration based on (Morchain and Kelsey, 2016[80]), Finding Ways Together to Build Resilience: The Vulnerability and Risk Assessment Methodology, https://policy-practice.oxfam.org/resources/finding-ways-together-to-build-resilience-the-vulnerability-and-risk-assessment-593491/.

Various tools have been developed to support assessment of climate risks and socio-economic contexts at sectoral levels (Table 3.10). For instance, the Energy Sector Management Assistance Program Hands-on Energy Adaptation Toolkit is a semi-quantitative risk assessment approach to prioritise hazards and risks to a country's energy sector. This toolkit also helps identify adaptation options (World Bank, n.d.[81]). Another tool called Confronting Climate Uncertainty in Water Resources Planning and Project Design can help demonstrate the robustness of a project to climate change in the water resource management sector. It is based on a bottom-up assessment of the project's vulnerabilities to climate hazards (Ray and Brown, 2015[82]). The Food and Agriculture Organization of the United Nations (FAO) has provided extensive climate risk assessment tools, e.g. for the fisheries and aquaculture sector and the agriculture sector (FAO, 2015[83]; FAO, 2007[84]).

Table 3.10. Assess the climate risks to a sector, and reflect them in the development plans for that sector: Guidance and tools

Guidance and tools	Focus	Audience
Climate and Disaster Risk Screening Tools (World Bank)	Climate and Disaster Risk Screening provides an extensive list of tools and resources to support a proactive approach to consider short- and long-term climate and disaster risks in project and sector planning processes. Various sector-specific tools are also available for agriculture, energy, finance, health, information and communication technologies, industry, transportation and water sectors, among others.	✓ Governments and development co-operation
Information Sources to Support ADB Climate Risk Assessments And Management (ADB)	This technical note is intended to support climate risk assessment experts by providing a compendium of relevant open access resources.	✓ Experts in climate risk assessment
Climate Risk Assessment at Community Level in the Agriculture Sector (FAO)	This document outlines methods needed for assessing climate-related risks at community level, focusing on the agriculture sector.	✓ National and sub-national governments and development co-operation providers
Assessing Climate Change Vulnerability in Fisheries and Aquaculture (FAO)	This document provides an overview of vulnerability assessment concepts and methodologies in fishery and aquaculture sectors.	✓ National and sub-national governments and development co-operation providers
Gender Analysis Toolkit for Coastal Management Practitioners (MFF, SEI, SEAFDEC)	This toolkit provides a practical compendium for coastal and fisheries management practitioners seeking to understand how gender can affect coastal ecosystems resource use and management and coastal resilience.	✓ Project developers

Note: ADB: Asian Development Bank; FAO: Food and Agriculture Organization of the United Nations; MFF: Mangroves for the Future; SEAFDEC: Southeast Asian Fisheries Development Center; SEI: Stockholm Environmental Institute.

Box 3.12. Identifying priority actions to improve sectoral plans on climate resilience

The Former Yugoslav Republic of Macedonia developed and issued a Climate Change Health Adaptation Strategy and Action Plan in 2011. The strategy and action plan envisage objectives and activities on climate resilience to be carried out by the country's health sector in co-operation with other relevant sectors. The strategy aims to create linkages with the climate-related strategies developed by other sectors to respond effectively to climate change risks for health and well-being. Specific goals include promoting a co-ordinated approach by the sectors and relevant institutions in terms of effective and efficient use of available resources; raising public awareness about climate change and its effect on health; establishing an integrated, efficient and effective approach for prevention; early warning and management of the health effects of heatwaves; and protection from climate change-related communicable diseases, among others (WHO, 2014[85]).

The country has conducted climate vulnerability and risk assessment and identified possible adaptation measures. These processes have informed prioritisation of focus areas of the strategy, including the following:

- raising awareness of climate change and its effects on health
- identifying, registering and monitoring climate change and health risks

- improving health system promotion, prevention and timely response to climate change and health risks
- allocating responsibility to the Ministry of Health for monitoring and implementation of the strategy and its action plan.

The strategy also sets out more detailed actions for individual priority areas, their implementation timeframes, roles and responsibilities, indicators for monitoring and evaluation, and financial implication (WHO, 2014[85]).

The Fiji Climate Vulnerability Assessment has identified 125 projects that could help build the country's climate resilience across different sectors. These projects were selected based on climate risks identified through the assessment, and on the national development priority and strategy. The government plans to translate the list of priorities into an investment plan for public assets and infrastructure that identifies costs and responsible public agencies. The exercise could also help the Ministry of Finance use it to estimate additional financing needs for climate change adaptation (Hallegatte, Rentschler and Rozenberg, 2020[68]).

3.2.5. Integrate climate resilience consideration into sector investment plans

A sectoral plan on climate resilience may be accompanied by an investment plan that includes information on the financial needs of planned measures. Examples of such needs include capital investments, operational expenditures and other expenses, such as for capacity building, policy development and feasibility studies (see also section 3.2.7). For instance, a tool called Climate Smart Agriculture (CSA) Investment Plans[2] aims to identify concrete actions for the government, both in the form of investment opportunities, as well as policy design and implementation. CSA Investment Plans aim to inform government, development co-operation providers and the private sector about promising CSA technologies, as well as their associated costs. Zambia's CSA Investment Plan has recommended investments in crop diversification, commercial horticulture, agroforestry and infrastructure to reduce post-harvest losses (World Bank, 2019[86]).

Many countries and development co-operation providers have applied a range of other approaches to consider climate resilience in their sectoral investment planning. For instance, the Rwanda Green Fund prioritises sector-specific projects on climate adaptation among its investment criteria (FONERWA, n.d.[87]). The Swiss Agency for Development and Cooperation (SDC) has also developed guidance for assessing climate, environment and disaster risks of strategies, programmes and projects by development co-operation providers (see Box 3.13). The Asian Development Bank has provided tools for climate-proofing investment projects and relevant technical guidelines (ADB, 2018[88]). These tools aim to help practitioners take a proactive approach to considering short- and long-term climate and disaster risks in sector planning processes, associated investment plans and relevant project development (see Box 3.14).

Infrastructure development often composes a major part of a sector-specific investment plan. Making infrastructure more resilient goes beyond questions of finance. It must also include good governance and the ability to make appropriate decisions on designs, operation and maintenance of the infrastructure. Such decisions should ensure infrastructure is resilient to current and future climate change. In particular, the early stages of infrastructure development (e.g. designing regulations, producing hazards data and developing master plans) can significantly improve its overall resilience with a relatively low resource requirement (Hallegatte, Rentschler and Rozenberg, 2020[68]).

For a systematic climate risk and vulnerability assessment for sectoral investment, governments can also greatly benefit from developing inventories of key infrastructure and assets. These could include power plants and energy networks, primary health care facilities, water utilities and schools, among others. Such an inventory helps government authorities identify facilities at risk or determine priorities for climate resilience investments (Hallegatte, Rentschler and Rozenberg, 2020[68]). The government of Viet Nam, for example, has an inventory of more than 750 health care facilities, detailing their georeferenced locations, types and capacities. This could inform development of climate-resilient investment plans for the sector (Hallegatte, Rentschler and Rozenberg, 2020[68]).

Climate resilience of infrastructure investments in a given sector can be pursued at three different levels (OECD, 2018[89]; Hallegatte, Rentschler and Rozenberg, 2019[90]). The first level is resilience of assets such as power plants, water supply and sanitation facilities, roads and bridges. The second is resilience of services such as interconnected networks, while the third is resilience of users such as people and supply chains. Governments and development co-operation therefore need to plan their investments, bearing in mind the resilience of both the assets and the broader infrastructure systems[3] to manage the climate risks to them (OECD, 2019[91]; Hall et al., 2019[92]; Hallegatte, Rentschler and Rozenberg, 2019[90]). Several tools for sector-specific investment planning in support of climate resilience have been developed, with some examples introduced in Table 3.11.

Table 3.11. Integrate climate resilience consideration into sector investment plans: Guidance and tools

Guidance and tools	Focus	Audience
Climate, Environment and Disaster Risk Reduction Integration Guidance (SDC)	This guidance consists of three modules that help development co-operation providers assess whether their strategies, programmes and projects are at risk from climate change and other environmental challenges.	✓ Development co-operation providers
Guidelines for Climate Proofing Investment (ADB) [Energy] [Agriculture] [Water] [Road infrastructure]	These guidelines present step-by-step methodological approaches to assist project teams in managing climate change risk in the context of the respective sectors.	✓ Project developers in governments and development co-operation
Sector Climate Change Adaptation Guidance Notes (IsDB) [Agriculture & rural development] [Energy] [Water] [Transport]	These guidelines aim to enable IsDB project teams to integrate information on climate risks into project design in the respective sectors. They outline the steps involved, such as climate risk screening, project impact and adaptation assessments, and project implementation.	✓ Primarily IsDB staff (with possible insights for other project developers in governments and development co-operation)
Framework and Principles for Climate Resilience Metrics in Financing Operations (Multilateral, regional and national development banks)	This framework sets out principles, including core concepts and other characteristics of climate resilience metrics.	✓ Development finance institutions
The Hydropower Sector Climate Resilience Guide (IHA)	This guide offers a methodology for identifying, assessing and managing climate risks to enhance the resilience of hydropower projects.	✓ Hydropower project developers

Note: ADB: Asian Development Bank; IsDB: Islamic Development Bank; SDC: Swiss Agency for Development and Cooperation; IHA: The International Hydropower Association.

Box 3.13. Climate, Environment and Disaster Risk Reduction Integration Guidance by Switzerland

The Swiss Agency for Development and Cooperation developed Climate, Environment and Disaster Risk Reduction Integration Guidance (CEDRIG) to help development co-operation providers assess whether their strategies, programmes and projects are at risk from climate change, environmental degradation and natural hazards. It also helps identify whether these interventions could further increase greenhouse gas emissions, environment degradation or disaster risks.

CEDRIG is divided into three modules:

- CEDRIG Light (taking about one hour) helps to decide on the need for a detailed risk and impact assessment.
- CEDRIG Strategic (taking about one day) supports analyses of strategies and programmes, covering i) risk perspectives (adaptation to climate change and degraded environments, and integration of disaster risk reduction); and ii) impact perspectives (avoiding negative impacts on the climate and on the environment and avoiding creation of new risks or exacerbation of existing ones).
- CEDRIG Operational (taking about two to three days) will systematically integrate climate change, environment and disaster risk reduction into an existing or planned project. It also covers the Light and Strategic perspectives.

CEDRIG has been applied to, for instance, programmes and projects on construction of a water treatment plant and improvement of horticulture value chains in Bolivia, Mozambique and Viet Nam.

Source: (SDC, n.d.[93]), The Climate, Environment and Disaster Risk Reduction Integration Guidance, www.cedrig.org/.

Box 3.14. Examples of criteria used by development banks to integrate climate resilience considerations into their sectoral investments

Seven multilateral development banks and members of the International Development Finance Club published a Framework and Principles for Climate Resilience Metrics in Financing Operations in 2019. The framework sets out principles, including core concepts and other characteristics of climate resilience metrics. Together with a high-level framework for such metrics in financing operations, the document also provides examples of approaches to the development and use of climate-resilience metrics, such as the following:

- The Asian Development Bank's Coastal Towns Environmental Infrastructure Project in Bangladesh used the bank's sector lending modality to support investments in a phased manner. The project included a performance-based allocation approach, with investments linked to improved governance criteria, including climate-resilient and participation processes.
- The World Bank's Resilience Transparency Rating System aims to operate at two levels. One would focus on the resilience of projects and the other on resilience achieved through projects. The rating system measures the quality of the inclusion of climate-related risks in the economic and financial assessment of projects. To assess the resilience of projects, methodologies can use climate resilience metrics to express the quality of project design that encompass diagnostics, inputs and activities. To assess resilience through projects, a hybrid approach can combine elements of both quality of project design and outcomes in terms of improved climate resilience of the wider system in which the project is located.
- The Inter-American Development Bank (IDB) has put in place a systematic assessment of disaster risk and climate change risks for its projects. It allows for the financing of USD 5 billion in climate change-related activities in Latin America and the Caribbean in 2019, accounting for 29% of total IDB Group annual approvals. This is in line with the group's goal to have financing for climate change reach 30% of total approvals by 2020.
- The European Bank for Reconstruction and Development is exploring the use of a shadow water price. This price would reflect the full economic value of the water saved in its water infrastructure project in Central Asia to address the region's worsening water stress because of climate change. The project, which was designed to reduce water losses, is estimated to deliver annual water savings of 2.8 million cubic metres per year compared to the pre-project baseline. This could amount to EUR 1.4 million per year as an estimate value of water saved using the abovementioned shadow water price.

Note: This report, published by the Inter-American Development Bank, was developed by African Development Bank; Asian Development Bank; Asian Infrastructure Investment Bank; European Bank for Reconstruction and Development; European Investment Bank; Inter-American Development Bank; International Development Finance Club; and Islamic Development Bank.
Source: (IDB, 2019[94]) A Framework and Principles for Climate Resilience Metrics in Financing Operations, http://dx.doi.org/10.18235/0002040.

3.2.6. Use environment assessments to enhance climate resilience of sector policies, plans and projects

Design of sectoral policies, plans and projects, including infrastructure development, should integrate climate resilience considerations from the outset (UNECE, n.d.[95]). Environment impact assessments (EIAs) and strategic environmental assessments (SEAs) have traditionally been applied to avoid negative environmental impacts of a particular policy, plan, programme or project (see Figure 3.3). Both EIAs (typically at the project level) and SEAs (at the policy, plan or programme level) also present opportunities for incorporating climate-resilience considerations into these different levels of activities.

Figure 3.3. An illustrative example of relations between strategic environmental assessment and environmental impact assessment

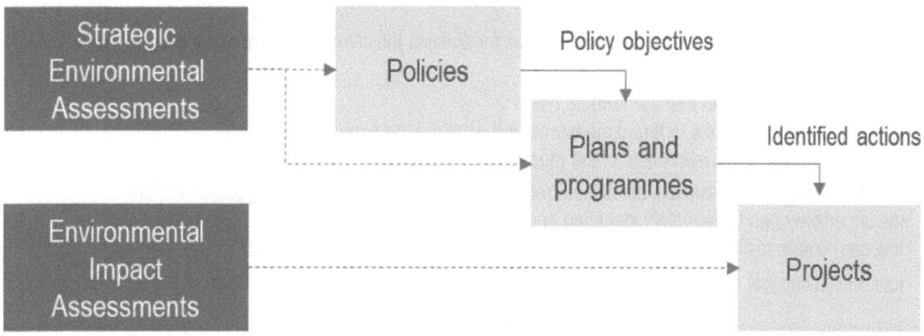

Source: Authors' elaboration based on (Rodrigo-Ilarri et al., 2020[96]) Advances in implementing strategic environmental assessment (SEA) techniques in Central America and the Caribbean, https://www.mdpi.com/2071-1050/12/10/4039/pdf, (EC, 2013[97]) Guidance on Integrating Climate Change and Biodiversity into Strategic Environmental Assessment, https://ec.europa.eu/environment/eia/pdf/SEA%20Guidance.pdf.

Despite the application of EIAs over the past decades, it is often challenging to systematically assess interdependencies of multiple hazards, including those associated with climate change (UNDRR, 2020[98]). An EIA should ideally be integrated into a project preparation process from the outset. This process can be supported through explicit consideration of climate-related risks, broad consultations with relevant stakeholders, and thorough examination of the potential risks of maladaptation (EC, 2013[97]). Potential steps for integrating climate resilience considerations into an EIA include the following:

- Identify a methodology to assess climate risk on the project and the project area.
- Use regional climate models and hazard maps, when available, as input to the EIA process.
- Assess implications of the identified climate risks for the long-term environmental impacts of the planned project.
- Ensure that measures to reduce the environmental impacts, environmental management plans and monitoring efforts within the EIA adequately consider the management of climate risks.
- Consider impacts of extreme weather impacts on the planned project and develop contingency plans (see (IISD, 2016[99]) for further details).

Complementing project-level EIAs, an SEA systematically evaluates the environmental implications of proposed plans or programmes, and possibly also policies, including those at the sector level (Fortun, 2020[100]). SEAs aim to explore ways to address identified climate- and environment-related risks at the early stage of decision making (EC, 2013[97]). Applying SEAs to the development of policies and plans can offer opportunities to enhance the climate resilience of the sector. At the same time, SEAs can prevent its policies and plans from causing adverse effect on the environment or the well-being of the people affected by the intervention (EC, 2013[97]). (see Table 3.12 for examples of steps and key considerations in an SEA).

Table 3.12. Steps and key considerations in Strategic Environmental Assessment processes

SEA steps	Key questions to consider
Screen	Is implementation of the policy, plan of programme likely to significantly affect climate resilience (or be affected by climate change)?
Scope	What are the key climate risks to the policy area in question? What is the current policy context of climate resilience in the country, and how will the planned intervention likely affect the context? Who are the relevant stakeholders and authorities for building the climate resilience of the sector, and how will they be involved in the SEA?
Consider alternatives and assess effects	What are the measures to manage climate risks? What is the feasibility of the different measures and what are the expected impacts? How can potential negative impacts of the measures be avoided?
Make decisions	Does the SEA report clearly explain climate resilience-related issues to support decision making? Has uncertainty been adequately identified and considered? How can climate resilience issues be integrated into a final policy/plan effectively?
Monitor and evaluate	How will the impacts on climate resilience be monitored along with the implementation of the selected policy or plan?

Source: Authors' elaboration based on (EC, 2013[97]) Guidance on Integrating Climate Change and Biodiversity into Strategic Environmental Assessment, https://ec.europa.eu/environment/eia/pdf/SEA%20Guidance.pdf.

Many developing countries have already conducted SEAs for their policies and plans, including those on climate change. In El Salvador, SEAs are applied to assess environmental risks related to its policies on biofuel, energy and metal mining, as well as marine coastal strips (Rodrigo-Ilarri et al., 2020[96]). The government of Montenegro, with support of the European Commission, also conducted an SEA of the country's National Climate Change Strategy (NCCS). The SEA aims to contribute to the reforms in the area of environment and climate change in Montenegro. It focuses on the impacts on the environment of climate change adaptation and mitigation measures proposed by the NCCS, including soft measures (e.g. use of fiscal instruments) (Palerm et al., 2015[101]). Further information on country- and sector-level SEAs to assess policies, plans and programmes are available at (Fortun, 2020[100]), while examples of tools and guides are outlined in Table 3.13.

Table 3.13. Use environment assessments to enhance climate resilience of sector policies, investment plans and projects: Guidance and tools

Guidance and tools	Focus	Audience
Guidance on Integrating Climate Change and Biodiversity into Strategic Environmental Assessment (EU)	This guidance aims to improve consideration of issues related to the integration of climate change and biodiversity into strategic environmental assessments carried out across EU member states.	✓ Governments of EU member states but may also inspire other countries
Guidance on Integrating Climate Change and Biodiversity into Environmental Impact Assessment (EU)	This guidance aims to improve consideration of issues related to integration of climate change and biodiversity into environmental impact assessments carried out across EU member states.	✓ Governments of EU member states but may also inspire other countries
Strategic Environmental Assessment (EU)	This webpage provides an overview of steps for SEAs and a list of tools for conducting SEAs, as well as country examples.	✓ Development co-operation providers
Strategic Environmental Assessment (WB)	This webpage provides several SEA-related documents and publications to promote SEA for incorporation of environmental considerations across plans, programmes and policies.	✓ Governments and development co-operation providers
Climate Change Adaptation and EIA (IISD)	This document summarises some key steps in integrating climate change adaptation into the EIA process.	✓ Governments and development co-operation providers

3.2.7. Enhance climate resilience of the financial sector

Apart from real economy sectors (e.g. agriculture, energy, tourism, water), the financial sector can also be affected by negative impacts of climate change and disasters through different, and overlapping, channels

(Feyen et al., 2020[102]). For instance, climate- and weather-related hazards can trigger losses and tighter liquidity conditions due to stricter risk premiums when a disaster occurs. Damages to infrastructure, higher prices of commodities and energy, and lower productivity, for instance, can negatively affect the repayment capacity of some borrowers, especially when their assets are uninsured. Physical risks of climate change can also impede the pricing accuracy of insurance liabilities. This challenge can cause losses to insurers, which could potentially raise premiums for policy holders, or even cause them to withdraw insurance covers. This may also increase fiscal costs as governments are forced to backstop losses (Feyen et al., 2020[102]; Hallegatte, Rentschler and Rozenberg, 2020[68]).

Central banks and other financial regulators can play a greater role in ensuring that policies, regulations and enabling measures (that guide financial actors across the financial system) address climate risks (Miller and Swann, 2019[103]). More central banks and financial regulators are exploring their roles in identifying and managing climate risks to the financial sector in their own country. As of December 2020, 83 central banks and financial regulators have become members of the Network of Central Banks and Supervisors for Greening the Financial System (NGFS). Of these, around 20% are from developing countries (NGFS, 2020[104]). The NGFS provides a forum for members to develop frameworks for financial policies and regulations in support of assessing climate risk in micro-supervision, integrating sustainability and climate risks into monetary policy frameworks and endorsing mandatory disclosure, among others. The Sustainable Banking Network (SBN) is another community of financial sector regulators and banking associations from emerging markets committed to work on sustainable finance, including for climate resilience (IFC, n.d.[105]).

Central banks and financial regulators have been rapidly developing their methodologies. A non-exhaustive list of examples of such approaches appears in the list below based on several sources (NGFS, 2020[106]; Hallegatte, Rentschler and Rozenberg, 2020[68]; Miller and Swann, 2019[103]; Feyen et al., 2020[102]; EU TEG, 2020[107]). These provide a range of tools developed over the past years, some of which are regularly updated (Table 3.14):

- Support financial institutions in raising awareness and developing internal technical and financial expertise to conduct analysis of climate risks and opportunities.
- Designate climate risk as a material risk for financial institutions, and encourage or require them to disclose information on climate-related risks to their assets and operations, using or based on robust and internationally consistent climate-related disclosure frameworks, including the framework developed by the Task Force on Climate-related Financial Disclosures.
- Integrate climate resilience considerations, informed by physical and transitional climate risk analyses, into relevant areas of the financial sector governance, including regulations, standards setting, incentives and monetary policy.
- For micro-supervision, map transition and physical climate risks (and their transmission channels) to better understand the impacts of climate risk on the financial system.
- Explore methodologies to integrating physical climate risk considerations into stress-testing methodologies for regulated financial institutions.
- Encourage domestic financial institutions to consider integrating enhanced understanding of climate resilience in all investments and lending via the employment of climate scenarios used for stress testing at the level of the financial system.
- Support development of a capital market that is also resilient to climate risks (e.g. credit enhancement issuances by municipalities, promotion of public-private partnership (PPP) projects related to climate-resilient infrastructure and climate resilience bonds).
- Scale up an appropriate use of catastrophe bonds and contingency funds to increase the country's fiscal resilience to the negative impacts of disasters.

Table 3.14. Enhance climate resilience of the financial sector: Guidance and tools

Guidance and tools	Focus	Audience
NGFS publications (The Network of Central Banks and Supervisors for Greening the Financial System)	This webpage gathers the publications and useful materials from the NGFS, including those on environmental risks analysis, monetary policies, climate scenario analysis and prudential supervision in the context of climate change.	✓ Central banks and other financial regulators, as well as development co-operation providers working with them
EU Platform on Sustainable Finance (EU)	This webpage provides information and materials on EU-level work on sustainable finance such as the EU taxonomy to determine environmentally sustainable economic activities; an EU Green Bond Standard; methodologies for EU climate benchmarks and disclosures; and guidance to improve corporate disclosure of climate-related information.	✓ Primarily for experts in sustainable finance, working with the European Union, but providing insights and tools to central banks and other financial regulators, as well as development co-operation providers working with them
TCFD Publications (Task Force on Climate-related Financial Disclosures, TCFD)	This webpage provides various materials on reporting on climate-related financial information, scenario analysis for non-financial companies and risk management integration, among others, developed under TCFD.	✓ Central banks and other financial regulators, as well as development co-operation providers working with them
Driving Finance Today for the Climate Resilient Society of Tomorrow (UNEP FI)	This report provides recommendations on incorporating physical climate risks into investment decision making by financial institutions.	✓ Central banks and other financial regulators
Sustainable Banking Network (IFC)	The SBN website provides key resources, tools, webinars and analytical papers to promote sustainable financing in emerging economies.	✓ Central banks and other financial regulators, as well as financial institutions
Macro-Financial Aspects of Climate Change (Feyen et al.)	This report examines interactions between macro-financial and climate-related risks, and policy.	✓ Central banks and other financial regulators, as well as financial institutions

Note: IFC: International Finance Corporation; NGS: Network of Central Banks and Supervisors for Greening the Financial System; TCFD: Task Force on Climate-related Financial Disclosures.

3.3. Financial management and instruments

3.3.1. Checklist for action

Actions	Actor(s)1
Identify necessary action on climate resilience and assess associated financial needs	
✓ Engage with state and non-state actors to better understand climate risks to target populations and ecosystems, explore suitable measures to address the risks, and collect information on associated costs of such measures.	Governments with support from dev-co[2]
✓ Examine methodological approaches to assessing costs of actions to strengthen climate resilience, and select the most suited one(s) for the purposes and capacities.	Governments with support from dev-co
✓ Engage development and commercial financial institutions to harness their financial expertise and private-sector perspectives, where relevant, for articulating assessments of financial needs.	Governments and dev-co
Integrate climate resilience into public financial management	
✓ Identify entry points to integrate climate resilience considerations into the public financial management system, and apply a gender budgeting approach where relevant.	Governments with support from dev-co
✓ Enhance collaboration between planning and finance ministries and other government bodies responsible for climate policies and sectoral development through the budgeting processes (see also section 3.2.5).	Governments
✓ Tag budgets and public expenditures to better understand where, how and how much public finance is allocated for climate resilience and potential gaps.	Governments with support from dev-co
✓ Develop and enhance social safety nets that are responsive to shocks, while encouraging public investments in reduction of disaster risks where possible.	Governments with support from dev-co
Elevate the role of finance ministries in enabling action on climate resilience	
✓ Link management of climate risks with the finance ministry's traditional mandates (e.g. managing fiscal risks and contingent liabilities, planning, managing and monitoring budget execution, supervising public procurement, developing financial protection strategies, etc.).	Governments with support from dev-co
✓ Integrate climate resilience considerations into policies for development of the domestic financial systems by working with central banks and other financial regulators, and foster coherence between financial sector development strategies and policies on climate resilience, as appropriate (see also section 3.2.7).	Governments with support from dev-co
✓ Encourage national development financial institutions to promote domestic investments in climate resilience, increase direct and indirect project origination, and identify and report on climate risks associated with financial operations of the institutions.	Governments with support from dev-co
Select and combine financial instruments for the management of climate risks	
✓ Take stock of available financial instruments (e.g. grants, debt instruments and risk transfer/sharing instruments), and select and combine them as part of a comprehensive approach to manage various climate risks.	Governments with support from dev-co
✓ Explore and pilot emerging financial instruments and solutions (e.g. parametric insurance, climate resilience bonds, and digital financial services) in support of climate resilience.	Governments and dev-co
✓ Identify and apply tools to support selection of financial instruments based on the uncertainty presented by climate change, as well as efficacy and broader socio-economic considerations such as gender and social inclusion.	Governments and dev-co
Maximise the benefits of risk insurance solutions	
✓ Further develop the insurance sector through capacity building and awareness raising for policy makers, domestic insurers and potential beneficiaries, building on public-private partnerships and pilot activities.	Governments with support from dev-co
✓ Invest in open-source models, and data generation needed for the models, to provide the private sector (insurers and policy holders) with a long-term view of climate risks.	Governments and dev-co
✓ Involve target beneficiaries, including women and marginalised groups, in an early stage of insurance deployment and create functioning partnerships to achieve scale.	Governments and dev-co
✓ Manage expectations among policy holders about benefits of the insurance products through model development and financial literacy programmes, among others.	Governments and dev-co
Link action on financial inclusion with action on climate resilience	
✓ Integrate climate risk consideration into action on financial inclusion, such as financial education and development of national financial inclusion programmes, while also integrating relevant aspects of gender-responsive financial inclusion.	Governments and dev-co
✓ Consider applying methodologies, such as the 4P (Provision, Promotion, Protection and Prevention) Framework, to link policy agendas on financial inclusions and sustainable/green finance.	Governments with support from dev-co
✓ Provide training on issues related to climate resilience to trainers in charge of financial education and inclusion.	Governments with support from dev-co

Further engage the private sector in climate-resilient investment	
✓ Set clear and bold policy targets on climate resilience to enhance the private sector's confidence in the co-benefits and risk-return profiles of climate-resilient investments.	Governments with support from dev-co
✓ Develop and enforce legal and regulatory frameworks that lower investment barriers and enhance economic incentives for private sector to invest in measures for climate resilience.	Governments with support from dev-co
✓ Make use of blended finance for projects with potential to deliver impacts on enhanced climate resilience but that cannot reach scale due to a high degree of risks or costs for the private sector.	Dev-co
✓ Harmonise domestic legal frameworks and standards for public-private partnerships with policies on climate resilience.	Governments with support from dev-co
Facilitate access to climate finance	
✓ Support and facilitate preparation of project/programme proposals by domestic actors, as well as the production, collection and analysis of data needed for climate risk assessment to be used in the proposals.	Governments and dev-co
✓ Engage target stakeholders, especially the most vulnerable to climate change, such as women, marginalised communities and Indigenous people, at an early stage of project development.	Governments and dev-co
✓ Identify the most relevant international financing sources based on the eligibility criteria, access modalities, programming priorities and logical frameworks of the financial sources in light of the country's own needs, priorities and capacities.	Governments with support from dev-co
✓ Support capacity development at the organisational level in accessing climate finance, especially national focal points and candidates for direct access entities where relevant.	Governments and dev-co

Note 1: Key actors (i.e. governments or development co-operation, or both) that play the primary role in promoting individual actions can greatly vary among countries and sectors. This column nevertheless indicates the likely leader in each of the actions. Some actions are led by governments but in many cases also supported by development co-operation (indicated as "Governments with support from dev-co").
Note 2: Dev-co: providers of development co-operation.
Note 3: Actions listed in this list are indicative and some may not be relevant to all countries or development co-operation providers.

3.3.2. Rationale

Governments, often in collaboration with development co-operation and the private sector, are the primary sources of finance for both structural (e.g. infrastructure investment) and non-structural (development of capacity, information and policies) measures. How and where a government invests will directly or indirectly contribute to the resilience of the country, its economy, people and ecosystems to climate change, either positively or negatively.

Infrastructure investments that strengthen the resilience of vulnerable sectors (e.g. agriculture, water supply and sanitation, tourism, transport, among others) create a structural foundation for achieving countries' sustainable development objectives. It is crucial to integrate climate resilience consideration into the development and operation of infrastructure systems to protect public and private assets and their services from impacts of climate change. Finance also needs to be allocated to cover the cost of operation and maintenance throughout the lifecycle of the assets (Mahul et al., 2019[108]); see also section 3.2.

Finance is also needed for development of capacity, information and policies. This includes establishing and operationalising effective institutional arrangements, formulating policies and plans, producing and disseminating climate data and information, building capacity, and monitoring and evaluating progress on action, to name a few (OECD, 2020[11]). Finance for those non-structural measures for action on climate resilience is needed at all levels of governance (e.g. national, municipal, local and community levels) for a wide range of stakeholders (public and private, as well as CSOs and across sectors.

When disasters occur, governments bear a large share of contingent liabilities for response and recovery (OECD and World Bank, 2019[109]). Even when some sort of insurance is available, a government may need to fund response measures if the insurance cannot cover an especially costly disaster. Finance is therefore needed to meet such liabilities and provide fiscal transfers to sub-national governments for rehabilitation of damaged assets, immediate relief and livelihood support, and assistance to uninsured households and businesses. (Mahul et al., 2019[108]). Growing macroeconomic impacts of disasters, including those caused by climate change and now the COVID-19 crisis, create a vicious cycle. They lower economic growth, increase debt and worsen financial vulnerability, especially of small and vulnerable countries (IMF, 2019[110]).

Financial resources can be delivered from various sources through different mechanisms and instruments. As illustrated in Figure 3.4, national and sub-national budgets, bilateral and multilateral development co-operation and private-sector finance – whether from financial institutions or companies' own balance sheets and savings – are all crucial sources of finance for strengthening climate resilience.

Decisions on how, when, to whom and by whom finance will be allocated, provided or mobilised to build climate resilience involves various factors. They include the acceptable level of residual risks for individual stakeholders despite efforts to adapt to climate change. They also involve the relative allocation of identified risks by reducing, transferring or retaining them.

Other factors not directly related to finance may also influence decisions. These could include capacities of stakeholders, political power dynamics and the cultural acceptability of the proposed measures. The psychological and emotional distress expected to be triggered by the impacts of climate change is another consideration.

Depending on the extent to which a country has integrated climate resilience consideration into its budget processes, gender-responsive budgeting can help ensure that allocations of public funds address the differentiated needs of women and men for enhancing their climate resilience. Gender-responsive budgeting can be based on gender analysis (see section 3.1.3), which enables better targeting of expenditures. A gender-responsive impact assessment of budgets and expenditures on climate resilience can also be effective [see for instance (Stephenson, 2018[111]; OECD, 2018[112]) for more information on gender budgeting]. Beyond domestic resources, mechanisms such as the Green Climate Fund, the Adaptation Fund and the Least Developed Country Fund have also integrated gender policies into the decision-making processes. The gender policies of these funds represent a key opportunity for countries to address gender consideration in their financing for activities in support of climate resilience.

Figure 3.4. Examples of financial sources for climate resilience

	Public	Private
Domestic	• National budgets • Sub-national budgets • National development financial institutions and funds	• Businesses and households • Commercial banks • Non-bank financial institutions (microfinance, funds, credit unions) • Philanthropy • Insurance companies
International	• Governments of providers of ODA and other official flows • Multilateral and bilateral development financial institutions • International climate funds and facilities	• Remittances • Multinational enterprises • Commercial banks and institutional investors (insurance companies, funds, etc.) • Philanthropy

Source: Authors based on (OECD, 2018[113]), Global Outlook on Financing for Sustainable Development 2019: Time to Face the Challenge, https://doi.org/10.1787/9789264307995-en, (Price-Kelly and Hammill, 2016[114]) sNAPshot: Domestic Public Finance for Implementation of NAPs, https://napglobalnetwork.org/resource/snapshot-domestic-public-finance-implementation-naps/

This section focuses on the issues listed below to outline approaches to allocating and accessing financial resources effectively to support structural and non-structural measures to manage different climate risks:

- Identify necessary action on climate resilience and assess associated financial needs
- Integrate climate resilience into public financial management
- Elevate the role of finance ministries in enabling action on climate resilience
- Select and combine financial instruments for the management of climate risks
- Maximise the benefits of risk insurance solutions
- Link action on financial inclusion with action on climate resilience
- Further engage the private sector in climate-resilient investment
- Facilitate access to climate finance

3.3.3. Identify necessary action on climate resilience and assess associated financial needs

A government must take several key initial steps to plan its financing for climate resilience. First, it must understand the nature of the climate risks to vulnerable people and ecosystems in the country. Second, it must assess possible approaches to manage those risks (e.g. policies, technologies, technical assistance and other types of activities) (Parry, Dazé and Dekens, 2017[115]; Financial Protection Forum, 2018[116]). Relevant government bodies then compare and prioritise the approaches based on their costs and benefits (or broader effectiveness or coherence criteria, or both – see also section 3.1.6). In many cases, however, it remains methodologically challenging to make reliable cost estimates of such approaches (Chapagain et al., 2020[117]; Hallegatte, Rentschler and Rozenberg, 2020[68]). A recent study identified 44 NDCs and NAPs from developing countries that indicated adaptation costs over 2020-30. It observed most estimates either lack any methodological description or simply add up the budget items in the proposed adaptation actions (Chapagain et al., 2020[117]).

Nevertheless, practitioners in government and development co-operation providers could refer to one of several suggested approaches to assess financial needs for action on climate resilience and broader SDGs (see Table 3.15). Countries are also increasingly using costing measures to support climate resilience, especially as part of the NAP processes (e.g. Guatemala, Fiji and South Africa) (Casado Asensio, Kato and Shin, forthcoming[13]; Government of Fiji, 2020[118]) For instance, Fiji's Ministry of Economy worked with the NAP Global Network on a rapid and comparable set of cost estimates. It has costed 160 priority measures in its NAP document for 2021-25 (Government of Fiji, 2020[118]).

A broad range of stakeholders is needed to understand climate risks, explore and prioritise approaches, and assess financial needs to implement them. While it may be resource-intensive, such processes can provide valuable input for discussion among various public- and private-sector stakeholders. These discussions can cover climate risks, drivers of vulnerabilities and priority actions on climate resilience in light of overall development objectives. Information on these issues obtained through stakeholder engagement can also provide a basis for further discussion on the scale of finance needed and potential sources of finance (Foss, 2017[119]; Parry, Dazé and Dekens, 2017[115]).

Central to this process are finance and economic planning ministries, other line ministries and agencies responsible for key areas. These areas include development, climate policies, disaster risk management and climate-sensitive sectors such as agriculture, fisheries, energy, transport and tourism. Co-ordination between these different ministries and agencies is crucial (see Box 3.15 for an example). The participation of sub-national governments, and representatives of local businesses and households that are particularly vulnerable, or that may be significantly affected by approaches, is also essential. Financial institutions can bring expertise and private-sector perspectives on building climate resilience into the process, and may provide financial solutions for implementation. These institutions could include insurance providers, development financial institutions, commercial banks and microfinance institutions.

Participation by bilateral and multilateral providers of development co-operation in the process may also provide opportunities. For example, they could help better align their country programmes and individual projects with the country's climate and overall development objectives. Such engagement could also help mobilise further resources through better donor co-ordination or catalysing private-sector finance. Development co-operation can also provide governments with technical support in assessing financial needs, identifying targeted beneficiaries and exploring potential sources and delivery mechanisms (OECD, 2015[120]).

Table 3.15. Identify necessary action on climate resilience and assess associated financial needs: Guidance and tools

Guidance and tools	Focus	Audience
Investment Needs to Achieve the Sustainable Development Goals (UN Sustainable Development Solutions Network)	This paper proposes an analytical framework for SDG needs assessments that translates the 17 SDGs into eight investment areas that include climate change adaptation and mitigation. The document outlines several needs assessment methodologies.	✓ Government officials and development co-operation practitioners
Financing National Adaptation Plan Processes: Contributing to the Achievement of Nationally Determined Contribution Adaptation goals: Guidance Note (IISD and GIZ)	This guidance note aims to assist countries with the development of strategies for securing funding throughout the National Adaptation Plan (NAP) processes. It provides a clear understanding from a financing perspective and presents the range of potential sources of finance.	✓ Government officials working on NAP processes, especially development and implementation of finance-related aspects
Costing Methodology for Fiji's National Adaptation Plan (Fiji and NAP Global Network)	This document provides tools for evaluation of the indicative costs required to implement the entire set of adaptation measures prioritised in the NAP documents. While this case study is on Fiji, the steps outlined to estimate costs could be applied to other countries.	✓ Officials of the government of Fiji, but potentially also those from other countries
Disaster Risk Finance: A Primer: Core Principles and Operational Framework (WB)	This framework provides an overview of an approach to financial planning, aiming to protect national budgets, as well as the lives and livelihoods of their residents from the impacts of disasters. The operational framework also provides technical steps for governments to pursue the financial planning.	✓ Government officials in charge of national-level disaster risk transfer mechanisms

Box 3.15. Engaging with sub-national governments for the budgeting of climate action in Ghana

In Ghana, the National Development Planning Commission co-ordinates development planning at the national and sub-national levels. Sub-national governments are required to elaborate climate policy statements and plans to receive budget allocation for needed action. To that end, the Commission also supports sub-national governments through the budget hearing and policy hearing processes. At the national level, the Commission collaborates closely with ministries, departments and agencies to ensure that climate change is well integrated into all planning and budget processes. For this process of engaging and supporting sub-national governments, the Commission shares responsibility with the Ministry of Local Government and Rural Development and the Ministry of Finance.

Source: (OECD, 2020[11]), Common Ground Between the Paris Agreement and the Sendai Framework, https://doi.org/10.1787/3edc8d09-en.

3.3.4. Integrate climate resilience into public financial management

Bilateral and multilateral development finance are likely to remain important sources for climate action, especially in lower income countries. However, national and sub-national budgets still play a crucial role in financing efforts to build climate resilience (Allan, Bahadur and Vidya, 2019[121]; OECD, 2018[113]). As shown in Figure 3.5, public finance can anticipate hazards (risk reduction and prevention) or react to their occurrence (response and recovery) (Hubert, Evain and Nicol, 2018[122]; GCA, 2019[64]). Having finance available for response and recovery also help a government absorb impacts of disasters on debt levels, costs of capital and overall fiscal stability in the country. Such finance could take the form of contingent credit, insurance or contingency reserves. Table 3.16 outlines tools for governments and development co-operation to integrate climate resilience consideration into public financial management (PFM), while the following paragraphs analyse some of these approaches.

Figure 3.5. Financial needs for different phases of strengthening climate resilience

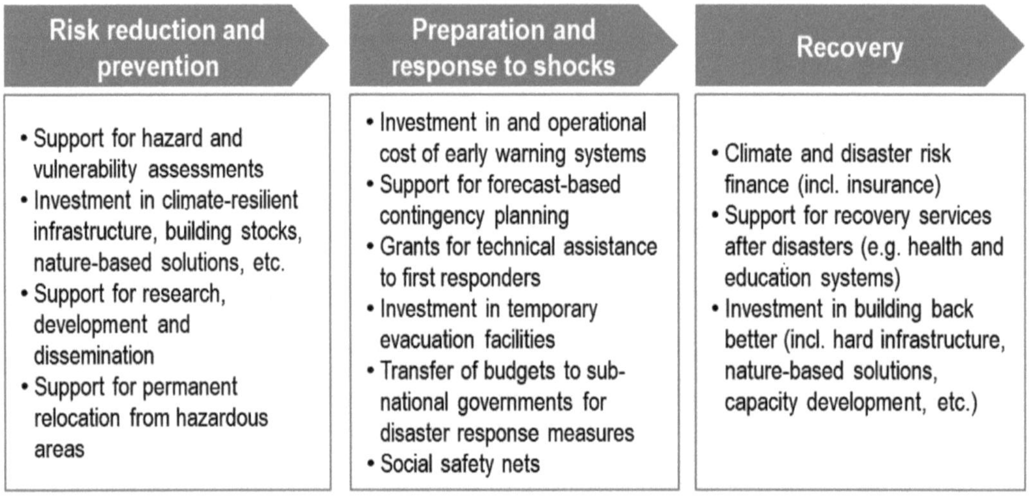

Note: The examples included in the figure are indicative and some could be related to more than one phase (e.g. results of vulnerability assessments could be used in all three phases).
Source: Authors' elaboration based on (GCA, 2019[64]) Adapt Now: A Global Call for Leadership on Climate Resilience, https://gca.org.

Governments can better manage various public spending in support of climate resilience, when they have better understanding of how the public finance is being spent, and when they consider climate risks in PFM (Mahul et al., 2019[108]; Financial Protection Forum, 2018[116]) (see Box 3.16. for a definition of PFM). Integration of climate resilience into PFM also requires closer collaboration between different government bodies. These include finance and planning ministries, as well as those in charge of climate policies and individual sectoral policies. As they do for other government functions, many countries conduct budgeting in siloes (Moser et al., 2019[123]).

On the expenditure side of PFM, budget allocations to sector ministries and agencies can strengthen climate resilience components of development plans in the sectors (see also section 3.2). Some measures may not be explicitly focused on climate resilience, but rather embedded in broader sector development projects (Price-Kelly and Hammill, 2016[114]). Budget allocations to ministries and agencies directly responsible for promoting climate resilience are also crucial for ensuring adequate resourcing of core functions. These functions include implementation of measures under NAPs, enforcement of related environmental regulations, and monitoring and evaluation of implementation (OECD, 2012[124]).

A government holds a fundamental responsibility to provide social safety nets to complement activities that reduce climate risks and help poor households cope with devastating impacts of disasters (Tenzing, 2020[125]; Aleksandrova, 2019[126]; Hallegatte, Rentschler and Rozenberg, 2020[68]). For instance, cash transfers can help households build resilience to climate-related hazards and their impacts on livelihoods. Governments can also create employment through public works. For example, beneficiaries could provide community services or build assets in support of climate resilience for cash or in-kind benefits (e.g. reforestation, irrigation, mitigating soil erosion and water security).

Social safety nets should not discourage risk reduction activities over the long term. For example, support to areas that are increasingly affected by natural hazards (e.g. droughts or floods) should not be designed in ways that lock people in those places (Hallegatte, Rentschler and Rozenberg, 2020[68]). Further, governments should recognise that approaches to social safety nets can have long-term benefits for human health, livelihoods, poverty and inequality, and social exclusion, which are root causes of the vulnerability to climate hazard. For these reasons, social safety nets must target the most disadvantaged groups (Tenzing, 2020[125]; Aleksandrova, 2019[126]).

Tagging budgets and reviewing public expenditures for activities that contribute to national, sub-national and sectoral targets on climate resilience can support integration of climate risks into PFM. Such a tagging exercise can help governments understand where, how and how much of the public budget is being allocated and disbursed for climate resilience measures through a broad selection of line ministries. Mapping the sources of finance available (i.e. domestic budgets, and where relevant, development finance provided to complement them) can also help planning and sectoral ministries see potential financing gaps (OECD, 2020[11]; UNDP, 2019[127]). Several countries have already introduced tools for tracking public budget allocation. These include Bangladesh, Cambodia, Ghana, Indonesia, Nepal, Pakistan, Peru, Philippines, Samoa, Thailand and Vanuatu (OECD, 2020[11]; UNDP, 2019[127]; NDC Cluster, n.d.[128]; Storey, 2016[129]).

Box 3.16. Public financial management systems

A public financial management (PFM) system is essentially the way a country decides how to raise financial resources (the revenue side) and where to allocate those resources (the expenditure side). Upstream components of the budget process include strategic planning, preparation of a medium-term expenditure framework and annual budgeting. Downstream components include revenue management, procurement, accounting, reporting, monitoring and evaluation, audit and oversight (OECD, 2012[124]).

The Public Expenditure and Financial Accountability (PEFA) Program has recently been developing the "PEFA Climate". This is a set of indicators building on the PEFA Framework to inform how PFM systems can support implementation of climate change actions by governments. Pilot testing of the PEFA Climate was expected to start in July 2020: further information was to be available on www.pefa.org/.

Another tool to improve PFM systems in support of climate resilience is the Post-Disaster Financial Management Review and Engagement Framework (PD-PFM Review), developed by the World Bank and Canada. It aims to help countries build resilient, responsive PFM systems by strengthening their capacity to respond more effectively to disasters and other catastrophic events. The PD-PFM Review focuses on four pillars: legal and institutional foundations, budget appropriation, financial management control and public procurement. Well-designed PFM systems can also help ministries of finance avoid difficult trade-offs between respect for due process and swift support to the population after a disaster (World Bank, 2019[130]).

Multi-annual cycles for policy planning and budgeting can be a useful tool for countries to increase predictability of their financing plans. Many countries have adopted a fiscal arrangement called a medium-term expenditure framework (MTEF). This allows them to extend the horizon of fiscal policies, thereby increase the predictability of budget outcomes (Martí, 2019[131]; Di Francesco and Barroso, 2015[132]). MTEF may also, in turn, inform annual sectoral-level budgeting that would ideally reflect the funding needed for strengthening climate resilience in the sector (Price-Kelly and Hammill, 2016[114]).

MTEF could also complement multi-year strategic and implementation plans on climate resilience (e.g. NDCs, NAPs, national disaster risk reduction strategies, among others) (Allan, Bahadur and Vidya, 2019[121]; Parry, Dazé and Dekens, 2017[115]). For instance, as part of its NAP process, Togo developed a practical guidebook on how to integrate climate change into different steps of its planning and budgeting cycle (Price-Kelly and Hammill, 2016[114]). Several other countries have developed climate-related budget planning processes along with their MTEFs. Cameroon and Thailand, for example, link their mid-term national development and climate change plans to the budgeting processes (GIZ, 2014[133]; Kohli, 2018[134]).

Table 3.16. Integrate climate resilience into public financial management: Guidance and tools

Guidance and tools	Focus	Audience
NAP Align: Recommendations for Aligning National Adaptation Plan Processes with Development and Budget Planning (GIZ)	NAP Align supplements the LDC Expert Group's NAP Technical Guidelines and highlights key steps to align a National Adaptation Plan (NAP) with development planning and financial issues. One of the key components is on links between annual and medium-term budgeting procedures with NAP.	✓ Officials in finance and/or planning ministries, and the lead ministries for climate change policy, especially those leading NAP processes
Knowing What You Spend: A Guidance Note for Governments to Track Climate Finance in their Budgets (UNDP)	This guidance note aims at those exploring ways to improve financial management of the response to climate change and to reduce long-term impacts on their countries. An annex provides a detailed account of approaches to budget tagging in several case study countries.	✓ Officials in finance and/or planning ministries, and the lead ministries for climate change policy
A Methodological Guidebook Climate Public Expenditure and Institutional Review (CPIER) (UNDP)	A CPEIR is a diagnostic tool to assess ways in which climate change concerns are integrated into the national and sub-national budget allocation and expenditure process. The CPEIR analytical framework consists of i) policy analysis; ii) institutional analysis; and iii) climate public expenditure analysis.	✓ Officials in finance and/or planning ministries, and the lead ministries for climate change policy
Words into Action: Developing National Disaster Risk Reduction Strategies (UNDRR)	This guidance outlines practical steps and examples to develop national disaster risk reduction strategies. This includes guides on how to evaluate the availability of financial resources, engage with finance ministries, understand budgets dedicated to various categories of risk reduction, and get an overview of the status of national reserves and public risk transfer mechanisms.	✓ Officials in finance and/or planning ministries, and the lead ministries for climate change policy
The Role of Domestic Budgets in Financing Climate Change Adaptation (Allan et al.)	This is an analytical study provides accessible accounts of different budget cycle phases and possible entry points to mainstream climate change adaptation, including medium-term expenditure framework. It also provides case studies on Afghanistan, Bangladesh, India and the Philippines.	✓ Officials in finance and/or planning ministries, and the lead ministries for climate change policy, especially those leading NAP processes
Integrating Gender in Climate Change Adaptation Proposals (USAID)	This book focuses on the front end of the project cycle, specifically proposal preparation for accessing climate change adaptation financing, by providing tools on incorporating gender considerations into project proposals.	✓ Officials in climate/sectoral ministries or private-sector actors
Booklet: Nepal's Citizens' Climate Budget (Government of Nepal)	This presentation on Nepal's "citizens' climate budget" provides an example of how information on a climate-related budget can be communicated to citizens. The booklet presents how the budget was allocated to address climate change and its effects in different sectors over the past years. It uses official information from the Ministry of Finance and other government agencies in Nepal.	✓ National and sub-national government officials and civil society organisations
Disaster Response: A Public Financial Management Review Toolkit (World Bank)	This tool provides an overview of the conceptual framework and core principles that underpin the design of the Post-Disaster Financial Management Review and Engagement Framework.	✓ Officials in finance and/or planning ministries and disaster management agencies
Social Protection and Climate Resilience (DFID)	This guidance identifies issues for consideration when integrating climate resilience concerns into the design of social protection programmes.	✓ Development co-operation

3.3.5. Elevate the role of finance ministries in enabling action on climate resilience

The role of finance ministries in supporting national strategies to address climate risk is increasingly recognised. This is exemplified by the number of countries that have joined the Coalition of Finance Ministers for Climate Action (World Bank, 2019[135]). The role of finance ministries in supporting action on climate resilience may be closely linked with their traditional mandates as shown in Table 3.17. Many finance ministries are already working to help build their countries' financial resilience to disasters, including those related to climate. To that end, they collaborate with government bodies responsible for economic planning, climate policies, and disaster risk reduction and management. Finance ministries in many countries have also led exercises in tracking climate finance over the past decade (OECD, 2020[11]; UNDP, 2019[127]; NDC Cluster, n.d.[128]; Storey, 2016[129]).

Finance ministries can also promote the use of national development banks and funds to address barriers to domestic investment in climate resilience (Miller and Swann, 2019[103]). They can do this, in part, by putting climate resilience at the core of strategic frameworks of those banks and funds. Developing criteria for their credit risk assessment and financial decision making may increase allocation of their financial resources to projects that support climate resilience. Finance ministries can also encourage the banks and funds to de-risk domestic investment in climate resilience (e.g. by using guarantees), to increase direct and indirect project origination, and to identify and report on climate risks associated with their operations.

Table 3.17. Examples of roles of financial ministries in climate resilience

Role	Approach
Manage fiscal risks	• Take climate risks into account in macroeconomic forecasts, debt sustainability analyses, fiscal risk assessments (to prevent an abrupt increase of public debts, and to improve governments' ability to raise new debt or refinance it). • Develop comprehensive disaster risk financing strategies. • Allocate public funding to bear top-tier risks (e.g. high-impact and low-probability events) so that climate and disaster insurance markets continue to exist.
Set financial targets	• Adopt a climate resilience related finance target for a country (e.g. in light of its NDC and/or NAP), and reflect the target in the formulation and implementation of fiscal plans, expenditure reviews and programme evaluations, which can also inform future fiscal policies.
Manage public investment programmes	• Integrate climate resilience considerations and policies into the guidance, procedures and methodologies used for selection and appraisal of programmes to be financed by public budget (e.g. social discount rates, multi-criteria assessments, etc.).
Support line ministries/agencies and sub-national governments in budget planning	• Integrate climate resilience aspects into annual budgeting reports and templates for planning, and into estimates of future resources available for climate-related expenditure where possible.
Incentivise policy makers to incorporate climate resilience considerations in their decisions	• Generate data on climate-related expenditures by introducing climate budget tagging and scoring systems, among others. • Strengthen capacity for better informed planning and improved transparency and monitoring.
Tailor fiscal instruments to shift investment behaviours and mobilise necessary financial resources	• Mobilise resources for climate resilience through environmental taxes, charges or subsidy reforms. • Use fiscal instruments such as grants, concessional loans and tax credits to actors that invest in research and development, production and diffusion of goods and services for strengthening climate resilience, or to those who purchase and use them.
Supervise procurement policies	• Integrate climate resilience considerations into the guidance, procedures and methodologies for public procurement.
Promote financial sector development that also supports climate resilience	• Promote voluntary disclosure of exposure of financial institutions and real sector companies to physical risks, among others (see also section 3.2.7). • Consider integration of climate resilience aspects into treasury or municipal bonds.
Encourage domestic public financial institutions or funds to promote investment in climate resilience	• Put climate resilience at the core of their key strategic frameworks and these institutions' investment risk assessment and decision-making criteria, and encourage them to de-risk domestic investments in climate resilience, increase direct and indirect project origination, and identify and report on climate risks associated their operations.
Support in accessing international climate finance	• Act as a focal point for international climate funds, or proactively engage with other ministries and agencies to understand, select and operationalise different modalities to access funds.

Source: Authors' elaboration, based on (OECD, 2020[11]) Common Ground Between the Paris Agreement and the Sendai Framework: Climate Change Adaptation and Disaster Risk Reduction, https://doi.org/10.1787/3edc8d09-en, (Mahul et al., 2019[108]), Boosting Financial Resilience to Disaster Shocks: Good Practices and New Frontiers, https://www.financialprotectionforum.org/publication/boosting-financial-resilience-to-disaster-shocks-good-practices-and-new-frontiers, (UNDP, 2019[127])Knowing What You Spend: A Guidance Note for Governments to Track Climate Change Finance in their Budgets, https://www.undp.org/content/undp/en/home/librarypage/climate-and-disaster-resilience-/knowing-what-you-spend.html.

Maintaining fiscal space in normal conditions is in many cases the most reliable way of managing unexpected shocks (Hallegatte, Rentschler and Rozenberg, 2020[68]) (see also section 3.3.6 for different financial instruments to support this). Finance ministries in many countries lead efforts and co-ordinate with other government bodies to manage explicit and implicit contingent liabilities to compensate for part of disaster losses. In so doing, they bear a significant share of the costs of responding to negative impacts of disasters (OECD and World Bank, 2019[109]). Relating to this, finance ministries also play a central role in developing and implementing financial protection strategies for managing residual risks. Such financial protection strategies help disaster-affected people to secure access to financing in advance of shocks. At the same time, the strategies protect the country's fiscal balance and budget when disasters strike. Ethiopia, Indonesia, Peru and the Philippines, for example, have developed their financial protection strategies (OECD and World Bank, 2019[109]; OECD, 2020[11]); (Mahul et al., 2019[108]). Financial protection strategies combine different financial instruments to address different types of climate and disaster risks. In this way, they help ensure that each instrument matches the funding needs during different phases of disaster response and recovery (Mahul et al., 2019[108]; UNDRR, 2020[136]). Those instruments include budgetary measures, contingent credit facilities and risk transfer instruments (e.g. insurance), among others (OECD and World Bank, 2019[109]).

Table 3.18. Elevate the role of finance ministries in enhancing climate resilience: Guidance and tools

Guidance and tools	Focus	Audience
Climate Action Peer Exchange (CAPE) (WB)	CAPE provides finance ministries and other relevant institutions with a platform for peer learning, knowledge sharing and mutual advisory support. It brings together ministers and senior technical specialists from finance ministries to discuss the fiscal challenges involved in implementing NDCs.	✓ Officials in finance and ministries, and the lead ministries for climate change policy, and development co-operation providers who work with those ministries
UNDP Governance of Climate Change Finance Programme (UNDP)	Established in 2012, this website provides an extensive list of tools and case studies, including on Climate Change Financing Frameworks (CCFFs) and Climate Public Expenditure and Institutional Reviews (CPEIRs).	✓ Officials in finance and ministries, and the lead ministries for climate change policy
A Guidance Note on Climate Change Financing Framework (UNDP)	This note aims to guide governments and institutions through the process of creating or refining a CCFF. It provides an overview of the elements, processes, workflows and outputs involved in a CCFF and how these fit together to create an effective framework.	✓ Officials in finance and ministries, and the lead ministries for climate change policy
Disaster Response: A Public Financial Management Review Toolkit (WB)	This tool aims to help countries quickly pinpoint specific elements of their public financial management systems that could be refined to optimise the allocation and execution of public resources to facilitate timely recovery from disasters. Specific elements here include policies, practices and procedures that can be strengthened to improve a government's capability to respond more efficiently and effectively.	✓ Officials in finance and ministries, and the lead ministries for disaster risk reduction
Fiscal Resilience to Natural Disasters: Lessons from Country Experiences (OECD and WB)	The research and analysis in this report aims to support government officials with practical lessons and insights in more proactive management of explicit and implicit liabilities in case of extreme events.	✓ Officials in finance and ministries, and the lead ministries for disaster risk reduction

3.3.6. Select and combine financial instruments for the management of climate risks

No single financial instrument can address all risks. Thus, the government and development co-operation providers normally combine different financial instruments to manage climate-related risks in the country efficiently (Financial Protection Forum, 2018[116]). Yet selecting the most effective financial instruments could also be a challenge in itself. This is due to the deep uncertainty associated with climate scenarios and their possible consequences, as well as complex and dynamic socio-economic circumstances surrounding target beneficiaries.

Governments and development co-operation are increasingly aware of the benefit of combining multiple types of financial instruments to pursue a more comprehensive approach to climate risk management (Martinez-Diaz, Sidner and McClamrock, 2019[137]). Various methodologies can guide the choice of instruments. These include the layering approach that uses frequency and severity of hazards as the key selection criteria along with other factors such as economic and social preferences of beneficiaries. [For more information on the layering approach, see for instance (Financial Protection Forum, 2018[116]) and section 5.2 of (GIZ, 2019[138])].

Box 3.19 outlines examples of several financial instruments for climate resilience, provided ex ante (i.e. before a disaster occurs) or ex post (after a disaster), and short descriptions of their characteristics. The table also shows activities for which these financial instruments may be used. The expected effectiveness of these instruments is assessed against various criteria. These include financial costs and benefits, timeliness, volume and discipline in terms of when and how resources can be available (see World Bank Group (2014[139])) for further information on approaches to the selection). There are also emerging financial instruments and mechanisms such as forecast-based financing, climate resilience bonds, application of blockchain technologies (see Box 3.17).

Table 3.20 gives examples of tools and guidance documents that help governments and development co-operation providers select and combine such financial instruments to support action on climate resilience. Apart from these instruments, equity and mezzanine finance has been used to finance projects in support of climate resilience, but their application is still at an early stage of development.

Table 3.19. Overview of financing instruments for action on strengthening climate resilience

Instrument (description)	Timing and examples	Examples of potential activities
Grants • A transfer in cash, goods or services for which no repayment is required, which can be used to cover up-front costs, subsidise return requirements, mitigate risks for high indebtedness to those affected by disasters, etc.	*Ex-ante*	• Financial support for improvement of climate and weather information (database, climate risks assessment, climate services etc.) • Concessional financing to infrastructure investment (seed funding, interest subsidies, etc.) • Technical assistance to improve policies, institutions, guidance and tools, public awareness, technical capacity (through trainings, analytical work, policy dialogues, etc.) • Forecast-based financing for disaster-prone areas (see Box 3.17)
	Ex-post	• Response measures after disasters (e.g. conditional and unconditional cash transfers, humanitarian aid for health systems, and basic goods and services, etc.) • Support to investment in reconstruction of critical infrastructure
Debt finance instruments • Typically loans and bonds that can be used to finance, such as climate-resilient infrastructure, nature-based solutions, etc. • Contingent credit lines that are negotiated and established before an event has occurred)	*Ex-ante* (Loans, green and climate bonds)	• Investment in climate-resilient infrastructure systems • Rehabilitation of existing infrastructure systems to make them more resilient • Refinancing for infrastructure assets • Purchase of goods and services supportive of climate resilience (e.g. early warning systems, water-efficient irrigation equipment, heat-tolerant crop seeds, etc.)
	Ex-post (Contingent credit lines, CAT-DDO*, state-contingent debt instruments)	• Response measures after disasters (e.g. humanitarian aid and activities to restore basic services and businesses) • Investment in reconstruction of critical infrastructure • Inclusion of disaster clauses in their sovereign bond contracts to enable changes in debt service payments in the event of an exogenous disaster
Risk sharing and transfer instruments • Instruments to share certain weather and climate-related risks (risk sharing and pooling) or to transfer risks to third parties in exchange for premium payments (risk transfer) • Guarantees to lower a lender's potential initial losses from default	*Ex-post* (disaster/climate risk insurance, re-insurance, catastrophe bonds, CAT-DDO, guarantees, regional risk-sharing facilities)	• Indemnity- and index-based insurance for business continuity management, recovery of livelihood, support to investment in resilient infrastructure, etc. • (Contribution to risk reduction through mapping, analysing, prioritising and pricing climate risks throughout the process of planning for and purchase of insurance products) • Loan guarantees (credit guarantees, risk guarantees, etc.) for lending to climate-resilient projects

Note: CAT-DDO (Catastrophe Deferred Drawdown Option) combines ex-ante and ex-post measures. While CAT-DDO disburses funding after a disaster, governments commit to preventive policy reforms that aim to reduce the disaster's impact before it strikes. Such an arrangement to promote preventive measures can also apply for certain insurance solutions, such as the African Risk Capacity that requires governments to develop pre-defined contingency.

Source: Authors based on (OECD, 2020[11]) Common Ground Between the Paris Agreement and the Sendai Framework: Climate Change Adaptation and Disaster Risk Reduction, https://doi.org/10.1787/3edc8d09-en, (OECD and World Bank, 2019[109]), Fiscal Resilience to Natural Disasters: Lessons from Country Experiences, https://doi.org/10.1787/27a4198a-en, (Sadler et al., 2016[140]), Making Climate Finance Work in Agriculture http://documents.worldbank.org/curated/en/986961467721999165/Making-climate-finance-work-in-agriculture.

Table 3.20. Select and combine financial instruments for the management of climate risks: Guidance and tools

Guidance and tools	Focus	Audience
Financial Instruments and Mechanisms for Climate Change Programs in Latin America and the Caribbean (IDB)	This guide, intended for ministries of finance, outlines financial mechanisms and instruments that could be used to channel resources into climate change programmes primarily in Latin America and the Caribbean. It offers lessons learnt and policy recommendations given in the countries' experience with different versions of these mechanisms.	✓ Officials in ministries of finance, but also ministries in charge of climate change
Disaster Risk Finance: A Toolkit (GIZ)	This toolkit provides a comprehensive overview of financial instruments for risk reduction, retention and transfer, offering guidance on how to choose instruments for different circumstances.	✓ Officials in governments and development co-operation providers
ASEAN Green Financial Instruments Guide (Climate Bonds Initiative)	This guide highlights financial instruments and mechanisms available from and for public and private entities in the ASEAN region looking to fund green assets. It also provides a step-by-step guide to green financing, giving an overview of the whole financing process. Annexes provide a detailed list of debt and equity instruments, credit enhancement mechanisms and risk transfer tools.	✓ Officials in governments and development co-operation providers

Note: ASEAN: Association of Southeast Asian Nations; GIZ: Deutsche Gesellschaft für Internationale Zusammenarbeitl (German Development Agency); IDB: Inter-American Development Bank.

Box 3.17. Examples of emerging financial instruments

Climate resilience bonds

Climate resilience bonds are an instrument whose proceeds will be used to finance projects that contribute to enhanced climate resilience. Examples include climate-resilient infrastructure (e.g. water, energy, transport, communications and urban infrastructure), nature-based solutions, climate-resilient business and commercial operations, climate-smart agriculture and ecological systems, among others. The European Bank for Reconstruction and Development, for instance, issued USD 700 million in climate resilience bonds in 2019 (Bennett, 2019[141]).

Forecast-based financing (FbF)

FbF aims to fill gaps in the humanitarian system by using weather and climate information to anticipate possible impacts in risk-prone areas and mobilise resources automatically before an event. Providers of humanitarian aid, National Meteorological and Hydrological Services and communities agree on selected actions that are worth carrying out once a forecast reaches a certain threshold of probability. In Uganda, the Uganda Red Cross activated a humanitarian action triggered by a forecast of flood risk in 2015. Nearly 400 families were provided 5 000 non-food items, including jerry cans and water-purification tablets (Jaime, n.d.[142]). The Anticipation Hub also provides further information on a range of institutions and initiatives that promote FbF. These include the Early Action Focus Task Force, FOREWARN, Risk Informed Early Action Partnership, the International Network on Multi-hazard Early Warning Systems, among others (German Red Cross and IFRC, 2020[143]). The Caribbean Disaster Emergency Management Agency and Agence Française de Développement (AFD) have also been collaborating. They wish to identify the challenges and opportunities for a regional forecast-based early action mechanism for the Eastern Caribbean under the AFD's Adapt'Action programme (ODI et al., 2019[144]).

Digital platform for blockchain-based insurance products

While not a financial instrument in itself, Blockchain Climate Risk Crop Insurance is a digital platform for standardised crop insurance for smallholder farmers in Africa. It aims to increase those farmers' resilience to climate change by enabling transparent, timely and fair payouts in extreme weather events. By creating templates for blockchain-based insurance products, this platform aims to provide third parties (insurers and beyond) with the tools to create their own index-based crop insurance products (Sprout Insure, 2019[145]). Blockchain and the distributed ledger technologies more broadly can improve transparency, accountability, efficiency and security of exchanging decentralised stores of information. These technologies can be used to deliver development finance and humanitarian aid for climate resilience, including those for post-disasters (Coppi and Fast, 2019[146]). For instance, a German start-up, Etherisc, has been developing a crop insurance solution that pays automatically in cases of droughts or floods in developing countries. Etherisc uses the blockchain technologies to help improve efficiency, hence economic margins, of parametric insurance products (Peverelli and de Feniks, 2017[147]). Many of these features, however, may not be absolute or intrinsic to the distributed ledger technologies. Intentional design choices therefore must be made to develop systems based on blockchain and other distributed ledger technologies to ensure the strengths above (Zwitter and Boisse-Despiaux, 2018[148]).

3.3.7. Maximise the benefits of risk insurance solutions

Insurance, as a type of risk transfer instrument, plays an important role in protecting individuals, businesses and countries against the negative impacts of climate change and other natural hazards. Insurance can operate at various levels: international (e.g. multi-country risk pools), national (e.g. sovereign disaster insurance, catastrophe bonds) and sub-national or local (e.g. indemnity- or index-based crop insurance, flood insurance) (InsuResilience Investment Fund, 2018[149]). Table 3.21 summarises major benefits of risk insurance products in promoting climate resilience (see also Box 3.18 for more examples).

Table 3.21. Key benefits of insurance in strengthening climate resilience

Benefits	Descriptions	Examples
Financial protection for people	Timely and reliable payouts can enable households and businesses to protect their livelihoods and avoid resorting to negative coping strategies. In some insurance products, payouts can happen even before a shock unfolds.	An index-based livestock insurance programme in Kenya led to an estimated reduction of 25–36% in the likelihood of distress livestock sales.
Complementing climate adaptation measures cost-effectively	Insurance and other risk financing instruments cover residual risks that could not be mitigated in a cost-effective manner through adaptation measures. For example, risk financing can reduce disaster-related contingent liabilities from public assets for high severity but low frequency impacts, where resilience investments into infrastructure are no longer cost-effective.	Mexico's Fondo de Desastres Naturales (FONDEN) is a financial vehicle through which the federal government allocates budget *ex-ante* for post-disaster relief, rehabilitation, and reconstruction of critical public infrastructure.
Financial resilience of governments	Insurance can help governments to protect their balance sheets, as it provides rapid liquidity for immediate post disaster relief. It supports the long-term fiscal stability of a state. Demonstrating preparedness, both financially and institutionally, could positively affect the assessment of the country's sovereign credit risk and hence its access to international capital.	Dominica received a payout of USD 9 million from the Caribbean Catastrophe Risk Insurance Facility relatively quickly (14 days) after Hurricane Maria struck in 2017.
Encouraging risk reduction	Well-designed insurance can incentivise policy holders to invest more in the insured assets during non-payout periods, encourage risk assessment to identify vulnerabilities of the assets and reduce risks. Some risk finance instruments require the design and implementation of a pre-defined emergency plan (contingency plan).	Farmers insured by the Agriculture and Climate Risk Enterprise (ACRE Africa) in Kenya, Rwanda and Tanzania invested 19% more and earned 16% more than their uninsured counterparts.
Co-benefits in data management and use	Tools such as data repositories, risk models and risk profiles, while initially designed to facilitate the insurance-buying process, can help governments and other actors better understand and manage the risks they face.	The Pacific Risk Information System and individual country risk profiles are used not only for insurance purchase but also for broader disaster risk reduction effort by governments in the Pacific region.

Source: Authors' elaboration based on (Väänänen et al., 2019[150]), Linking climate risk insurance with shock-responsive social protection, https://www.insuresilience.org/wp-content/uploads/2019/03/insuresilience_policybrief_1-2019_190312_web.pdf, (Martinez-Diaz, Sidner and McClamrock, 2019[137]), The future of disaster risk pooling for developing countries: Where do we go from here?, http://www.wri.org/publication/disaster-risk-pooling.

Box 3.18. Examples of initiatives in promoting insurance for climate risk

At the international level, several multi-country insurance facilities are already in place, often led by governments with support of development co-operation. Examples include the African Risk Capacity (ARC), the Caribbean Catastrophe Risk Insurance Facility, the Pacific Catastrophe Risk Assessment and Financing Initiative and the Southeast Asia Disaster Risk Insurance Facility. Insurance for climate and disaster risk financing is also often provided or supported by national governments, domestic insurance companies, and bilateral and multilateral development financial institutions. Support of development co-operation spans wide areas. It includes contribution to the initial capital base for the disaster insurance pools, as well as grants for premiums, support for pilot projects and development of policy frameworks and knowledge base such as risk modelling.

Several development co-operation providers have been involved in development and dissemination of insurance instruments for climate risks. Examples include the Disaster Risk Financing and Insurance Program led by the World Bank Group. This aims to help countries develop and implement tailored financial protection strategies through financial and technical support (World Bank, n.d.[151]).

The InsuResilience Global Partnership (IGP) is a multi-stakeholder platform to scale up climate and disaster risk finance and insurance in developing countries. The aim is to strengthen financial and fiscal resilience of poor and vulnerable communities in the face of climate and disaster risks. The IGP fosters dialogue between representatives of these countries and a broad variety of other IGP members (multilateral organisations, development banks, private sector, CSOs and academia). The IGP plays a central role within the international resilience community in ensuring coherence and co-ordination of implementation and donor contributions on climate and disaster risk finance. Further, the IGP addresses challenges to applying insurance products. These include low consumer risk awareness; and demand and insufficient ability of insurers to provide low-cost coverage given data gaps and lack of sufficient pooling, among others (IGP, 2018[152]).

Insurance solutions should be embedded in broader measures for climate resilience. This means that the expansion of insurance instruments should be accompanied by a broader range of risk transfer and retention instruments by governments. This, in turn, may receive support of development co-operation (e.g. contingency funds, catastrophe bonds, cash transfers and concessional loans) and investments in risk reduction and preparedness (e.g. early warning systems and resilient infrastructure) (GIZ, 2019[138]). Insurance has shown to provide benefits for strengthening climate resilience. However, it is generally more suitable for weather events that occur with low frequency but high intensity than those that occur with high frequency (e.g. recurrent excessive rainfall leading to floods). Insurance that covers the latter type of events could lead to disproportionately high insurance premiums (Väänänen et al., 2019[150]). To address these issues, public funding from governments, possibly with support from development co-operation, may be necessary. Such funding would bear top-tier disaster risks so that climate and disaster insurance markets or schemes continue to exist. Technical and political challenges still limit the uptake of insurance for climate risks, including the following (Martinez-Diaz, Sidner and McClamrock, 2019[137]; Väänänen et al., 2019[150]; OECD, 2020[11]):

- limited willingness by policy makers to pay the premium due to lack of awareness of the benefit of such disaster risk insurance schemes
- competing development priorities for potential beneficiaries, making it difficult to justify the relatively high up-front premiums with uncertain returns
- poor management of unmet expectations (and the lack of confidence among stakeholders towards insurance), which result from gaps between modelled losses and actual losses, or from instances of non-payouts where the catastrophe models worked properly but policy holders still anticipated a payout
- risk of increase in premiums and decrease in the viability of insurance mechanisms due to increased frequency and intensity of climate-related disasters in the mid- to long-term
- insufficient uptake of a risk-layering approach in developing countries despite the importance of combining risk transfer instruments to address the various "layers" of risks.

Various practices and studies provide valuable insights into how to overcome the barriers and maximise the benefits of insurance for countries' efforts to strengthen climate resilience and pursue inclusive and sustainable development (Väänänen et al., 2019[150]; InsuResilience Investment Fund, 2018[149]; Martinez-Diaz, Sidner and McClamrock, 2019[137]; Jarzabkowski et al., 2019[153]). Such efforts can target various areas including comprehensive management of climate risks; enhancement of data and information; engagement with policy makers, target beneficiaries and insurers; and improvement of affordability of insurance solutions.Box 3.19 provides some examples of such approaches, while Table 3.22 provides examples of relevant tools and guides.

Table 3.22. Maximise the benefits of risk insurance solutions: Guidance and tools

Guidance and tools	Focus	Audience
Knowledge Hub: the InsuResilience Global Partnership for Climate and Disaster Risk Finance and Insurance Solutions(InsuResilience Global Partnership)	This knowledge hub provides an extensive list of tools, data and analytical work on climate and disaster risk finance, prepared under the Partnership, among others.	✓ Governments and development co-operation
A Multi-Criteria Assessment Framework and Key Performance Indicators (Munich Re)	Building on a Multi-Criteria Cost Effectiveness Analysis, this paper aims to develop an assessment framework that facilitates the comprehensive understanding of cost-effective climate risk insurance approaches for vulnerable populations.	✓ Governments and development co-operation
Linking Climate Risk Insurance with Shock-responsive Social Protection (InsuResilience Global Partnership)	Drawing from experiences, this document examines the opportunities and challenges that arise to link climate risk insurance with social protection measures.	✓ Governments and development co-operation
Applying a Gender Lens to Climate Risk Finance and Insurance (InsuResilience Global Partnership)	This paper aims to explore the link between gender and disaster risk financing and insurance and set out recommendations to strengthen the linkages.	✓ Governments and development co-operation

Box 3.19. Examples of approaches to promoting insurance solutions for climate risks

Comprehensive management of climate risks

- Combine insurance with measures to reduce vulnerabilities or exposures to hazards, or both. Examples of such measures include higher yielding seeds and fertilizers, climate-related policies, economic incentives for risk reduction and access to finance for those measures.
- Integrate insurance products into social protection. Combining insurance and social protection (e.g. grants for social safety nets, labour market interventions and social services) can support poverty reduction in the most vulnerable communities. Promoting risk-layering approaches would be helpful.
- Develop or adjust the PFM system to deliver payouts to beneficiaries in an effective and timely manner.

Engagement

- Promote capacity building and awareness raising for policy makers.
- Involve target beneficiaries at an early stage of insurance deployment and create functioning partnerships to achieve scale. Increasing understanding for insurance products and their mechanics is essential for their acceptance.
- Deploy effective measures to manage unmet expectations. This will require continual investment to improve climate risk model quality, as well as constant education for and communication with beneficiaries.
- Encourage insurers to improve their awareness of gender differences in designing their products and distribution channels, and gather sex-disaggregated industry data.

Affordability

- Continue to work to reduce costs of insurance products – both operational costs and the cost of insurance to beneficiaries – while avoiding moral hazards (e.g. imposition of conditions on policy holders to promote risk reduction).

- Deploy targeted support for premium to assist beneficiaries who need the insurance product most. Development co-operation providers and governments play an important role in providing concessional finance for such support.

Data and information

- Invest in analytics and research institutions to develop and improve models that provide a long-term view of climate risk and link to insurance solutions.
- Invest in open-source models that are open and widely available. This can ensure use of models to support public and private insurance mechanisms.

Source: (Väänänen et al., 2019[150]), Linking climate risk insurance with shock-responsive social protection, https://www.insuresilience.org; (InsuResilience Investment Fund, 2018[149]), Climate insurance schemes for poor and vulnerable households and micro, small and medium enterprises, https://www.insuresilienceinvestment.fund; (Martinez-Diaz, Sidner and McClamrock, 2019[137]), The future of disaster risk pooling for developing countries: Where do we go from here?, http://www.wri.org/publication/disaster-risk-pooling; (Jarzabkowski et al., 2019[153]), Insurance for Climate Adaptation: Opportunities and Limitations, https://cdn.gca.org.

3.3.8. Link action on financial inclusion with action on climate resilience

Effective approaches to improving financial inclusion can promote further savings by households and businesses and access to formal financial products, including insurance. Financial inclusion means "individuals and enterprises can access and use a range of different financial services offered in a well-regulated environment" (UNCDF, n.d.[154]). A greater level of savings and access to finance can in turn help these actors strengthen their abilities to reduce risks, and cope with and recover from climate-related hazards. Key targets are low-income households, small businesses, women, and other vulnerable groups (IPA, n.d.[155]; Moore et al., 2019[156]; Calderone, Weingärtner and Kroessin, 2019[157]). Access to credit can also allow households to finance investments in climate resilience measures they could not afford through their own savings. In many cases, loan repayments cost less than what households would have paid in repairs or coping with impacts of disasters (Hallegatte, Rentschler and Rozenberg, 2020[68]).

Key pillars for the promotion of financial inclusion include: i) provision of financial consumer protection; ii) development of national financial inclusion strategies; and iii) promotion of financial education (GPFI, 2010[158]). Increasing formal savings accounts, for instance, has been shown to encourage productive investments. They do this by providing a more secure means of storing money than informal savings methods (e.g. investment in livestock) (Moore et al., 2019[156]). Enhanced access to credit with appropriate consumer protection may also enable farmers and small businesses to invest in climate resilience (e.g. more resilient crops and agroforestry practices). For rural households, enhancing financial inclusion may require specific measures such as mobile banking to access savings and credit. This is especially the case for women given their roles within their households.

Good practices in financial education have also helped strengthen climate resilience through improved financial inclusion (Moore et al., 2019[156]). For instance, a study shows that a financial education programme in India increased the adoption of rainfall insurance from 8% to 16% (Gaurav, Cole and Tobacman, 2011[159]). Purchase of insurance products can mitigate losses caused by extreme weather events (IPA, n.d.[155]). At the same time, it can encourage farmers to increase spending on productive inputs such as water-efficient irrigation equipment that could contribute to their resilience to climate change.

A number of tools to facilitate financial education in general could also be useful for building climate resilience. These tools include some developed under the International Network on Financial Education and the Alliance for Financial Inclusion (AFI). Examples include development of nationally co-ordinated frameworks for financial education policies, and related mechanisms for co-ordination between government, civil society and the private sector (Bel and Eberlein, 2015[160]).

There has been some work to link the promotion of green finance and financial inclusion. For policy makers in financial regulators and finance ministries, AFI (2019[161]) proposes the "4P Framework for Inclusive Green Finance" (Table 3.23). A broader range of tools and guides to help governments link financial inclusion with climate resilience can be found in Table 3.24.

Table 3.23. 4P Framework and its implication for climate resilience

Policies from AFI's 4P Framework	Implication for climate resilience
Provision	Provision policies help to ensure financial services are provided to qualified beneficiaries, whether through targeted lending for reducing vulnerability or increasing adaptive capacity to climate change, or through (re)financing recovery and reconstruction efforts.
Promotion	Promotion policies create incentives for the private sector to offer financial services to qualified beneficiaries, for example, through moral suasion, awareness raising and capacity building for green lending, or data collection and dissemination on green finance.
Protection	Protection policies reduce financial risk through insurance or social payments, or by giving one early access to their assets in a time of crisis, among others.
Prevention	Prevention policies aim to avoid undesirable outcomes by lowering financial, social and environmental risks.

Source: Authors' elaboration based on (AFI, 2019[161]), Inclusive Green Finance: A Survey of the Policy Landscape, https://www.afi-global.org/publications/3036/Inclusive-Green-Finance-A-Survey-of-the-Policy-Landscape.

Table 3.24. Link action on financial inclusion with action on climate resilience: Guidance and tools

Guidance and tools	Focus	Audience
Inclusive Green Finance: From Concept to Practice (AFI)	This note provides a conceptual framework of how financial inclusion can enable and support climate change adaptation and mitigation. It also approaches inclusive green finance from a policy maker's perspective.	✓ Officials in financial regulators and other related ministries working on climate resilience
National Financial Inclusion Strategies: A Toolkit (AFI)	This toolkit provides practical guidance on formulating and implementing national financial inclusion strategies, and then systematically and efficiently monitoring and evaluating progress over time.	✓ Officials in financial ministries and financial regulators working on financial inclusion, and ministries working on climate resilience
OECD/INFE Toolkit for Measuring Financial Literacy and Financial Inclusion (OECD)	This toolkit aims to help institutions collect information about the country's financial literacy and inclusion, which can be used to identify target groups and prioritise initiatives, while giving an important signal that national financial education efforts are following international good practices.	✓ Officials in financial ministries and financial regulators working on financial inclusion, and ministries working on climate resilience
Financial Inclusion Support Framework (FISF)	The website of the FISF provides a number of case studies and knowledge products that can help accelerate and increase the effectiveness of reforms and other country-led actions to achieve national financial inclusion goals.	✓ Officials in financial ministries and financial regulators working on financial inclusion, and ministries working on climate resilience

3.3.9. Further engage the private sector in climate-resilient investment

The role of the private sector in financing climate resilience is increasingly recognised, as discussed in section 3.1 (see also Table 3.2). On the one hand, private-sector actors have been adjusting their operations in response to changes in their business environments, including a changing climate, for decades or centuries. On the other, they generally do not invest in action for climate resilience unless the investment generates acceptable risk-adjusted returns, or is required by law.

Various factors can prevent private sector investment in climate resilience. They include uncertainty in the expected impacts of climate change on individual businesses; regulatory frameworks that do not adequately consider social costs of climate change; and limited knowledge among businesses about climate risks and potential solutions as well as opportunities. These challenges, in turn, increase uncertainty in the financial viability of investments in climate resilience (Crawford and Church, 2019[162]; UNDP, n.d.[163]; UNEP DTU Partnership, 2018[164]).

Clear and bold policy goals set by national or sub-national governments in support of building climate resilience can enhance private sector confidence in the co-benefits and risk-return profiles of projects that aim to support climate resilience (UNDRR, 2020[98]). Those goals, in turn, can drive market interest and foster stronger partnership between public and private sectors (UNDRR, 2020[98]).

Laws and regulations can also provide private-sector actors with greater predictability in the quality of goods and services they should supply or purchase (e.g. material that meets building standards). There are various approaches to laws and regulations (Hallegatte, Rentschler and Rozenberg, 2019[90]; UNDRR, 2020[98]; Sudo, 2019[165]; Moser et al., 2019[123]; Casado Asensio, Kato and Shin, forthcoming[13]). Market regulations, for example, can be used in sectors such as water, electricity, agriculture and financial markets. Business registration processes, such as granting of business permits, is another option. Other approaches are procurement rules that consider climate resilience, and disclosure principles on physical risks of climate change to financial institutions. The private sector can also develop and promote its own quality standards for better climate resilience. Energy performance standards, for example, could consider climate risks. With these standards in place, it can then help clients become more resilient.

Financing models through PPPs can help transfer risks that the private sector cannot bear, such as default, to public partners better placed to handle them. The private sector may better address risks associated with, for instance, management and operations of infrastructure systems than the public sector can. By transferring such risks, PPPs can decrease downside risks of investment, provide strengthened resilience capacities to beneficiary communities and reduce burden on the government's balance sheet (Hallegatte, Rentschler and Rozenberg, 2019[90]; UNDRR, 2020[98]). Many governments still hold great potential to further improve legal frameworks and institutional arrangements to ensure that climate resilience is incorporated into the countries' PPP projects. For instance, many countries have their own disaster risk framework and PPP legal framework, but these two policy frameworks often do not interact sufficiently (Hallegatte, Rentschler and Rozenberg, 2019[90]).

Blended finance, defined as the strategic use of development finance to mobilise additional finance towards sustainable development (OECD, 2018[166]), has great potential to scale up private-sector investment in climate resilience. Pilots may have good potential to deliver impacts on climate resilience and generate a revenue stream or other benefits, for example. However, they may be unable to reach scale due to a high degree of risks or costs for the private sector. Blended finance can act as a bridge from reliance on grants and other donor financing towards more self-sustaining financing approaches to climate resilience (OECD, 2019[167]). The OECD Development Assistance Committee (DAC) endorsed the following Blended Finance Principles for Unlocking Commercial Finance for the Sustainable Development Goals as a policy tool for all providers of development finance (OECD, 2018[166]). The Principles are complemented by the Blended Finance Guidance, a practical tool for donors to design and implement quality blended finance approaches, adopted by the DAC in 2020 (OECD, 2020[168]).

- Principle 1: Anchor blended finance use to a development rationale.
- Principle 2: Design blended finance to increase the mobilisation of commercial finance.
- Principle 3: Tailor blended finance to local context.
- Principle 4: Focus on effective partnering for blended finance.
- Principle 5: Monitor blended finance for transparency and results.

Most multilateral development financial institutions, as well as many bilateral donors, deploy blended finance approaches to strengthen climate action (Miller and Swann, 2019[103]). There have already been applications of blended finance to projects for climate resilience in sectors such as water supply, sanitation, agriculture and energy sectors. See Box 3.20 on the use of blended finance to strengthen climate resilience in the water supply and sanitation sector.

Box 3.20. Using blended finance for water supply and sanitation

There are emerging cases where blended finance has supported action to enhance climate resilience, including in the water supply and sanitation sector (OECD, 2019[167]). In Latin America, the Water Funds promote the pooling of public and private financing to support sustainable watershed management through nature-based solutions. They create incentives for the private sector to engage in biodiversity conservation and climate adaptation (OECD, 2019[167]).

Development partners also often provide guarantees (e.g. credit risk and political risk guarantees) to limit the risk exposure of commercial lenders. These guarantees aim to mobilise commercial finance for climate-resilient projects in the water supply and sanitation sector through the mitigation of financial risk. This process can then lower the cost of capital.

Apart from guarantees, grants for capacity development also play an important role in improving the technical and financial performance of utilities, hence enhancing their creditworthiness. Grants for capacity development could also help commercial banks and investors build their internal capacities to adjust their financing practices. In addition, such grants could help create financial products targeting the needs of the water supply and sanitation sector. These needs might include longer tenors with a sufficient grace period, and reduced collateral requirements (OECD, 2019[167]).

Table 3.25. Further engage the private sector in climate-resilient investment: Guidance and tools

Guidance and tools	Focus	Audience
Engaging the Private Sector (UNDP)	Based on UNDP's "3 Cs" (Convening, Catalysing and Capitalising) framework, this website provides a range of information on interventions, financial instruments and case studies, which can help practitioners learn from good practices and lessons.	✓ Officials in governments and development co-operation providers working on climate change and/or private sector development
OECD DAC Blended Finance Guidance (OECD)	The OECD DAC Blended Finance Guidance, adopted in September 2020, is a practical policy tool to help donors put the Blended Finance Principles into practice. The Guidance provides policy recommendations, as well as practical steps and elements to facilitate understanding and good practice on the design and implementation of blended finance programmes. The Guidance also provides good practice examples and key references for blended finance implementers to follow.	✓ Governments and development co-operation providers
Toolkit for Engaging the Private Sector in National Adaptation Plans (NAPs) (NAP Global Network)	This toolkit aims to help governments develop strategies for the effective engagement of private-sector actors in the NAP process.	✓ Officials in governments, especially those leading NAP processes, as well as private sector development
Business Sector Prioritization and Engagement Tool (UNDP, UNEP and WRI)	This tool aims to help micro and small enterprises learn how to prioritise areas or investments in measures on climate change adaptation, examine drivers and barriers, and identify policy interventions.	✓ Businesses and officials in governments and development co-operation providers working on climate change and/or private sector development
Driving Finance Today for the Climate Resilient Society of Tomorrow (UNEP FI)	Part of this analytical work, prepared for the Global Commission on Adaptation, looks into roles of financial ministries and their related financial system governing bodies in promoting and accelerating adaptation investment.	✓ Officials in finance ministries and financial market regulators

EU Taxonomy Technical Report (TEG)	This document is a basis for the EU classification system for environmentally sustainable economic activities (EU Taxonomy), a tool that can enable financial sector and capital markets to identify investment opportunities that contribute to environmental policy objectives. The report provides a list of adaptation activities.	✓ Government officials and development co-operation practitioners
Climate Resilient Public Private Partnerships: A Toolkit for Decision Makers (IDB)	The toolkit aims to provide professionals with pragmatic, practical solutions to integrate the assessment of climate risks and resilience-related opportunities into the preparation of infrastructure projects through public-private partnerships (PPPs).	✓ Professionals working on PPPs

DAC: Development Assistance Committee; IDB: Inter-American Development Bank; UNDP: United Nations Development Programme; UNEP: United Nations Environment Programme; WRI: World Resources Institute.

3.3.10. Facilitate access to climate finance

Article 2.1c of the Paris Agreement requires ratifying Parties to make finance flows consistent with a pathway towards low greenhouse gas emissions and climate-resilient development (UNFCCC, 2015[2]). There is emerging evidence of effective co-ordination in building climate resilience on the ground between providers of development finance, national governments and sub-national actors, as well as non-state actors (e.g. civil society and the private sector) (LIFE-AR, 2019[4]).

Box 3.21. Evolution of climate finance provided and mobilised

An OECD report, *Climate Finance Provided and Mobilised by Developed Countries in 2013-18,* shows how climate finance has evolved over that period in the following four categories: bilateral public climate finance, multilateral climate finance (attributed to developed countries), climate-related officially supported export credits, and private finance mobilised by developed countries public finance interventions.

Climate finance targeting climate change adaptation and mitigation objectives was on the rise on a year-by-year basis over the period. Adaptation finance grew by an annual average of 29%, from USD 10.1 billion in 2016 to USD 16.8 billion in 2018. Mitigation finance increased from USD 42.2 billion in USD 55 billion in 2018. Finance for cross-cutting objectives (i.e. targeting both adaptation and mitigation) decreased from USD 6.2 billion in 2016 to USD 5.5 billion in 2017 but rose to USD 7.1 billion in 2018. The focus of climate finance in low income countries (LICs) differs substantially than for developing countries on average. Adaptation, grant financing, and the water and sanitation and agriculture sectors represent higher shares of climate finance in LICs.

The analysis included in the report builds upon three main data sources: biennial reports submitted by Annex I Parties to the United Nations Framework Convention on Climate Change; OECD Development Assistance Committee (DAC) statistics on development finance; and OECD export credit statistics. To fill in a limited number of remaining gaps, the OECD collected complementary ad hoc data from climate finance providers or developed estimates based on publicly available sources.

Source: (OECD, 2020[169]) Climate Finance Provided and Mobilised by Developed Countries in 2013-18 https://doi.org/10.1787/f0773d55-en.

Accessing climate finance nevertheless remains a challenge for governments of many developing countries (Shine, 2017[170]). It is also challenging to ensure that climate finance reaches stakeholders at the local level where action on climate resilience is needed most (LIFE-AR, 2019[4]) and those who are particularly vulnerable to climate risks. For instance, a study shows that only 11% of climate finance flowed to the local level between 2003 and 2015 (Soanes and Shakya, 2016[171]). Small-scale agriculture actors encounter a number of technical, political and commercial barriers to accessing climate finance. Only a small percentage of climate finance has been targeted at small-scale producers [see (Chiriac and Naran, 2020[172]) for more information]. Further, women also often face greater challenges in accessing climate finance. Further engagement of women's organisations, feminist advocates and gender-related groups in climate finance is important for ensuring their access to funding for gender-responsive action on climate resilience (WEDO, 2019[173]).

Accessing climate finance is resource- and time-intensive for governments, creating several practical barriers to accessing climate finance. For example, governments need to obtain data on climate risks facing people and ecosystems in the country to develop project proposals. They must also understand costs of needed measures to manage the risks and promote the development of project pipelines. In addition, they must identify appropriate financial sources and solutions. It is even harder to obtain such information in a disaggregated way by gender or social group. The architecture of climate finance sources is complex for many developing countries. Navigating it can often be resource-intensive, especially for countries with constrained capacity (OECD, 2015[120]). Further, different ministries and agencies are often in charge of different international funding channels. Thus, information can be fragmented across those different government institutions (NDC Partnership, 2018[174]).

Understanding and meeting procedures and standards required by providers of finance can also be a challenge. Some countries seeking climate finance lack sufficient in-country institutional structures or capacities. Many potential beneficiaries, including governments and non-state actors, often struggle to design well-articulated proposals. These proposals must demonstrate effectiveness and transformational impacts on climate resilience, while meeting standards for economic, environmental and social due diligence. As a result, many stakeholders with project ideas lack confidence about whether their projects are good enough to receive international funding (NDC Partnership, 2018[174]; OECD, 2015[120]). Countries that pursue direct access modalities to the Green Climate Fund or the Adaptation Fund also need strong national institutions that can meet robust fiduciary standards, and environmental and social safeguards, among other factors.

There has been accumulating experience of dealing with these challenges and enhancing access to climate finance by both governments' own efforts and support of development co-operation to strengthen the needed capacities. While the tools and guides that can be useful to facilitate access to climate finance are summarised in Table 3.26, some examples of recommended actions are also outlined in Box 3.22.

Table 3.26. Facilitate access to development finance: Guidance and tools

Guidance and tools	Focus	Audience
Accessing Climate Finance: A Step-by-Step Approach for Practitioners (ClimaSouth)	This guide provides a practical set of tools for key government and other stakeholders in partner countries to access climate finance. The tools present concrete step-by-step approaches to the preparation and assessment of project applications.	✓ Staff in governments and their domestic stakeholders
Supporting Access to Finance for Climate Action (Sida)	This guide primarily aims to provide guidance to Sida staff on different sources of finance for climate action in support of dialogue with, and support to, partner organisations in their implementation of the Paris Agreement.	✓ Staff in development co-operation providers
Toolkit to Enhance Access to Adaptation Finance (OECD)	This toolkit outlines a spectrum of "tools" that could help countries navigate the evolving architecture of climate finance and seize opportunities for accessing finance for adaptation.	✓ Government officials primarily in LDCs, SIDS and landlocked developing countries
Online Sourcebook: Integrating Gender In Climate Change Adaptation Proposals (USAID)	This sourcebook aims to enable project proponents to design gender-responsive climate change adaptation measures and projects, particularly in developing countries, by providing targeted, sector-specific guidance and real-life examples.	✓ Individuals and teams who prepare large-scale climate change adaptation
The NDC Funding and Initiatives Navigator (NDC Partnership)	The NDC Funding and Initiatives Navigator is a searchable database of financial and technical support that can help countries plan and implement their NDCs.	✓ Staff in governments working on NDC implementation

Elaboration of the Sources of and Modalities for Accessing Financial Support for Addressing Loss and Damage (UNFCCC)	This document provides a comprehensive overview of existing sources of financial support, including the financial mechanism of UNFCCC and a broader set of funds and institutions that channel financial support relevant for addressing loss and damage associated with climate change impacts.	✓	Staff in governments and development co-operation
A Resource Guide to Climate Finance (ACT Alliance)	This guide aims to provide an orientation to the available multilateral and bilateral funds that may be relevant for financing climate-related programmes and projects.	✓	Primarily ACT Alliance members and partners, as well as other faith-based organisations, CSOs and public institutions in developing countries

Note: CSOs: civil society organisations; LDCs: Least Developed Countries; NDC: Nationally Determined Contributions; Sida: Swedish International Development Cooperation Agency; SIDS: Small Island Developing States; UNFCCC: United Nations Framework Convention on Climate Change; USAID: United States Agency for International Development.

Box 3.22. Examples of recommended actions to enhance access to climate finance

Support and facilitate preparation of project and programme proposals

- Support effort to enhance capacities of government agencies and other relevant non-state actors in obtaining, generating, analysing and maintaining data needed for project development (e.g. for climate risk assessments, as well as economic and financial analysis).
- Raise political awareness and technical capacities to prepare project proposals for funding in light of the country's priorities on climate resilience and sustainable development.
- Engage a range of stakeholders, especially the most vulnerable to climate change, at an early stage of project proposal development in a transparent way that captures adequate information and expertise, as well as social considerations.

Identify the most relevant international financing channels

- Familiarise with practical sources of information on providers of climate finance [see for instance (OECD, 2020[175]; ODI, 2019[176]; UNFCCC, 2019[177]; Shine, 2017[170])].
- Understand and identify the most relevant climate finance sources and channels, based on their eligibility criteria, access modalities, programming priorities and logical frameworks in light of the country's priorities, needs and capacities.

Support capacity development at the organisational level

- Identify needs and opportunities for strengthening the institutional capacity (especially that of national focal points for climate funds such as the GCF and the GEF) in understanding the modalities of potential funding sources, and co-ordinate with stakeholders.
- If the country aims to accredit a domestic organisation as a direct access entity, identify candidates, familiarise them with accreditation procedures, help them collect evidence to meet accreditation criteria (e.g. fiduciary standards and environmental and social safeguards), among other actions, potentially with support of development co-operation.

Enhance domestic enabling environments to attract private and public finance

- Develop robust and predictable regulatory frameworks and well-designed economic incentives that are more likely to attract domestic and international finance or co-finance for climate-related projects, which can strengthen scalability and replicability potential of the project proposal.

Source: (OECD, 2015[120]), Toolkit to enhance access to adaptation finance, http://www.oecd.org/environment/cc; (Tippmann et al., 2016[178]) ClimaSouth E-Handbook N.8. Accessing Climate Finance, https://www.climamed.eu; (NDC Partnership, 2018[174]) Navigating International Climate Finance", webpage, https://ndcpartnership.org/node/15/.

3.4. Monitoring, evaluation and learning (MEL)

3.4.1. Checklist for action

ACTIONS	ACTOR(S)
Identify the objectives of the MEL framework to determine the most suitable approach	
✓ Identify through stakeholder consultation the key questions the MEL framework will address and develop a portfolio of complementary MEL tools to address those questions.	Climate resilience lead ministry or agency potentially w/ support from dev-co, academic institutes or CSOs
✓ Determine through stakeholder consultation data and information (including Indigenous knowledge and local understanding) available, existing gaps and approaches to address them.	Climate resilience lead ministry or agency w/ support from dev-co, academic institutes or CSOs
✓ Engage stakeholders in assessing emerging findings from monitoring and evaluation to facilitate learning and an iterative and adaptive approach to climate resilience.	Climate resilience lead ministry or agency potentially w/ support from dev-co, academic institutes or CSOs
✓ Explore opportunities for aligning climate resilience MEL frameworks with established guidelines and standards that may provide opportunities for aggregating data and information across sectors or levels of government.	Ministry or agency in charge of MEL, potentially w/ dev-co
✓ Align MEL frameworks with local capacities, and where possible use local MEL systems to further develop capabilities.	Ministry or agency in charge of MEL and dev-co
Develop indicators consistent with human and financial capacities that can inform monitoring and evaluation	
✓ Assess what data are monitored on a regular basis (including common socio-economic and sectoral data) that can inform a MEL framework for climate resilience.	Ministry or agency in charge of MEL and dev-co
✓ Identify data and information gaps for effective MEL for climate resilience and develop indicators commensurate with the human and financial resources available.	Ministry or agency in charge of MEL and dev-co
✓ Complement quantitative indicators with qualitative assessment to monitor changes in climate risks and to assess how those changes have come about.	Ministry or agency in charge of MEL and dev-co
✓ Draw on information from monitoring and evaluation for learning that can guide adjustments of the climate resilience initiative over time.	Ministry or agency in charge of MEL and dev-co
Conduct climate resilience portfolio and allocation analysis	
✓ Conduct a portfolio analysis to determine if the allocation of financial commitments reflect national or organisational priorities on climate change and the needs of partner countries.	Dev-co in particular

Note: Key actors (i.e. governments or development co-operation, or both) with the primary role in promoting individual actions can greatly vary among countries and sectors; the "Key actors" column nevertheless indicates the likely leaders in each of the actions. Some actions are led by governments but in many cases also supported by development co-operation (indicated as "Governments with support from dev-co").
CSOs: civil society organisations; Dev-co: providers of development co-operation; MEL: Monitoring, evaluation and learning.
Actions listed in this list are indicative and some may not be relevant to all countries or development co-operation providers. Section 3.4. is informed by (Noltze et al., forthcoming[179]) developed by the German Institute for Development Evaluation as input to this Guidance.

3.4.2. Rationale

As countries across levels of governance and sectors are identifying, prioritising, developing and implementing climate resilience interventions (strategies, policies, plans and programmes), they need mechanisms that facilitate assessments of progress made, impacts achieved and lessons learnt. Most countries have reporting mechanisms to monitor domestic policy processes. Many also have auditing mechanisms. These assess the compliance of domestic expenditures with agreed national and international goals and targets, and the extent to which expenditure is allocated cost-effectively in accordance with rules, regulations and principles of good governance (OECD, 2015[180]). The global agendas on development, climate change and disaster risk reduction further call for national and global stocktakes of progress, including on climate adaptation and resilience. Monitoring and evaluation has also been recognised as a critical phase of the NAP process, playing an important role in defining progress and evaluating effectiveness (see Box 3.23 for an example from Ghana).

Box 3.23. National climate reporting mechanisms in Ghana

In Ghana, every government implementing agency is mandated to monitor and evaluate its respective policies, programmes and projects. These are guided by national indicators, baselines and targets identified in the National Medium Term Policy Framework and in the Sector and District Planning. This process, in turn, is overseen by the National Development Planning Commission (NDPC). Rather than propose new reporting processes, Ghana's Nationally Determined Contributions (NDC), National Climate Change Policy, National Climate Change Adaptation Strategy and National Adaptation Plan Framework therefore all refer to existing reporting frameworks. Guidelines integrate NDC priorities into local medium-term development plans, which ensures that climate issues are monitored and evaluated through standard NDCP processes.

Source: (OECD, 2020[11]) Common Ground Between the Paris Agreement and the Sendai Framework: Climate Change Adaptation and Disaster Risk Reduction, https://doi.org/10.1787/3edc8d09-en.

The wealth of data available can inform domestic monitoring, evaluation and learning (MEL) frameworks for climate resilience. Ongoing monitoring of progress in implementing agreed deliverables must be complemented by evaluations of the extent and the efficiency by which outputs, outcomes and impacts have been achieved. Regular assessments of the nature of climate risks and an understanding of how these change over time can also guide discussions. Changes in the climate risk profile, for example, can be due to emerging hazards, changes in the exposure or vulnerability to those hazards, a reflection of the response taken to manage them or something else entirely (OECD, 2015[180]). For this information to guide subsequent approaches, mechanisms must be in place that encourage and facilitate learning (see Box 3.24). This is particularly important given the uncertain nature of current and projected climate impacts.

Approaches to strengthening climate resilience may result in varying impacts to different groups of society, including women, men, Indigenous people and other socially marginalised populations. By monitoring and evaluating the impacts of interventions on the climate resilience of marginalised groups, MEL systems can contribute towards a more inclusive process and access to any emerging benefits (Dazé and Church, 2019[6]). For example, a focus in MEL on gender differences in participation and benefits can help redress observed imbalances and track progress on gender equality and women's empowerment. Over time, this can lead to increased levels of ambition (Dazé and Church, 2019[6]).

Box 3.24. Definitions of monitoring, evaluation and learning (MEL) of climate resilience

Monitoring examines on an ongoing basis progress in implementing planned initiatives that directly or indirectly contribute to climate resilience. It entails a continuous assessment of the enabling environment in place and of the capacities to develop and implement climate resilience policies, plans and strategies. It further includes the identification of climate resilience outcomes, outputs, activities and inputs, as well as of the indicators to assess progress, and manage and analyse data.

Evaluation is an independent assessment of progress in reducing climate risks and vulnerabilities and an analysis of how the change came about. Evaluations are based on the data monitored, but they also draw on other relevant information, such as stakeholder consultations and expert reviews. An important focus is on evaluations that determine the effectiveness or impact of an intervention.

Learning requires the development of systems and procedures to reflect and act on the information generated by monitoring and evaluation. This must be complemented by a learning environment that is inclusive and participatory. The deep uncertainty of climate change and the context specificity of climate resilience measures makes learning a particularly important component of a climate resilience reporting system.

Source: (OECD, 2015[180]) National Climate Change Adaptation: Emerging Practices in Monitoring and Evaluation, https://dx.doi.org/10.1787/9789264229679-en.

Climate change is inherently uncertain. It interacts with other risks and the diverse set of drivers that determine nature's and society's response to climate change. This means that climate resilience interventions are often based on a range of *ex ante* assumptions. An effective MEL framework needs to identify, reflect on and deal with these sometimes implicit assumptions (Dinshaw, 2018[181]). This uncertainty in the evolution of climate risks and how best to approach climate resilience highlights the importance of a flexible and iterative approach. Further challenges in developing MEL frameworks are noted by several other researchers are highlighted below (Dinshaw et al., 2014[182]; Bours, 2014[183]; AF-TERG, 2020[184]; Noltze et al., forthcoming[179]):

- **Long-time horizons**: the objective of climate resilience measures to strengthen the resilience of sectors or communities to current and future climate variability and change is a long-term process. Outcomes and impacts will often become evident only years or potentially decades after the introduction of a resilience measure. Progress will in some cases be difficult to assess in the absence of an event. Examples include the effectiveness of coastal protection measures or nature-based solutions in reducing the impacts of sea-level rise. Success in some cases will mean no observable changes but instead maintaining status quo.
- **Moving baselines and targets**: baseline data collected at the start of an intervention provide a reference point for assessing progress. Given the uncertain nature of climate change, simply comparing the situation before and after a climate resilience intervention may not be sufficient for assessing its effectiveness or impact. Instead, the baseline may have to be revised to provide a more accurate understanding of what would have happened in the absence of the intervention.
- **Attribution**: the challenge of the long timeframes is compounded by changes in social, economic and environmental variables. Multiple drivers (e.g. behavioural or technological change) may also contribute towards a desired outcome, which makes it challenging to attribute the outcome to a particular intervention.

Given these challenges, the focus to date has primarily been on monitoring progress in implementing climate resilience interventions rather than evaluating their impact. While the interactions between climate and development are not fully understood, the MEL and climate resilience communities also need to further examine the lessons learnt from past performance. In so doing, they can build more systematically on lessons in both the design and implementation but also in the associated MEL approaches (Barrett et al., 2019[185]).

Providers of development co-operation and dedicated climate finance mechanisms increasingly recognise the challenges of MEL for climate resilience and the importance of taking this agenda forward. This, for example, is reflected in recent discussions of the Adaptation Fund Board (AF-TERG, 2020[184]) and by the OECD DAC Network on Development Evaluation. This section outlines key elements to be considered when developing MEL frameworks for climate resilience:

- Identify the objectives of the MEL framework to determine the most suitable approach.
- Develop indicators consistent with human and financial capacities that can inform monitoring and evaluation.
- Conduct climate resilience portfolio and allocation analysis.

3.4.3. Identify the objectives of the MEL framework to determine the most suitable approach

A MEL framework will be guided by the objectives of the intervention, whether a strategy, policy, plan or programme (see discussion in sections 3.1 and 3.2). These, in turn, may be informed by international commitments on climate change and disaster risk reduction, among others (see Box 3.25 on defining objectives for climate change adaptation interventions). The impact or contribution of the intervention can be assessed against these objectives. Indicators provide the basis against which the intervention is monitored and evaluated. In the context of climate resilience, the time horizon (i.e. impacts today versus impacts in future) and the coverage (i.e. impacts at the place of implementation versus in areas indirectly affected by the intervention) must be carefully considered when choosing the MEL approach.

Box 3.25. Defining objectives for climate change adaptation interventions

The Paris Agreement provides a goal on adaptation of "enhancing adaptive capacity, strengthening resilience and reducing vulnerability to climate change, with a view to contributing to sustainable development and ensuring an adequate adaptation response [...]" (Article 7.1) (UNFCCC, 2015[2]). The adaptation goal itself, however, remains vague. Countries define their own national goals, targets and indicators, for example, through their Nationally Determined Contribution (NDC) and National Adaptation Plan (NAP) processes. The Sendai Framework details a global goal on disaster risk reduction with 7 outcome-based targets, 38 associated indicators and standardised reporting mechanisms of which several contribute to climate resilience (UNDRR, 2015[186]).

MEL frameworks for climate resilience must factor in the potential impact of climate variability and change to be supportive of an adaptive management approach that facilitates learning (AF-TERG, 2020[184]) (see also section 3.1.5). This requires a good understanding of climate risks and the broader socio-economic context. It can be challenging for MEL frameworks to address this complexity while remaining simple and operational tools (Douxchamps et al., 2017[187]). Selecting the most appropriate MEL approach requires good understanding of climate resilience priorities and the questions the MEL framework aims to answer. Examples of potential questions are listed below, each requiring a different approach and focus:

- Whose resilience was strengthened and which climate risks were addressed? Which segments of society did not benefit, or potentially were harmed by the initiative? Did the initiative fail to address certain risks?

- How were the particular causes of climate vulnerability affecting women and men, and marginalised groups, addressed?
- Taking into account the socio-economic context in which the initiative was implemented, how effective was it in strengthening resilience?
- What elements of the initiative were effective in addressing climate risks and how was that impact brought about?
- What are the impacts of the initiative in the near- and medium-term? Locally, nationally, regionally? For women and for men?

MEL frameworks for climate resilience will in most cases include multiple objectives, highlighting the need for tailored frameworks that draw on different MEL methods. The objectives can broadly be grouped in three ways. Formative objectives focus on the evolving nature of an intervention, with the aim of learning and improving over the course of implementation. Summative objectives summarise the results of an intervention and provide final assessments of its success. Participatory objectives focus on the importance of inclusive and participatory approaches to enhance transparency and buy-in. In the context of development co-operation, an additional objective may be that of accountability. See (Noltze et al., forthcoming[179]) for an overview of different MEL methods and approaches.

Box 3.26. Theory-based evaluation of the African Risk Capacity

The African Risk Capacity (ARC), a specialised agency of the African Union, is an index-based weather risk insurance pool and early response mechanism. In 2015, the United Kingdom commissioned an independent evaluation of ARC for 2015-24. It sought to identify and feed lessons learnt into ARC's programme management; assess its effectiveness with the aim of contributing to the global evidence base; and provide accountability. The evaluation includes a formative component that tests ARC's Theory of Change (ToC) and assesses whether ARC is on track to achieve agreed outcomes. This is complemented by a summative component assessing ARC's contribution to the outcomes identified in the ToC.

Complexity of the intervention is driven and augmented by: i) high levels of uncertainty around how the programme will evolve and where and when it will achieve results; ii) high degrees of interdependence across multiple stakeholder levels; iii) emergent conditions in implementation of the programme and in the manifestation of droughts and other natural hazards; and iv) the co-evolutionary nature of applying ARC's contingency planning frameworks to implementation as interacting and adaptive agents organise themselves.

Source: (Scott et al., 2017[188]) Independent Evaluation of African Risk Capacity (ARC): Final Inception Report https://www.africanriskcapacity.org/wp-content/uploads/2018/03/Formative-Phase-1-ARC-Evaluation_merged.pdf (in Noltze et al. (forthcoming[179])).

OECD (2015[180]) analysis of country approaches to monitoring and evaluation of climate change adaptation highlighted the potential of a portfolio of tools. Individual tools only capture distinct components, while a combination of tools sheds light on progress in strengthening climate resilience. The applicability of the tools will vary across countries and over time:

- ***Climate risk and vulnerability assessments*** at the outset of a national focus on climate resilience (e.g. with the introduction of a related strategy or plan) can contribute to a baseline understanding of the nature of climate vulnerability and exposure against which changes in the country's climate resilience can be assessed. When such assessments are repeated regularly, they point to changes in the risk and vulnerability profile over time. These must be complemented by analysis of how those changes have come about.

- ***Indicators to monitor agreed climate resilience priorities*** over time and between locations are resource-intensive to identify, collect and use. It is therefore important to define a manageable set of qualitative and quantitative indicators that capture the climate resilience priorities. At the same time, the indicators must reflect data already available and the capacity to monitor them. Sampling strategies for data collection or focus group interviews may also be useful to improve efficiency. Further, indicators alone will not provide adequate insights into, and understanding of, the changes observed.
- ***Project and programme evaluations*** can help identify approaches to climate resilience that are effective in achieving agreed objectives. They can further contribute to a better understanding of the role of the broader socio-economic contexts in determining the outcomes of such initiatives.
- ***National audits and climate expenditure reviews*** can help answer several questions related to public expenditures. Are the expenditures aligned with national and international climate resilience objectives? Do they respect rules, regulations and principles of good governance? Are they cost-effective? Audits and expenditure reviews can also support accountability where resources from development co-operation may be earmarked for specific initiatives.

Climate resilience often will be mainstreamed across sectoral policies, plans and programmes. Consequently, a MEL framework may not aim to show how strengthened resilience can be attributed to individual interventions. Rather, it may point to how they have contributed to national climate resilience objectives over time (OECD, 2015[180]). This is particularly the case when evaluations are conducted before the full outcomes or impacts have manifested (EEA, 2020[189]).

Engagement with different non-state actors can play an important role in pointing to, and sharing, data and information that can inform monitoring and evaluation. Examples include the role of Indigenous groups in providing knowledge and local understanding of the natural environment and traditional approaches to manage risks (AF-TERG, 2020[184]). Stakeholder engagement can play an equally important role to support translation of findings from monitoring and evaluation into learning. To that end, stakeholder should be incorporated in subsequent decision-making processes (EEA, 2020[189]). Communicating the findings to a broader audience through established mechanisms can also contribute to a strengthened evidence base (Dinshaw, 2018[181]). The credibility of MEL frameworks, in fact, relies on the consent and participation of the people and institutions the intervention aims to support (AF-TERG, 2020[184]). In practice, top-down approaches continue to be prevalent where the target groups of an intervention will not necessarily participate actively in the MEL process (AF-TERG, 2020[184]).

Guidelines and standards at international, national, sectoral or programme levels will also inform MEL frameworks for climate resilience. Examples include reporting requirements agreed upon internationally, e.g. for the SDGs or the Sendai Framework for Disaster Risk Reduction; national or sectoral priorities in key strategy documents; or reporting requirements by providers of development co-operation. Those guidelines may facilitate some aggregation across comparable thematic interventions. However, in all cases, ensuring the framework reflects local capacities will be a priority; where possible, it should use local systems to further develop that capacity (Noltze et al., forthcoming[179]).

A range of knowledge products have been developed that can guide efforts to identify the objectives of the MEL framework and determine the approach, some of which are summarised in Table 3.27.

Table 3.27. Identify the objectives of the MEL framework and determine the approach: Guidance and tools

Guidance and tools	Focus	Audience
Impact Evaluation Guidebook for Climate Adaptation Projects (GIZ)	This guidebook supports project managers by providing an overview of different impact evaluation methods and how they can be applied to climate change adaptation projects.	✓ Development practitioners
Participatory Monitoring, Evaluation, Reflection and Learning (PMERL) (CARE)	This manual helps practitioners measure, monitor and evaluate changes in local adaptive capacity, for better decision making in community-based adaptation activities. The approach provides an ongoing platform for local stakeholders to articulate their own needs and preferences beyond the lifetime of a project.	✓ Project managers and field staff, communities and local partners engaged in designing and implementing community-based adaptation projects
Tracking Adaptation and Measuring Development (IIED)	This document provides a conceptual framework that countries can use to i) evaluate how far, and how well, climate risks are managed at international, national and sub-national scales; and ii) use vulnerability and development indicators to assess whether development outcomes bring better local climate resilience, and whether that aggregates at larger scales to contribute to climate-resilient development.	✓ Staff in government agencies and development co-operation providers
Guidebook for Monitoring and Evaluating Ecosystem-based Adaptation Interventions (GIZ, UNEP-WCMC and FEBA)	This guidebook provides an overview of the process needed for designing and implementing effective monitoring and evaluation for ecosystem-based adaptation. It describes key considerations and components for each step and points to additional tools and methodologies that provide more specific instructions.	✓ Development practitioners
Adaptation Made to Measure (GIZ)	This guide seeks to equip officials and practitioners for a systematic, step-by-step approach to developing adaptation projects and results-based monitoring systems.	✓ Representatives of governments, bilateral donors and non-governmental organisations
AdaptMe Toolkit (UKCIP)	This toolkit aims to provide practical support in evaluating adaptation progress and performance. It highlights the challenges of evaluating adaptation initiatives, and provides tools for design a robust evaluation.	✓ Officials and practitioners in organisations that have undertaken adaptation initiatives
PPCR Monitoring and Reporting Toolkit 2018 (Climate Investment Funds)	This toolkit offers practical guidance to in-country stakeholders of the Pilot Program for Climate Resilience (PPCR) on enabling the monitoring and reporting system review. It establishes a basis for monitoring and evaluation of the impact, outcomes and outputs of PPCR-funded activities. The logic model depicts the cause-and-effect chain of results from inputs and activities through to project outputs, programme outcomes and national/international impacts.	✓ Government focal points for PPCR-funded activities and their MEL counterparts
Magenta Book: Central Government Guidance on Evaluation (UK Government)	This book provides a comprehensive overview of evaluation in government in general rather than in the context of climate resilience in particular. It highlights the role of scoping, design, management, use and dissemination of evaluation and the capabilities required of government evaluators.	✓ Policy, delivery and analysis professions; all of which are responsible for securing and using good evidence

3.4.4. Develop indicators consistent with human and financial capacities that can inform monitoring and evaluation

Climate resilience initiatives will often be closely aligned with and directly contribute to broader development objectives. Most national-level indicators for monitoring and evaluating climate resilience interventions will therefore be informed by socio-economic or sectoral data systematically collected by most countries (Hallegatte, Rentschler and Rozenberg, 2020[68]). Different types of indicators can be considered (e.g. process, output, outcome and impact indicators; qualitative and quantitative; indicators and indices) (Lamhauge, Lanzi and Agrawala, 2012[190]). Gender-disaggregated data can contribute to a better understanding of whether and how the impacts differ among women and men. Over time it can shed light on the effectiveness of different approaches in addressing those aspects of the risks that are gender-specific.

Determining how to use the data available, identifying gaps and potentially collecting new data for monitoring is resource-intensive. This highlights the importance of setting priorities that match the human and financial resources available to support MEL. Drawing on established indicators provides opportunities for aggregating information across levels of reporting. Examples include initiatives that cut across sectors or levels of government, national or global processes (e.g. countries' NDCs or NAPs or reporting on resilience-related SDG or Sendai indicators). In practice, such exchanges of information have often proven difficult or limited in value given the context-specific nature of climate resilience initiatives (Leiter and Pringle, 2018[191]) (EEA, 2020[189]).

Regular monitoring of indicators provides a good basis for assessing progress made but also where it may be lagging. To understand changes, quantitative assessments must be complemented by qualitative information that explores different factors contributing to the outcome (Lamhauge, Lanzi and Agrawala, 2012[190]) (see an example from development co-operation in Box 3.27). When learning is an integral part of the process, regular monitoring can also guide course corrections in the implementation of the initiative. In this way, adjustments need not be considered admissions of failure (Hallegatte, Rentschler and Rozenberg, 2020[68]). This is important in the context of climate change where the risk landscape changes or where scientific or technological advances facilitate a better understanding of the risks and enable more targeted approaches (Hallegatte, Rentschler and Rozenberg, 2020[68]).

The inclusion of milestones and triggers can also facilitate an adaptive approach to climate resilience and learning. For example, new information on climate risks (e.g. new climate projections) or the reaching of certain milestones (e.g. sea-level rise) provides an opportunity to assess if the approach is still appropriate (Haasnoot, van 't Klooster and van Alphen, 2018[192]; DEFRA, 2020[193]). In some cases, adjustments may suffice; in others, more fundamental changes may be needed (see section 3.1.5 on adaptive pathway approaches). Table 3.28 points to some guidelines and tools that can inspire the development of indicators for climate resilience.

Box 3.27. InsuResilience Global Partnership – A collaborative effort towards development of a holistic, multidimensional MEL framework

In 2019, the InsuResilience Global Partnership for Climate and Disaster Risk Finance and Insurance Solutions introduced a new MEL framework in support of "Vision 2025". The framework consists of six result areas, corresponding targets and indicators. Each result area has a prominent lead indicator and the result areas track progress on, respectively: i) total risk covered and number of people protected; ii) number of countries with comprehensive disaster risk finance strategy; iii) number of countries adopting climate and disaster risk finance and insurance solutions; iv) increased cost-effectiveness; v) development/human impact; and vi) increase in evidence.

The InsuResilience Secretariat collects data annually to estimate the number of beneficiaries, coverage volumes in relation to average annual losses and other quantitative indicators across all contributing programmes and projects. This information is complemented by desk research on, for example, the availability of countries' disaster risk financing strategies.

Source: (InsuResilience Global Partnership, 2019[194]). InsuResilience Global Partnership Vision 2015, www.insuresilience.org.

Box 3.28. Integrating new types of data and analysis into MEL

MEL systems are increasingly reliant on new types of data generated through mobile technologies, social media and satellite data. Geophysical data, for example, can improve warning and climate-related disaster preparedness. They can also monitor changes to an ecological system. As well, they can set a baseline by assessing the state of the ecosystem or assess impacts after a specific climate or weather event, such as fluvial flooding. Such remote forms of data collection and analysis can also support MEL in contexts of high fragility or even conflict.

Machine learning predicts trends and patterns based on the processing of large datasets. Use of machine learning can monitor and evaluate large-scale policy interventions targeting transformation and behavioural change e.g. via newspaper or social media comments. Data on mobile phone usage, for instance, can help predict the spread of diseases, including those spreading increasingly due to a climate change. New and larger datasets are not a panacea, however. Often, they only reflect major trends and probabilities and fail to address cause-and-effect relationships. There is, however, enormous potential in using both big data and machine learning for complex evaluations and assessing ever more empirical data.

Source: (Noltze et al., forthcoming[179]) Monitoring, evaluation and learning for climate resilience, https://doi.org/10.1787/22220518.

Table 3.28. Develop indicators consistent with human and financial capacities that can inform monitoring and evaluation: Guidance and tools

Guidance and tools	Focus	Audience
Adaptation Support Tool (Climate ADAPT)	This tool aims to assist policy makers and co-ordinators at the national level to develop, implement, monitor and evaluate climate change adaptation strategies and plans. It includes a discussion on indicators and mixed-method approaches for monitoring and evaluation. This includes a brief overview of issues to consider when developing indicators for climate adaptation.	✓ National and sub-national actors responsible for developing adaptation strategies and plans
NAP Global Network Resource Library (NAP Global Network)	This resource library includes a wealth of knowledge products produced by the NAP Global Networks and others that can inform the NAP process. This includes guidance and examples of country approaches to MEL that can inspire emulation. Guidance for incorporating gender considerations into the MEL process is also available.	✓ Stakeholders leading or supporting national NAP processes
Adaptation Principles: A Guide for Designing Strategies for Climate Change Adaptation and Resilience (World Bank)	This report offers practical guidance to the design, implementation and monitoring of national adaptation strategies. It specifies six guiding principles consistent with common policy domains. The report includes an annex with an illustrative list of indicators for the actions outlined in the guidance.	✓ Providers of development co-operation

3.4.5. Conduct climate resilience portfolio and allocation analysis

For providers of development co-operation, a good understanding of the portfolio and the patterns of the allocation of financial resources is useful. This can provide an overview of whether financial commitments reflect national or organisational priorities on climate finance. A portfolio analysis can shed light on the relevance, complementarity and coherence of financial commitments for climate resilience. This can also inform discussions on the allocation of resources, say between bilateral and multilateral channels, or between programme- and project-based support. Moreover, it can highlight the contributions of core development partners, including civil society, academia and the private sector in achieving set objectives (Noltze et al., forthcoming[179]).

Complementary analysis on the determinants of allocation patterns can examine a country's vulnerability to climate change or the capacities of local implementing partners. This, in turn, can shed light on past allocation decisions to identify room for improvement. Further analysis may entail qualitative content analysis of strategy documents and expert interviews. These could help determine whether allocation patterns are consistent with global development agendas and national priorities. Finally, results should be triangulated with an investigation of different development partner perspectives. These include government, CSOs, the private sector and the beneficiaries themselves (Noltze et al., forthcoming[179]) (see example in Box 3.29).

Box 3.29. A global portfolio and allocation analysis of Germany's adaptation finance 2011-17

In accordance with the Paris Agreement, Germany has set an objective of supporting partner countries and people most affected by climate change. The German Institute for Development Evaluation (DEval) examined if the allocation of Germany's adaptation finance over 2011-17 reflected this objective. Specifically, it examined if increasing climate vulnerability affected a country's probability of receiving adaptation finance and the amount of funds committed. Further, it analysed if the poorest countries and small island states benefited from Germany's adaptation support.

DEval employed a mixed-method approach to the allocation analysis:

- ***theory-building*** that operationalises the research interest through empirically verifiable expectations or assumptions
- ***theory-testing*** that confirms or refutes the identified expectations and forms the basis for this evaluation module's conclusions and recommendations.

The cross-cutting nature of the analysis meant it touched on different thematic or sectoral strategies. Consequently, DEval combined statistical data analysis with document analysis and qualitative interviews with development co-operation providers, implementing organisations and civil society.

Source: (Noltze and Rauschenbach, 2019[195]), Evaluation of Climate Change Adaptation Measures. Portfolio and Allocation Analysis, https://www.deval.org/en/evaluation-reports.html.

Table 3.29. Conduct climate resilience portfolio and allocation analysis: Guidance and tools

Guidance and tools	Focus	Audience
Evaluation of Climate Change Adaptation Measures: Portfolio and Allocation Analysis (DEval)	This report analyses the portfolio of the German federal government's allocation for climate-related development finance over 2011-17. It includes a number of overarching evaluation questions that can be considered when conducting such portfolio and allocation analysis.	✓ Independent evaluation units of development co-operation providers or other bilateral or multilateral providers of climate-related development finance

References

ACHPR (2018), *State Reporting Guidelines and Principles on Articles 21 and 24 of the African Charter relating to Extractive Industries, Human Rights and the Environment*, African Commission on Human and Peoples' Rights, Banjul, The Gambia, https://www.achpr.org/legalinstruments/detail?id=1. [75]

ADB (2018), "Information sources to support ADB climate risk assessments and management", *Technical Note*, Asian Development Bank, Manila, https://www.adb.org/sites/default/files/publication/458756/adb-climate-risk-assessments-info-sources.pdf. [88]

AFI (2019), *Inclusive Green Finance: A Survey of the Policy Landscape*, Alliance for Financial Inclusion, Kuala Lumpur, https://www.afi-global.org/publications/3036/Inclusive-Green-Finance-A-Survey-of-the-Policy-Landscape. [161]

AF-TERG (2020), *Evaluating Adaptation: Common Challenges Identified across Three Studies Commissioned by the Adaptation Fund Technical Evaluation Reference Group*, Adaptation Fund Technical Evaluation Reference Group, Washington, DC, https://www.adaptation-fund.org/wp-content/uploads/2020/10/AFB.EFC_.26.b.Inf_.2_Common-challenges-across-three-studies.pdf. [184]

Aleksandrova, M. (2019), "Social protection as a tool to address slow onset climate events: Emerging issues for research and policy", *Discussion Paper*, No. 16, German Development Institute / Deutsches Institut für Entwicklungspolitik, Bonn, http://dx.doi.org/10.23661/dp16.2019. [126]

Allan, A., S. Bahadur and S. Vidya (2019), *The Role of Domestic Budgets in Financing Climate Change Adaptation:*, Global Commission on Adaptation, Rotterdam and Washington, DC, https://cdn.gca.org/assets/2020-01/The_Role_of_Domestic_Budgets_in_Financing_Paper__Final.pdf. [121]

Aryal, J. et al. (2015), *Framework Guidelines and Governance for Designing Local Adaptation Plans of Action to Mainstream Climate Smart Villages in India*, CGIAR Research Program on Climate Change, Agriculture and Food Security, https://cgspace.cgiar.org/bitstream/handle/10568/68326/LAPA.pdf?sequence=1&isAllowed=y. [71]

Aytur, S., J. Hecht and P. Kirshen (2015), "Aligning Climate Change Adaptation Planning with Adaptive Governance: Lessons from Exeter, NH", *Journal of Contemporary Water Research & Education*, Vol. 155/1, pp. 83-98, http://dx.doi.org/10.1111/j.1936-704x.2015.03198.x. [45]

Baird, R. (2008), "The impact of climate change on minorities and Indigenous peoples", *Briefing Paper*, Minority Rights Group International, London, https://gsdrc.org/document-library/the-impact-of-climate-change-on-minorities-and-indigenous-peoples/. [24]

Barrett, S. et al. (2019), "Measuring climate resilience by linking shocks to development outcomes", *Climate and Development*, Vol. 12/7, pp. 677-688, http://dx.doi.org/10.1080/17565529.2019.1676689. [185]

Bebbington, A. et al. (2018), "Resource extraction and infrastructure threaten forest cover and community rights", *Proceedings of the National Academy of Sciences of the United States of America*, Vol. 115/52, pp. 13164-13173, http://dx.doi.org/10.1073/pnas.1812505115. [74]

Bel, S. and J. Eberlein (2015), "Why financial literacy matters for development", *OECD Observer Special offprint* July, https://oecdobserver.org/news/fullstory.php/aid/4967/Why_financial_literacy_matters_for_development.html. [160]

Bennett, V. (2019), "World's first dedicated climate resilience bond, for US$ 700m, is issued by EBRD", 20 September, European Bank for Reconstruction and Development, London, https://www.ebrd.com/news/2019/worlds-first-dedicated-climate-resilience-bond-for-us-700m-is-issued-by-ebrd-.html. [141]

Bours, D. (2014), "Twelve reasons why climate change adaptation M&E is challenging", *Guidance Note*, No. 1, SEA Change CoP, Phnom Penh and UKCIP, Oxford, https://ukcip.ouce.ox.ac.uk/wp-content/PDFs/MandE-Guidance-Note1.pdf. [183]

Buechler, S. et al. (2016), "Re-linking governance of energy with livelihoods and irrigation in Uttarakhand, India", *Water*, Vol. 8/10, p. 437, http://dx.doi.org/10.3390/w8100437. [77]

Calderone, M., L. Weingärtner and M. Kroessin (2019), "Investing in financial inclusion for climate resilience and adaptation The role of Islamic financial services", *Briefing Note*, No. May, Overseas Development Institute, London and Islamic Relief Worldwide, Birmingham, https://www.odi.org/sites/odi.org.uk/files/resource-documents/12685.pdf. [157]

Canales, N. (2011), "Civil Society and the Integration of Climate Change Risks into Planning and Policy-making", webpage, https://www.wri.org/our-work/project/world-resources-report/civil-society-and-integration-climate-change-risks-planning (accessed on 27 July 2020). [28]

Casado Asensio, J., T. Kato and H. Shin (forthcoming), *Private-sector Engagement in Strengthening Climate Resilience*, OECD Publishing, Paris. [13]

Chapagain, D. et al. (2020), "Climate change adaptation costs in developing countries: Insights from existing estimates", *Climate and Development*, Vol. 12/10, pp. 934-942, https://doi.org/10.1080/17565529.2020.1711698. [117]

Chingarande, D. et al. (2020), "Background paper on mainstreaming gender into national adaptation planning and implementation in Sub-Saharan Africa", *CFAS Working Paper*, No. 23, CGIAR Research Program on Climate Change, Agriculture and Food Security, Wageningen, The Netherlands, https://hdl.handle.net/10568/110699. [7]

Chiriac, D. and B. Naran (2020), "Examining the Climate Finance Gap for Small-Scale Agriculture", webpage, http://www.climatepolicyinitiative.org (accessed on 8 January 2021). [172]

Clar, C. and R. Steurer (2019), "Climate change adaptation at different levels of government: Characteristics and conditions of policy change", *Natural Resources Forum*, Vol. 43/2, pp. 121-131, https://doi.org/10.1111/1477-8947.12168. [76]

Coppi, G. and L. Fast (2019), *Blockchain and Distributed Ledger Technologies in the Humanitarian Sector*, Overseas Development Institute, London, https://www.odi.org/publications/11284-blockchain-and-distributed-ledger-technologies-humanitarian-sector. [146]

Crawford, A. and C. Church (2019), *Engaging the Private Sector in National Adaptation Planning Processes*, NAP Global Network, Winnipeg, http://www.napglobalnetwork.org. [162]

Crawford, A., C. Church and C. Ledwell (2020), *Toolkit for Engaging the Private Sector in National Adaptation Plans (NAPs): Supplement to the UNFCCC Technical Guidelines for the NAP process*, NAP Global Network & United Nations Framework Convention on Climate Change Adaptation Committee, International Institute for Sustainable Development. Winnipeg, http://napglobalnetwork.org/wp-content/uploads/2020/06/napgn-en-2020-Toolkit-for-engaging-the-private-sector-in-NAPs.pdf. [33]

Dazé, A. (2019), "Why gender matters in climate change adaptation", IISD blog (6 June 2019), https://www.iisd.org/library/gender-climate-change. [3]

Dazé, A. (forthcoming), *Integrating Climate Change Adaptation across Sectors: Lessons from the National Adaptation Plan (NAP) Process*, International Institute for Sustainable Development, Winnipeg. [73]

Dazé, A. and C. Church (2019), *Toolkit for a Gender-Responsive Process to Formulate and Implement National Adaptation Plans (NAPs): Supplement to the UNFCCC Technical Guidelines for the NAP Process*, International Institute for Sustainable Development, Winnipeg, https://napglobalnetwork.org/resource/toolkit-for-gender-responsive-national-adaptation-plans/. [6]

Dazé, A., H. Price-Kelly and N. Rass (2016), *Vertical Integration in National Adaptation Plan (NAP) Processes: A Guidance Note*, International Institute for Sustainable Development, Winnipeg, https://www4.unfccc.int/sites/NAPC/Documents%20NAP/Supplements/Vertical-Integration-in-NAP-Processes-Guidance-Note.pdf. [38]

DEFRA (2020), *Accounting for the Effects of Climate Change: Supplementary Green Book Guidance*, Department for Environment, Food & Rural Affairs, United Kingdom, https://www.gov.uk/government/publications/green-book-supplementary-guidance-environment. [193]

Dekens, J. and A. Dazé (2019), *Conducting Gender Analysis to Inform National Adaptation Plan (NAP) Processes: Reflections from six African countries*, NAP Global Network, Winnipeg, http://napglobalnetwork.org/wp-content/uploads/2019/04/napgn-en-2019-conducting-gender-analysis-to-inform-nap-processes.pdf. [21]

Di Francesco, M. and R. Barroso (2015), "Bottom-up costing within medium term expenditure frameworks: A survey of practices in selected OECD countries", *Public Budgeting & Finance*, Vol. 35/3, pp. 44-67, https://doi.org/10.1111/pbaf.12069. [132]

Dinshaw, A. (2018), "Monitoring and evaluating mainstreamed adaptation to climate change: A synthesis study on climate change in development cooperation", *IOB Evaluation*, No. 426, Policy and Operations Evaluation Department, Ministry of Foreign Affairs, The Netherlands, http://www.oecd.org/derec/netherlands/IOB-Monitoring-Evaluating-Mainstreamed-Adaptation-Climate-Change.pdf. [181]

Dinshaw, A. et al. (2014), "Monitoring and Evaluation of Climate Change Adaptation: Methodological Approaches", *OECD Environment Working Papers*, No. 74, OECD Publishing, Paris, https://dx.doi.org/10.1787/5jxrclr0ntjd-en. [182]

Douxchamps, S. et al. (2017), "Monitoring and evaluation of climate resilience for agricultural development – A review of currently available tools", *World Development Perspectives*, Vol. 5, pp. 10-23, http://dx.doi.org/10.1016/j.wdp.2017.02.001. [187]

Dunford, S. (2018), *Attributes of Good Governance for Effective Adaptation Action, and Regional Transitions*, National Climate Change Adaptation Research Facility, Australia, https://nccarf.edu.au/wp-content/uploads/2019/05/S3-5470-Dunford-_Attributes-of-Good-Governance.pdf (accessed on 6 February 2021). [42]

EC (2013), *Guidance on Integrating Climate Change and Biodiversity into Strategic Environmental Assessment*, European Commission, Brussels, https://ec.europa.eu/environment/eia/pdf/SEA%20Guidance.pdf. [97]

EC (2005), *The SEA Manual: A Sourcebook on Strategic Environmental Assessment of Transport Infrastructure Plans and Programmes*, European Commission, Brussels, https://ec.europa.eu/environment/archives/eia/sea-studies-and-reports/pdf/beacon_manuel_en.pdf. [78]

EEA (2020), "Monitoring and evaluation of national adaptation policies throughout the policy cycle", *EEA Report*, No. 6, European Environment Agency, Luxembourg, http://dx.doi.org/10.2800/83221. [189]

Ensora, J. et al. (2016), "Can community-based adaptation increase resilience?", *Climate and Development*, pp. 134-151, http://dx.doi.org/10.1080/17565529.2016.1223595. [41]

EU TEG (2020), "Technical Expert Group on Sustainable Finance: Overview", webpage, https://ec.europa.eu/info/publications/sustainable-finance-technical-expert-group_en (accessed on 22 December 2020). [107]

FAO (2015), "Assessing climate change vulnerability in fisheries and aquaculture: Available methodologies and their relevance for the sector", *Fisheries and Aquaculture Technical Paper*, No. 597, Food and Agriculture Organization of the United Nations, Rome, http://www.fao.org/3/a-i5109e.pdf. [83]

FAO (2007), "Climate risk assessment at community level in the agriculture sector", *Module*, No. 4, Food and Agriculture Organization of the United Nations, Rome, http://www.fao.org/3/a1247e/a1247e03.pdf. [84]

Feyen, E. et al. (2020), *Macro-Financial Aspects of Climate Change*, World Bank, Washington, DC., http://dx.doi.org/10.1596/1813-9450-9109. [102]

Financial Protection Forum (2018), *Disaster Risk Finance: A Primer: Core Principles and Operational Framework*, Disaster Risk Financing & Insurance Program, World Bank Group, Washington DC, https://www.financialprotectionforum.org/publication/disaster-risk-finance-a-primercore-principles-and-operational-framework. [116]

FONERWA (n.d.), *About FONERWA*, webpage, http://www.fonerwa.org/about (accessed on 2020 November 11). [87]

Fortun, P. (2020), "Strategic Environmental Assessment", webpage, https://europa.eu/capacity4dev/public-environment-climate/wiki/strategic-environmental-assessment (accessed on 14 November 2020). [100]

Foss, M. (2017), "Direct access to climate finance builds capacity and credibility of national institutions", 10 November, Adaptation Fund, Washington, DC, https://www.adaptation-fund.org/direct-access-climate-finance-builds-capacity-credibility-national-institutions/. [119]

Fünfgeld, R. (2012), "Local climate change adaptation planning: A guide for government policy and decision", *VCCCR Project: Framing Adaptation in the Victorian Context*, Victorian Centre for Climate Change Adaptation Research, Melbourne, http://www.vcccar.org.au/sites/default/files/publications/VCCCAR%20Local%20Climate%20Change%20Adaption%20Planning-WEB.pdf. [51]

Gaurav, S., S. Cole and J. Tobacman (2011), "Marketing complex financial products in emerging markets: Evidence from rainfall insurance in India", *Journal of Marketing Research*, Vol. 48, pp. S150-S162, https://doi.org/10.1509%2Fjmkr.48.SPL.S150. [159]

GCA (2019), *Adapt Now: A Global Call for Leadership on Climate Resilience*, Global Commission on Adaptation, https://gca.org/global-commission-on-adaptation/report. [64]

German Red Cross and IFRC (2020), "Anticipation Hub", webpage, https://www.forecast-based-financing.org/de/anticipationhub/ (accessed on 27 September 2020). [143]

GIZ (2019), *Disaster Risk Finance – A Toolkit*, Deutsche Gesellschaft für Internationale Zusammenarbeit, Bonn and Eschborn, https://indexinsuranceforum.org/sites/default/files/Publikationen03_DRF_ACRI_DINA4_WEB_190617.pdf. [138]

GIZ (2014), *NAP Align Recommendations for Aligning National Adaptation Plan Processes with Development and Budget Planning*, Deutsche Gesellschaft für Internationale Zusammenarbeit, Bonn and Eschborn, https://www.adaptationcommunity.net/?wpfb_dl=235. [133]

GNDR (2019), *Coherence Cookbook: Building Resilience in an Integrated Way*, Global Network of Civil Society Organisations for Disaster Reduction, London, https://sustainabledevelopment.un.org/content/documents/24342Coherence_cookbook_EN_web.pdf. [30]

Gogoi, E., A. Bahadur and C. Rumbaitis del Rio (2017), "Mainstreaming adaptation to climate change within governance systems in South Asia: An analytical framework and examples from practice", *Learning Paper*, No. October, Action on Climate Today, http://www.acclimatise.uk.com/wp-content/uploads/2018/02/OPM_ACT_LP_Governance_Paper_final.pdf. [15]

Government of Canada (2017), "Gender Analysis", webpage, https://www.international.gc.ca/world-monde/funding-financement/gender_analysis-analyse_comparative.aspx?lang=eng (accessed on 28 July 2020). [22]

Government of Fiji (2020), *Costing Methodology for Fiji's National Adaptation Plan*, Government of Fiji and NAP Global Network/International Institute for Sustainable Development, https://napglobalnetwork.org/wp-content/uploads/2020/09/napgn-en-2020-costing-methodology-for-Fiji-NAP.pdf (accessed on 11 January 2021). [118]

Government of India (2008), *National Action Plan on Climate Change*, The Prime Minister's Council on Climate Change, http://www.nicra-icar.in/nicrarevised/images/Mission%20Documents/National-Action-Plan-on-Climate-Change.pdf. [72]

GPFI (2010), *G20 Principles for Innovative Financial Inclusion - Executive Brief*, Global Partnership for Financial Inclusion, https://gpfi.org/publications/g20-principles-innovative-financial-inclusion-executive-brief. [158]

GWP-Med (2019), "The Nexus Approach: An Introduction", webpage, https://www.gwp.org/en/GWP-Mediterranean/WE-ACT/Programmes-per-theme/Water-Food-Energy-Nexus/the-nexus-approach-an-introduction/ (accessed on 26 June 2020). [61]

Haasnoot, M. et al. (2013), "Dynamic adaptive policy pathways: A method for crafting robust decisions for a deeply uncertain world", *Global Environmental Change*, Vol. 23, pp. 485-498, http://dx.doi.org/10.1016/j.gloenvcha.2012.12.006. [47]

Haasnoot, M., S. van 't Klooster and J. van Alphen (2018), "Designing a monitoring system to detect signals to adapt to uncertain climate change", *Global Environmental Change*, Vol. 52, pp. 273-285, http://dx.doi.org/10.1016/j.gloenvcha.2018.08.003. [192]

Hallegatte, S., J. Rentschler and J. Rozenberg (2020), *Adaptation Principles : A Guide for Designing Strategies for Climate Change Adaptation and Resilience*, World Bank, Washington, DC, https://openknowledge.worldbank.org/handle/10986/34780. [68]

Hallegatte, S., J. Rentschler and J. Rozenberg (2019), *Lifelines: The Resilient Infrastructure Opportunity: Sustainable Infrastructure*, World Bank, Washington, DC, http://hdl.handle.net/10986/31805. [90]

Hall, J. et al. (2019), *Adaptation of Infrastructure Systems: Background Paper for the Global Commission on Adaptation*, Environmental Change Institute, University of Oxford, Oxford, https://cdn.gca.org/assets/2019-12/GCA-Infrastructure-background-paperV11-refs_0.pdf. [92]

Handicap International (2017), *Inclusive Disaster Risk Deduction Post 2015*, Handicap International, Geneva, https://handicap-international.ch/sites/ch/files/documents/files/inclusive_disaster_risk_reduction_post201_hi_expertise.pdf. [19]

Hardoy, J. et al. (2018), *Implementation Guide for Local Disaster Risk Reduction and Resilience Strategies*, United Nations Office for Disaster Risk Reduction, Geneva, https://www.undrr.org/publication/words-action-guidelines-implementation-guide-local-disaster-risk-reduction-and. [48]

HelpAge International (2019), *Age Inclusive Disaster Risk Reduction – A Toolkit*, HelpAge International, London, https://www.preventionweb.net/files/68082_ageinclusivedisasterriskreductionat.pdf. [20]

Hubert, R., J. Evain and M. Nicol (2018), "Getting started on physical climate risk analysis in finance - Available approaches and the way forward", *CLIMInvest Research Work Package*, No. 1, 14CE Institute for Climate Economics, Paris, https://www.i4ce.org/wp-core/wp-content/uploads/2018/12/I4CE-ClimINVEST_2018_Getting-started-on-physical-climate-risk-analysis.pdf. [122]

IDB (2019), *A Framework and Principles for Climate Resilience Metrics in Financing Operations*, Inter-American Development Bank, Washington, DC, http://dx.doi.org/10.18235/0002040. [94]

IDB (2019), *Governments and Civil Society Advancing Climate Agendas*, Inter-American Development Bank, Washington, DC, https://publications.iadb.org/publications/english/document/Governments_and_Civil_Society_Advancing_Climate_Agendas_en_en.pdf (accessed on 27 July 2020). [29]

IDB and NDF (2020), *Private Markets for Climate Resilience Global Report*, Inter-American Development Bank, Washington, DC and the Nordic Development Fund, Helsinki, https://ndf.fi/sites/default/files/news_attach/pmcr_global_report.pdf. [34]

IFC (n.d.), "Sustainable Banking Network", webpage, https://www.ifc.org/wps/wcm/connect/topics_ext_content/ifc_external_corporate_site/sustainability-at-ifc/company-resources/sustainable-finance/sbn (accessed on 22 December 2020). [105]

IGP (2018), "The Insuresilience Global Partnership", (flyer), Insuresilience Global Partnership, Bonn, https://www.insuresilience.org/wp-content/uploads/2018/11/Flyer_InsuResilienceGlobalPartnership_2018.pdf. [152]

IISD (2016), "Climate change adaptation and EIA", *EIA Learning Platform*, International Institute for Sustainable Development, Winnipeg, https://www.iisd.org/learning/eia/wp-content/uploads/2016/05/CCA.pdf. [99]

ILO (2017), *Indigenous Peoples and Climate Change: From Victims to Change Agents through Decent Work*, International Labour Organization, Geneva, https://www.ilo.org/wcmsp5/groups/public/---dgreports/---gender/documents/publication/wcms_551189.pdf. [23]

IMF (2019), "Building resilience in developing countries vulnerable to large natural disasters", *Policy Paper*, No. 19, International Monetary Fund, Washington, DC, https://www.imf.org/en/Publications/Policy-Papers/Issues/2019/06/24/Building-Resilience-in-Developing-Countries-Vulnerable-to-Large-Natural-Disasters-47020. [110]

InsuResilience Global Partnership (2019), *InsuResilience Global Partnership Vision 2015*, 6 June, InsuResiliance Global Partnership, Bonn, https://www.insuresilience.org/wp-content/uploads/2019/09/InsuResilience-Global-Partnership_Vision-2025-with-Workplan1.pdf. [194]

InsuResilience Investment Fund (2018), "Climate insurance schemes for poor and vulnerable households and micro, small and medium enterprises", Success Stories, InsuResilience Investment Fund, Luxembourg, https://www.insuresilienceinvestment.fund/wp-content/uploads/2018/News/Climate%20Insurance%20Success%20Stories.pdf. [149]

IPA (n.d.), *Financial Inclusion and Climate Change*, Innovations for Poverty Action, Washington, DC, https://www.poverty-action.org/sites/default/files/publications/Climate-Change-Financial-Inclusion_Final.pdf. [155]

IPCC (2019), "Annex I: Glossary", in van Diemen, R. (ed.), *Climate Change and Land*, Intergovernmental Panel on Climate Change, Geneva, https://www.ipcc.ch/site/assets/uploads/sites/4/2019/11/11_Annex-I-Glossary.pdf. [1]

IPCC (2014), "Adaptation planning and implementation", in Mimura, N. et al. (eds.), *Climate Change 2014: Impacts, Adaptation, and Vulnerability. Part A: Global and Sectoral Aspects. Contribution of Working Group II to the Fifth Assessment Report of the Intergovernmental Panel on Climate Change*, Cambridge University Press, Cambridge, https://www.ipcc.ch/site/assets/uploads/2018/02/WGIIAR5-Chap15_FINAL.pdf. [8]

Jaime, C. (n.d.), "Forecast-based Financing", webpage, https://understandrisk.org/forecast-based-financing/ (accessed on 30 July 2020). [142]

Jarzabkowski, P. et al. (2019), *Insurance for Climate Adaptation: Opportunities and Limitations*, Global Centre on Adaptation, Rotterdam and Washington, DC, https://cdn.gca.org/assets/2019-12/Insurance%20for%20climate%20adaptation_Opportunities%20and%20Limitations.pdf. [153]

Jeuland, M. and D. Whittington (2013), "Water resources planning under climate change: A 'real options' application to investment planning in the Blue Nile", *Discussion Paper Series*, No. EFP-DP 1305, Environment for Development Initiative, Gothenburg, https://www.rff.org/publications/working-papers/water-resources-planning-under-climate-change-a-real-options-application-to-investment-planning-in-the-blue-nile/. [57]

Kohli, R. (2018), "Integrating climate change adaptation into planning and budgeting", presentation, regional dialogue on climate reslience growth and development, United Nations Development Programme, 21 February, https://www.climatefinance-developmenteffectiveness.org/regional-dialogue-event/img/day2/S3-Integrating-CCA-into-Planning-and-Budgeting.pdf. [134]

Lamhauge, N., E. Lanzi and S. Agrawala (2012), "Monitoring and Evaluation for Adaptation: Lessons from Development Co-operation Agencies", *OECD Environment Working Papers*, No. 38, OECD Publishing, Paris, https://dx.doi.org/10.1787/5kg20mj6c2bw-en. [190]

LDC Expert Group (2012), *National Adaptation Plans: Technical Guidelines for the National Adaptation Plan Process*, Least Developed Countries Expert Group of UNFCCC, Bonn, https://unfccc.int/topics/adaptation-and-resilience/workstreams/national-adaptation-plans-naps/guidelines-for-national-adaptation-plans-naps. [69]

Leiter, T. and P. Pringle (2018), "Pitfalls and potential of measuring climate change adaptation through adaptation metrics", in *Adaptation Metrics: Perspectives on Measuring, Aggregating and Comparing Adaptation Results*, UNEP DTU Partnership, Copenhagen. [191]

LIFE-AR (2019), *Delivering our Climate-Resilient Future: Lessons from a Global Evidence Review*, LDC Initiative for Effective Adaptation and Resilience, http://www.ldc-climate.org/wp-content/uploads/2019/09/web_LDCevidencereview.pdf. [4]

LIFE-AR (2019), *LDC 2050 Vision: Towards a climate-resilient future*, LDC Initative for Effective Adaptation and Resilience, http://www.ldc-climate.org/wp-content/uploads/2019/09/2050-Vision.pdf. [39]

Mahul, O. et al. (2019), *Boosting Financial Resilience to Disaster Shocks: Good Practices and New Frontiers*, World Bank Technical Contribution to the 2019 G20 Finance Ministers' and Central Bank Governors' Meeting,World Bank Group, Washington, DC, https://www.financialprotectionforum.org/publication/boosting-financial-resilience-to-disaster-shocks-good-practices-and-new-frontiers. [108]

Martí, C. (2019), "Performance budgeting and medium-term expenditure frameworks: A comparison in OECD central governments", *Journal of Comparative Policy Analysis: Research and Practice*, Vol. 21/4, pp. 313-331, https://doi.org/10.1080/13876988.2018.1526492. [131]

Martinez-Diaz, L., L. Sidner and J. McClamrock (2019), "The future of disaster risk pooling for developing countries: Where do we go from here?", *Working Paper*, No. August, World Resources Institute, Washington, DC, http://www.wri.org/publication/disaster-risk-pooling. [137]

McDermott, T. and S. Surminski (2018), "How normative interpretations of climate risk assessment affect local decision-making: An exploratory study at the city scale in Cork, Ireland", *Philosophical Transactions of the Royal Society A*, Vol. 376/2121, https://doi.org/10.1098/rsta.2017.0300. [54]

Mereu, V. et al. (2018), "Robust decision making for a climate-resilient development of the agricultural sector in Nigeria", in Lipper, L. et al. (eds.), *Climate Smart Agriculture*, Springer, Cham. [56]

Miller, A. and S. Swann (2019), *Driving Finance Today for the Climate Resilient Society of Tomorrow*, UNEP Financial Initiative (Contribution to Global Commission on Adaptation), https://www.unepfi.org/wordpress/wp-content/uploads/2019/07/GCA-Adaptation-Finance.pdf. [103]

MINEDD (2018), *Pour un processus de Plan National d'Adaptation (PNA) qui réponde aux questions de genre en Côte d'Ivoire*, Ministère de l'Environnement et du Développement Durable (MINEDD) de la République de la Côte d'Ivoire et Réseau Mondial de PNA/Institut International, http://www.environnement.gouv.ci/img/1553085982ivory-coast-briefing-note-fr_MASTER.pdf. [26]

Ministry of Food and Agriculture (2015), *National Cliamte-Smart Agriculture and Food Security Action Plan*, Ministry of Food and Agriculture of Ghana, Accra, https://ccafs.cgiar.org/publications/national-climate-smart-agriculture-and-food-security-action-plan-ghana-2016-2020#.X6r3IGj0mUI (accessed on 2 February 2021). [79]

Minority Rights Group International (2019), *Minority and Indigenous Trends 2019: Focus on Climate Justice*, Minority Rights Group International, London, http://www.minorityrights.org (accessed on 4 January 2021). [25]

Moore, D. et al. (2019), *Building Resilience through Financial Inclusion A Review of Existing Evidence and Knowledge Gaps*, Financial Inclusion Program, Innovations for Poverty Action, Washington, DC, https://www.poverty-action.org/sites/default/files/publications/Building-Resilience-through-Financial-Inclusion-English.pdf. [156]

Morchain, D. and F. Kelsey (2016), *Finding Ways Together to Build Resilience: The Vulnerability and Risk Assessment Methodology*, Oxfam GB, Oxford, https://policy-practice.oxfam.org/resources/finding-ways-together-to-build-resilience-the-vulnerability-and-risk-assessment-593491/. [80]

Moser, S. et al. (2019), "Adaptation finance archetypes: Local governments' persistent challenges of funding adaptation to climate change and ways to overcome them", *Ecology and Society*, Vol. 24/2, https://doi.org/10.5751/ES-10980-240228. [123]

Munaretto, S., E. Siciliano and M. Turvani (2014), "Integrating adaptive governance and participatory multicriteria methods: A framework for climate adaptation governance", *Ecology and Society*, Vol. 19/2, http://dx.doi.org/10.5751/ES-07704-200411. [35]

NDC Cluster (n.d.), *Climate Budget Tagging*, webpage, https://www.ndc-cluster.net/tool/climate-budget-tagging (accessed on 10 February 2021). [128]

NDC Partnership (2018), "Navigating International Climate Finance", webpage, https://ndcpartnership.org/node/15/ (accessed on 22 July 2020). [174]

NGFS (2020), "Membership", webpage, https://www.ngfs.net/en/about-us/membership (accessed on 21 December 2020). [104]

NGFS (2020), "NGFS Publications", webpage, https://www.ngfs.net/en/liste-chronologique/ngfs-publications (accessed on 19 December 2020). [106]

Noltze, M. et al. (forthcoming), *Monitoring, evaluation and learning for climate risk management*, OECD Publishing, Paris, https://doi.org/10.1787/22220518. [179]

Noltze, M. and M. Rauschenbach (2019), *Evaluation of Climate Change Adaptation Measures. Portfolio and Allocation Analysis*, German Institute for Development Evaluation, Bonn, https://www.deval.org/en/evaluation-reports.html (accessed on 9 February 2021). [195]

ODI (2019), *Climate Funds Update*, webpage, https://climatefundsupdate.org/the-funds/ (accessed on 10 February 2020). [176]

ODI et al. (2019), *Strengthening Forecast-based Early Action in the Caribbean*, Overseas Development Institute, the Red Cross Red Crescent Climate Centre and Ramboll, https://www.climatecentre.org/downloads/files/EarlyAction_V9_Digital.pdf. [144]

OECD (2020), *Blended Finance Principles Guidance*, OECD, Paris, http://www.oecd.org/officialdocuments/publicdisplaydocumentpdf/?cote=DCD/DAC(2020)42/FINAL&docLanguage=En. [168]

OECD (2020), *Climate Change: OECD DAC External Development Finance Statistics*, webpage, http://www.oecd.org/dac/financing-sustainable-development/development-finance-topics/climate-change.htm (accessed on 10 February 2021). [175]

OECD (2020), *Climate Finance Provided and Mobilised by Developed Countries in 2013-18*, OECD Publishing, Paris, https://dx.doi.org/10.1787/f0773d55-en. [169]

OECD (2020), *Common Ground Between the Paris Agreement and the Sendai Framework : Climate Change Adaptation and Disaster Risk Reduction*, OECD Publishing, Paris, https://dx.doi.org/10.1787/3edc8d09-en. [11]

OECD (2020), *Development Assistance Committee Members and Civil Society*, The Development Dimension, OECD Publishing, Paris, https://dx.doi.org/10.1787/51eb6df1-en. [27]

OECD (2020), "What does "inclusive governance" mean? : Clarifying theory and practice", *OECD Development Policy Papers*, No. 27, OECD Publishing, Paris, https://dx.doi.org/10.1787/960f5a97-en. [5]

OECD (2019), *Good Governance for Critical Infrastructure Resilience*, OECD Reviews of Risk Management Policies, OECD Publishing, Paris, https://dx.doi.org/10.1787/02f0e5a0-en. [91]

OECD (2019), *Making Blended Finance Work for Water and Sanitation: Unlocking Commercial Finance for SDG 6*, OECD Studies on Water, OECD Publishing, Paris, https://dx.doi.org/10.1787/5efc8950-en. [167]

OECD (2019), "Recommendation of the Council on Policy Coherence for Sustainable Development", (flyer), OECD Publishing, Paris, https://www.oecd.org/gov/pcsd/oecd-recommendation-on-policy-coherence-for-sustainable-development.htm. [62]

OECD (2018), "Climate-resilient infrastructure", *OECD Environment Policy Papers*, No. 14, OECD Publishing, Paris, https://dx.doi.org/10.1787/4fdf9eaf-en. [89]

OECD (2018), *Global Outlook on Financing for Sustainable Development 2019: Time to Face the Challenge*, OECD Publishing, Paris, https://dx.doi.org/10.1787/9789264307995-en. [113]

OECD (2018), *Integration of the Gender Perspective in All Phases of the Budget Cycle*, webpage, https://www.oecd.org/gender/governance/toolkit/government/integration-in-budget-cycle/ (accessed on 10 February 2021). [112]

OECD (2018), *OECD DAC Blended Finance Principles for Unlocking Commercial Finance for the Sustainable Development Goals*, OECD Publishing, Paris, http://www.oecd.org/dac/financing-sustainable-development/development-finance-topics/OECD-Blended-Finance-Principles.pdf. [166]

OECD (2015), *Climate Change Risks and Adaptation: Linking Policy and Economics*, OECD Publishing, Paris, https://dx.doi.org/10.1787/9789264234611-en. [55]

OECD (2015), *Climate Change Risks and Adaptation: Linking Policy and Economics*, OECD Publishing, Paris, https://dx.doi.org/10.1787/9789264234611-en. [58]

OECD (2015), *National Climate Change Adaptation: Emerging Practices in Monitoring and Evaluation*, OECD Publishing, Paris, https://dx.doi.org/10.1787/9789264229679-en. [180]

OECD (2015), "Toolkit to enhance access to adaptation finance: For developing countries that are vulnerable to adverse effects of climate change, including LIDCs, SIDS and African states", Report to the G20 Climate Finance Study Group prepared by the Organisation for Economic Co-operation and Development in collaboration with the Global Environment Facility, http://www.oecd.org/environment/cc/Toolkit%20to%20Enhance%20Access%20to%20Adaptation%20Finance.pdf. [120]

OECD (2012), *Greening Development: Enhancing Capacity for Environmental Management and Governance*, OECD Publishing, Paris, https://dx.doi.org/10.1787/9789264167896-en. [124]

OECD (2009), *Integrating Climate Change Adaptation into Development Co-operation: Policy Guidance*, OECD Publishing, Paris, https://dx.doi.org/10.1787/9789264054950-en. [12]

OECD and World Bank (2019), *Fiscal Resilience to Natural Disasters: Lessons from Country Experiences*, OECD Publishing, Paris, https://doi.org/10.1787/27a4198a-en. [109]

Palerm, J. et al. (2015), *Strategic Environmental Assessment (SEA) of Montenegro's National Climate Change Strategy*, Ministry of Sustainable Development and Tourism of Montenegro, https://europa.eu/capacity4dev/public-environment-climate/documents/strategic-environmental-assessment-sea-montenegros-national-climate-change-strategy. [101]

Parry, J., A. Dazé and J. Dekens (2017), "Financing National Adaptation Plan (NAP) Processes: Contributing to the achievement of nationally determined contribution (NDC) adaptation goals", *Guidance Note*, NAP Global Network Secretariat, Winnipeg, https://www4.unfccc.int/sites/NAPC/Documents/Supplements/napgn-en-2017-financing-nap-processes.pdf. [115]

Peverelli, R. and R. de Feniks (2017), "Etherisc: Decentralized insurance leveraging blockchain", 16 October, Digital Insurance Agenda, Utrecht, The Netherlands, https://www.digitalinsuranceagenda.com/159/etherisc-decentralized-insurance-leveraging-blockchain/. [147]

Porthin, M. et al. (2013), "Multi-criteria decision analysis in adaptation decision-making:a flood case study in Finland", *Regional Environmental Change volume 13, pages1171–1180 (2013)*, http://dx.doi.org/DOI 10.1007/s10113-013-0423-9. [53]

Price-Kelly, H. and A. Hammill (2016), *sNAPshot: Domestic Public Finance for Implementation of NAPs*, NAP Global Network, Winnipeg, http://napglobalnetwork.org/wp-content/uploads/2016/10/napgn-en-2016-snapshot-domestic-public-finance-for-implementation-of-naps.pdf. [114]

Ray, P. and C. Brown (2015), *Confronting Climate Uncertainty in Water Resources Planning and Project Design: The Decision Tree Framework*, World Bank, Washington, DC, https://openknowledge.worldbank.org/handle/10986/22544. [82]

Rocha Menocal, A. et al. (2018), *Thinking and Working Politically through Applied Political Economy Analysis: A Guide for Practitioners*, United States Agency for International Development, Washington, DC, https://usaidlearninglab.org/sites/default/files/resource/files/pea_guide_final.pdf. [18]

Rodrigo-Ilarri, J. et al. (2020), "Advances in implementing strategic environmental assessment (SEA) techniques in Central America and the Caribbean", *Sustainability*, Vol. 12/10, https://www.mdpi.com/2071-1050/12/10/4039/pdf. [96]

Roelich, K. and J. Giesekam (2019), "Decision making under uncertainty in climate change mitigation: Introducing multiple actor motivations, agency and influence", *Climate Policy*, Vol. 19/2, pp. 175-188, https://doi.org/10.1080/14693062.2018.1479238. [52]

Sadler, M. et al. (2016), *Making Climate Finance Work in Agriculture*, World Bank Group, Washington, DC, http://documents.worldbank.org/curated/en/986961467721999165/Making-climate-finance-work-in-agriculture. [140]

Schaer, C. and N. Kuruppu (2018), *Private-sector Action in Adaptation: Perspectives on the Role of Micro, Small and Medium-size Enterprises*, UNEP DTU Partnership, Copenhagen, https://unepdtu.org/publications/private-sector-action-in-adaptation-perspectives-on-the-role-of-micro-small-and-medium-size-enterprises/. [31]

Scherr, S., S. Shames and F. Rachel (2013), "Defining integrated landscape management for policy makers", *EcoAgriculture Policy Focus*, No. 10, EcoAgriculture Partners, Washington, DC, https://www.un.org/esa/ffd/wp-content/uploads/sites/2/2015/10/IntegratedLandscapeManagementforPolicymakers_Brief_Final_Oct24_2013_smallfile.pdf. [67]

Scott, Z. et al. (2017), *Independent Evaluation of African Risk Capacity (ARC): Final Inception Report*, Oxford Policy Management, Oxford, https://www.africanriskcapacity.org/wp-content/uploads/2018/03/Formative-Phase-1-ARC-Evaluation_merged.pdf (accessed on 2 February 2020). [188]

SDC (n.d.), *The Climate, Environment and Disaster Risk Reduction Integration Guidance*, webpage, https://www.cedrig.org/ (accessed on 2 February 2021). [93]

Seddon, N. et al. (2020), "Understanding the value and limits of nature-based solutions to climate change and other global challenges", *Philosophical Transactions of the Royal Society B*, Vol. 375/1794, http://dx.doi.org/10.1098/rstb.2019.0120. [66]

Shepherd, T. (2019), "Storyline approach to the construction of regional climate change information", *Proceedings of the Royal Society A*, Vol. 475/20190013, http://dx.doi.org/10.1098/rspa.2019.0013. [59]

Shine, T. (2017), *Supporting Access to Finance for Climate Action*, Swedish International Development Cooperation Agency, Stockholm, https://www.sida.se/contentassets/1df42ce0c6924fedb2b11325fd255ff2/supporting_access_to_finance_for_climate_action_webb.pdf. [170]

Soanes, M. and C. Shakya (2016), "Six steps to local climate finance", IIED blog (6 November 2016), https://www.iied.org/six-steps-local-climate-finance. [171]

Sprout Insure (2019), *Blockchain Climate Risk Crop Insurance*, webpage, https://www.climatefinancelab.org/project/climate-risk-crop-insurance/ (accessed on 1 February 2021). [145]

Stephenson, M. (2018), *A Guide to Gender-Responsive Budgeting*, Oxfam GB, Oxford, http://DOI: 10.21201/2017.1848. [111]

Storey, D. (2016), "National-level climate finance tracking can help countries meet NDC goals effectively", CPI blog (10 November 2016), https://www.climatepolicyinitiative.org/2016/11/10/robust-tracking-of-climate-finance-at-the-national-level-will-help-countries-meet-their-ndc-goals-more-effectively/. [129]

Sudo, T. (2019), "Financing adaptation roadmap", in Anbumozhi, V. and S. Wesiak (eds.), *Towards a Resilient ASEAN Volume 2: Advancing Disaster Resilience and Climate Change Adaptation: Roadmaps and Options for Implementation*, Economic Research Institute for ASEAN and East Asia, Jakarta. [165]

Tenzing, J. (2020), "Integrating social protection and climate change adaptation: A review", *WIREs Climate Change*, Vol. 11/2, http://dx.doi.org/10.1002/wcc.626. [125]

Tippmann, R. et al. (2016), *ClimaSouth E-Handbook N.8. Accessing Climate Finance: A Step-by-Step Approach for Practitioners*, ClimaSouth project, Rabat, Cairo, Brussels, https://www.climamed.eu/wp-content/uploads/files/Accessing-climate-finance.pdf (accessed on 1 February 2021). [178]

Tonmoy, F., D. Rissik and J. Palutikof (2019), "A three-tier risk assessment process for climate change adaptation at a local scale", *Climatic Change*, Vol. 153, pp. 539–557, http://dx.doi.org/10.1007/s10584-019-02367-z. [36]

UCS (2016), *Toward Climate Resilience A Framework and Principles for Science-Based Adaptation*, Union of Concerned Scientists, Cambridge, MA, US, https://www.ucsusa.org/resources/toward-climate-resilience#ucs-report-downloads. [10]

UNCDF (2020), "Financing local climate change adaptation – LoCAL 2020", (brochure), UN Capital Development Fund, New York, https://www.uncdf.org/article/5713/local-2020-brochure. [46]

UNCDF (2019), "Financing local adaptation to climate change: Experiences with performance-based climate resilience grants", 8 April, Newsletter, UN Capital Development Fund, New York, https://www.uncdf.org/article/4468/uncdfs-subnational-climate-resilience-publication-integrated-into-nap-technical-guidelines-of-unfccc. [43]

UNCDF (n.d.), *Financial Inclusion*, webpage, https://www.uncdf.org/financial-inclusion (accessed on 2 February 2021). [154]

UNDP (2019), *Knowing What You Spend: A Guidance Note for Governments to Track Climate Change Finance in their Budgets*, Governance of Climate Change Finance Team of the UNDP, Bangkok, https://www.undp.org/content/undp/en/home/librarypage/climate-and-disaster-resilience-/knowing-what-you-spend.html. [127]

UNDP (2018), *UNDP Climate Change Adaptation: Engaging Private Sector*, webpage, https://www.adaptation-undp.org/privatesector/ (accessed on 2 February 2021). [32]

UNDP (n.d.), "Engaging the Private Sector", webpage, https://www.adaptation-undp.org/privatesector/ (accessed on 9 August 2020). [163]

UNDRR (2020), *Disaster Risk Reduction in Africa: A Summary of Findings from 16 Risk-sensitive Budget Reviews*, United Nations Office for Disaster Risk Reduction – Regional Office for Africa, Nairobi, https://www.undrr.org/publication/disaster-risk-reduction-africa-summary-findings-16-risk-sensitive-budget-reviews. [136]

UNDRR (2020), "Options for addressing infrastructure resilience", *Working Paper*, United Nations Office for Disaster Risk Reduction, Regional Office for Europe, Brussels, https://www.undrr.org/publication/working-paper-options-addressing-infrastructure-resilience. [98]

UNDRR (2015), *Sendai Framework for Disaster Risk Reduction 2015 – 2030*, United Nations Office for Disaster Risk Reduction, Geneva, https://www.undrr.org/publication/sendai-framework-disaster-risk-reduction-2015-2030. [186]

UNECE (n.d.), "Environmental Assessments for Climate Change Adaptation", webpage, https://www.unece.org/unece-and-the-sdgs/climate-change/sustainable-developmentclimate-changeunece-and-climate-change/environmental-assessments-for-climate-change-adaptation.html (accessed on 2 February 2021). [95]

UNEP (2019), "Maladaptation to climate change", in *UNEP Frontiers 2018/19 Emerging Issues of Environmental Concern*, United Nations Environment Programme, Nairobi, http://www.unenvironment.org. [63]

UNEP DTU Partnership (2018), *Private-sector Action in Adaptation: Perspectives on the Role of Micro, Small and Medium Size Enterprises*, UNEP DTU Partnership, Copenhagen, https://orbit.dtu.dk/ws/files/162053774/MSME_Adaptation_updated_WEB.pdf. [164]

UNFCCC (2019), "Elaboration of the sources of and modalities for accessing financial support for addressing loss and damage", *Technical Paper*, United Nations Framework Convention on Climate Change, Bonn, https://unfccc.int/sites/default/files/resource/tp2019_1_advance.pdf. [177]

UNFCCC (2019), "Supplementary Materials to the NAP Technical Guidelines", webpage, https://www4.unfccc.int/sites/NAPC/Guidelines/Pages/Supplements.aspx (accessed on 17 November 2020). [70]

UNFCCC (2017), "Opportunities and options for integrating climate change adaptation with the Sustainable Development Goals and the Sendai Framework for Disaster Risk Reduction 2015–2030", *Technical Paper*, United Nations Framework Convention on Climate Change Secretariat, Bonn, https://unfccc.int/sites/default/files/resource/techpaper_adaptation.pdf. [65]

UNFCCC (2015), "What is the Paris Agreement?", webpage, https://unfccc.int/process-and-meetings/the-paris-agreement/the-paris-agreement (accessed on 24 January 2020). [2]

USAID (2019), "USAID's RISE Challenge", webpage, https://competitions4dev.org/risechallenge (accessed on 2 February 2021). [40]

USAID (2018), "Thinking and Working Politically through Applied Political Economy Analysis", webpage, https://www.usaid.gov/documents/1866/thinking-and-working-politically-through-applied-political-economy-analysis (accessed on 10 September 2020). [17]

Väänänen, E. et al. (2019), "Linking climate risk insurance with shock-responsive social protection", *Policy Brief*, No. 1, Secretariat of InsuResilience, Bonn, https://www.insuresilience.org/wp-content/uploads/2019/03/insuresilience_policybrief_1-2019_190312_web.pdf. [150]

Vallejo, L. and M. Mullan (2017), "Climate-resilient infrastructure: Getting the policies right", *OECD Environment Working Papers*, No. 121, OECD Publishing, Paris, https://dx.doi.org/10.1787/02f74d61-en. [50]

Vermeulen, S. et al. (2013), "Addressing uncertainty in adaptation planning for agriculture", *Proceedings of the National Academy of Sciences of the United States of America*, Vol. 110/21, pp. 8357-8362, http://dx.doi.org/10.1073/pnas.1219441110. [37]

Walch, C. (2017), "Adaptive governance in the developing world: Disaster risk reduction in the State of Odisha, India", *Climate and Development*, Vol. 11/3, https://doi.org/10.1080/17565529.2018.1442794. [60]

WEDO (2019), *Women's Organizations and Climate Finance: Engaging in Processes and Accessing Resources*, Women's Environment and Development Organization, New York, https://wedo.org/womens-orgs-climate-finance/. [173]

WEF (2012), *Global Risks 2013*, World Economic Forum, Cologny/Geneva, http://reports.weforum.org/global-risks-2013/?doing_wp_cron=1596008407.8742570877075195312500. [49]

WHO (2014), *WHO Guidance to Protect Health from Climate Change through Health Adaptation Planning*, World Health Organization, Geneva, https://www4.unfccc.int/sites/NAPC/Documents/Supplements/WHO%20H-NAP%202014.pdf. [85]

Woor, S. (2017), "Engaging stakeholders and building ownership for climate adaptation: Best practice from Southern Egypt", 8 August, World Food Programme, Rome, https://www.weadapt.org/knowledge-base/climate-adaptation-training/engaging-stakeholders-and-building-ownership-for-climate-adaptation. [14]

Worker, J. (2017), *National Climate Change Governance: Topic Guide*, GSDRC, University of Birmingham, https://gsdrc.org/topic-guides/national-climate-change-governance/ (accessed on 10 September 2020). [16]

Worker, J. and E. Northrup (2018), *Assessing and Addressing Climate Governance Challenges in Low- And Middle-Income Countries*, Agence Française de Développement, Paris, https://www.afd.fr/en/ressources/assessing-and-addressing-climate-governance-challenges-low-and-middle-income-countries. [9]

World Bank (2019), "Climate smart agriculture investment plans: Bringing CSA to life", 4 December, World Bank, Washington, DC, https://www.worldbank.org/en/topic/agriculture/publication/climate-smart-agriculture-investment-plans-bringing-climate-smart-agriculture-to-life. [86]

World Bank (2019), *Coalition of Finance Ministers for Climate Action: An Overview*, World Bank and International Monetary Fund, Spring Meeting, World Bank, Washignton DC, http://pubdocs.worldbank.org/en/646831555088732759/FM-Coalition-Brochure-final-v3.pdf. [135]

World Bank (2019), *Disaster Response: A Public Financial Management Review Toolkit*, World Bank, Washington, DC, https://www.pefa.org/resources/disaster-response-public-financial-management-review-toolkit. [130]

World Bank (n.d.), "Disaster Risk Financing and Insurance (DRFI) Program", webpage, https://www.worldbank.org/en/programs/disaster-risk-financing-and-insurance-program (accessed on 22 July 2020). [151]

World Bank (n.d.), "Hands-on Energy Adaptation Toolkit (HEAT)", webpage, https://esmap.org/aboutthetoolkit (accessed on 17 January 2021). [81]

World Bank Group (2014), *Financial Protection Against Natural Disasters: An Operational Framework for Disaster Risk Financing and Insurance*, World Bank, Washington, DC, https://openknowledge.worldbank.org/handle/10986/21725. [139]

Ziervogel, G. et al. (2019), "Vertical integration for climate change adaptation in the water sector: Lessons from decentralisation in Africa and India.", *Regional Environmental Change*, Vol. 19/8, pp. 2729-2743, https://doi.org/10.1007/s10113-019-01571-y. [44]

Zwitter, A. and M. Boisse-Despiaux (2018), "Blockchain for humanitarian action and development aid", *Journal of International Humanitarian Action*, Vol. 3/16, http://dx.doi.org/10.1186/s41018-018-0044-5. [148]

Notes

[1] Colombia, Kenya, Nicaragua, South Africa, Philippines and Viet Nam.

[2] African Agriculture Initiative, the International Center for Tropical Agriculture (CIAT), the International Institute for Applied Systems Analysis and the World Bank have conducted a joint programme to promote the development of CSA Investment Plans in their partner countries. For more information, see (World Bank, 2019[86]).

[3] Infrastructure systems include energy, water, waste management, transport, telecommunications and building stocks. Broader definitions could also include social infrastructure, such as social protection systems, health-care systems, financial and insurance systems, education systems, and law enforcement and justice (Hall et al., 2019[92]).

4. Enablers for action on climate resilience

This chapter explores three enablers that play a critical role in strengthening climate resilience through checklists, tools and guidance. It begins with data and information, examining the role of regional and international weather and climate service initiatives, as well as National Meteorological and Hydrological Services. It moves on to the need for greater awareness and capacity at both individual, organisational and systemic levels. Several examples highlight the role of different stakeholders in strengthening capacity, as well as pilot projects by development co-operation providers that focus on long-term sustainability. The final enabler of technology highlights the different steps to develop and disseminate technology to strengthen climate resilience; the economic and non-economic barriers that prevent these steps; and the institutional arrangements and networks that could help overcome obstacles.

4.1. Data and information for implementation

4.1.1. Checklist for action

ACTIONS		ACTOR(S)[1]
Strengthen the institutional capacity of National Meteorological and Hydrological Services (NMHSs)		
✓	Strengthen the capacity of NMHSs to facilitate collaboration among national institutions engaged in the development, dissemination and application of weather, water and climate services.	Governments with support from dev-co[2]
✓	Ensure that NMHSs are located in a ministry or agency where they can deliver on their mandate through co-ordination, access to data and information, and human and technical capacity.	Governments, potentially with support from dev-co
✓	Strengthen policy environments, human and technical capacities, and financing models supportive of weather and climate services that are national-regional-global in scale, through established international processes and build on progress to date.	Governments with support from dev-co, academia, research funders
✓	Align international support with domestic NMHS priorities and strive for a co-ordinated approach supportive of existing public- and private-sector initiatives.	Dev-co
Improve observations and modelling capabilities as a basis for strengthened weather and climate services		
✓	Assess gaps in weather, water and climate observations and formulate national and regional strategies to address these gaps with associated implementation plans through established national and international processes.	Governments, potentially with international organisations, academia and dev-co
✓	Invest in human and technical capacity to collect, process and share weather, water and climate observations in a digital format nationally, regionally and globally.	Governments through established international processes and potentially with dev-co
Conduct climate risk assessments to inform decision-making processes for climate resilience		
✓	Determine the parameters of the risk assessment informed by related socio-economic variables and the resources available.	Governments, possibly with support from dev-co
✓	Consider approaches that combine quantitative and qualitative risk assessments to get an overview of both the possible economic and non-economic impacts.	Governments, possibly with support from dev-co
✓	Complement identification of the risks with a prioritisation of the risks, response measures and their implementation, monitoring, evaluation and learning.	Governments, possibly with support from dev-co
✓	Support partner countries in enhancing their capacity to conduct risk assessments, e.g. through staff exchange, peer learning and ongoing interaction.	Dev-co
Prioritise investments in forecasting and early warning systems and ensure user friendly platforms		
✓	Regularly assess the status of the key elements of the EWSs (i.e. hazard, vulnerability and exposure data and information, dissemination and communication, preparedness to respond) and the partnerships necessary to operate and maintain them and target investments accordingly.	Governments, possibly with support from dev-co
✓	Facilitate co-ordination and collaboration between national, regional and global systems and support mechanisms and enhance the capacity of EWSs and the accuracy of the information.	Governments, possibly with support from dev-co
Facilitate participatory approaches and tailor the data and information to the capacities and constraints of users		
✓	Facilitate participatory approaches to understand local climate risks and identify needs and possible solutions.	Governments & dev-co
✓	Implement mechanisms that facilitate engagement by holders of Indigenous and local knowledge to decision-making processes on climate resilience.	Governments & dev-co
✓	Tailor the format and language of the warning messages to the needs, capacities, constraints and priorities of different users.	Governments, possibly with support from dev-co

Note 1: Key actors (i.e. governments or development co-operation, or both) that play the primary role in promoting individual actions can greatly vary among countries and sectors. This column nevertheless indicates the likely leader in each of the actions. Some actions are led by governments but in many cases also supported by development co-operation (indicated as "Governments with support from dev-co").
Note 2: Dev-co: providers of development co-operation.
Note 3: Actions in this list are indicative and some may not be relevant to all countries or development co-operation providers.

4.1.2. Rationale

Efforts to strengthen climate resilience rely on the availability of weather, water and climate data and information to policy makers and other state- and non-state actors. Weather and climate services, collectively categorised as meteorological services, provide information and advice on past, present and future states of the atmosphere across different timescales. These range from minutes and weeks (weather) to months, years, decades and even centuries (climate). Complementing meteorological services are i) hydrological services that focus on surface and sub-surface inland waters and cover areas such as energy and water resource management; and ii) oceanographic and marine services that address the oceans and related sectors (Luther et al., 2019[1]). The term weather and climate services broadly refers to different types of climate data products and information as summarised in Table 4.1. These can, for example, be in the form of web platforms, smartphone apps or seasonal forecasts, all with the shared goal of being easily accessible to intended users.

Table 4.1. Data and information: Terms and examples

Terms	Examples
Climate data	Series of measured and constructed climate variables such as temperature, rainfall and wind from e.g. remote sensing, earth observations, field gauges and automatic weather stations (past) combined with model projections (future).
Climate data product	Analysis or processing of climate data such as maps of average rainfall, average wind speed and direction, or an outlook for next month's rainfall.
Climate information	A more general term for any combination of data, data product, knowledge and expert advice.

Source: (WMO, n.d.[2]), Climate Knowledge for Action: A Global Framework for Climate Services - Empowering the Most Vulnerable. Frequently Asked Questions, https://gfcs.wmo.int//sites/default/files/FAQ/HLT/HLT_FAQ_en.pdf.

Weather and climate services and the underlying infrastructure that supports them are critical to guide decision making on climate resilience, as recognised by over 40 developing countries in their Nationally Determined Contributions (NDCs) (Allis et al., 2019[3]). This infrastructure includes equipment to collect data, preserve and manage data records; and processes for developing and delivering weather and climate services. Development of the services must demonstrate a good understanding of the needs of decision makers and society more broadly to understand, anticipate and manage climate-related risks. They must also deliver information in a format that is relevant, accessible and credible (WMO & GFCS, 2019[4]). For decision makers, for example, information that sheds light on the impacts of climate change on their thematic or geographic areas of management will often be more valuable than data on the meteorological quantities per se (e.g. projected precipitation and temperature changes) (Hansen et al., 2019[5]).

Early and sustained engagement with different users can help ensure that data and information are decision-relevant. They must be compatible with the capacities of intended users, increasing their understanding of the issues, and in turn their confidence in using them (Weaver et al., 2017[6]; Butler et al., 2015[7]; Street et al., 2019[8]). Centralised platforms, such as the Global Framework for Climate Services (GFCS) spearheaded by the World Meteorological Organization (WMO), can facilitate support tailored to user needs (see Box 4.1). The GFCS provides access to weather and climate data and information, including observations, forecasting, risk modelling and the latest academic findings.

Box 4.1. Global Framework for Climate Services (GFCS)

Established by the international community at the World Climate Conference-3 in 2009, and spearheaded by the World Meteorological Organization, GFCS aims to "enable society to better manage the risks and opportunities arising from climate variability and change [...] through the development and incorporation of science-based climate information and prediction into planning, policy and practice" (WMO & GFCS, 2016, p. 12[9]). Observations, technology and scientific understanding serve as inputs to the development of climate services focused on meeting user requirements.

GFCS is structured around five pillars that must interact to make the production, delivery and application of climate services fully effective (WMO & GFCS, 2016[9]):

- **User Interface Platform**: a platform where users of climate services can make their needs understood to the producers of those services.
- **Climate Services Information System (CSIS)**: the production and distribution system for climate data and information products that address user needs:
    - **Regional Climate Centres (RCCs)**: provide national climate centres and other regional users online access to their services. The RCCs are also a component of the WMO **Global Data-processing and Forecasting System.**
- **Observations and Monitoring**: the essential infrastructure for generating climate data.
- **Research, Modelling and Prediction**: advances the science needed for improved climate services that meet user needs.
- **Capacity Development**: supports the systematic development of the institutions, infrastructure and human resources needed for effective climate services.

The priority for the third phase (2019-23) of GFCS is to strengthen the sustainability and financial investments of the five pillars and to further support the institutional mechanisms for climate service delivery and uptake. These are key elements of the broader climate services value chain (see Figure 4.1), of which the CSIS is one component (Hewitt et al., 2020[10]).

Coverage of hazard, exposure and vulnerability data and information is not always available at a level of granularity suitable for national or local decision-making processes. The governance of data and information generation and dissemination can also limit access and use. This is especially the case when the cost of acquiring data falls on several individual ministries or agencies rather than a central government entity, such as a National Meteorological and Hydrological Service (NMHS) (OECD, 2020[11]).

Housing the NMHS in a ministry or agency with limited authority or capacity to co-ordinate stakeholders can also affect access and use. In some countries, one agency is responsible for weather, water and climate; in others, it may be two or more separate agencies. NMHSs can also play a critical role in supporting different stakeholders affected by climate risks (e.g. agriculture, energy, transport, health and water). They can also help provide solutions for climate resilience (e.g. infrastructure developers and insurance providers) to complement use of weather and climate data and information with that on associated socio-economic variables. Further, they can facilitate access and co-ordination with regional and global stakeholders. These could include members of the United Nations system, other international organisations, economic commissions, financial institutions and the private sector (Hewitt et al., 2020[10]) (see examples of global and regional initiatives in Box 4.2).

In addition to the production and delivery of weather and climate services, the so-called climate services value chain also includes stakeholder actions and outcomes, and evaluations of associated economic costs and benefits (see Figure 4.1). Value chains of weather and climate services that are national-regional-global in scale require continued investments across all levels. This allows them to build on progress over the past decade both to develop weather and climate services and to overcome the "last mile" barriers that can limit their use and benefits (WMO & GFCS, 2019[4]). The benefits of investing in such a national-regional-global system have been estimated to outweigh the costs by around 80:1 (Kull, Graessle and Aryan, 2016[12]). For such benefits to materialise, however, supportive policy environments, as well as human and technical resources, must be available to put the systems in place and keep them operational; this is not the case for all developing countries (Kull, Graessle and Aryan, 2016[12]). In fact, it has often proven challenging to scale up weather and climate service interventions. Some obstacles include capacity constraints, inadequate institutions and difficulties in maintaining systems beyond the pilot project stage (IPCC, 2018[13]). Overcoming these challenges requires a shift towards a long-term financing model supportive of a system that spans national, regional and global scales.

Figure 4.1. Weather and climate services value chain

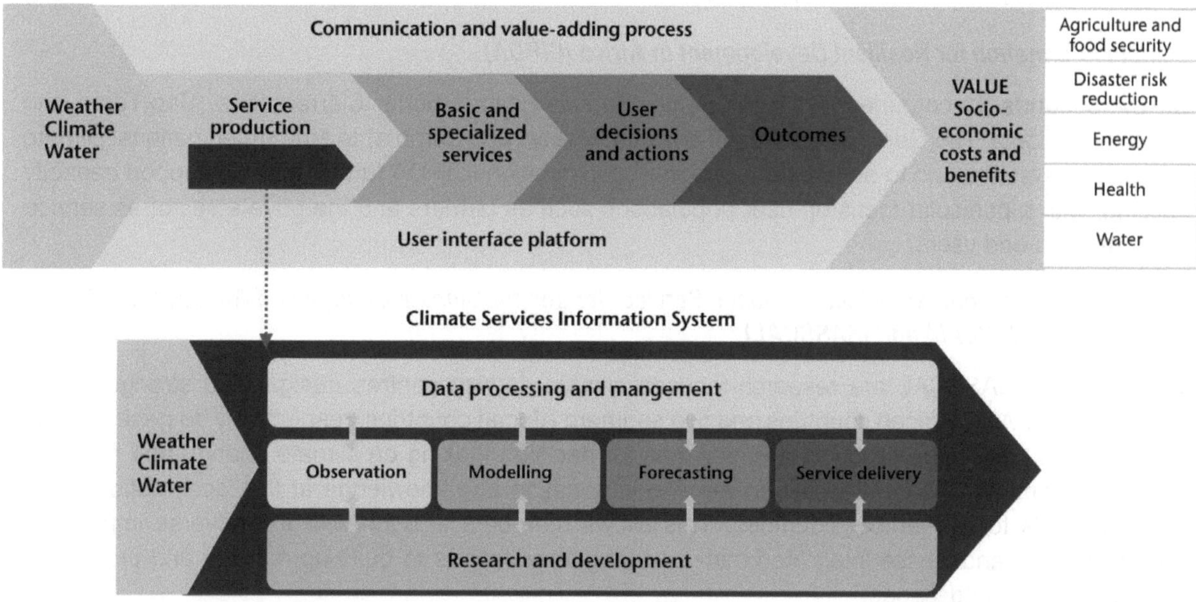

Note: World Meteorological Organization (WMO), in collaboration with the United Nations Educational, Scientific and Cultural Organization (UNESCO), the United Nations Environment Programme (UNEP), the Food and Agriculture Organization of the United Nations (FAO), the International Science Council (ISC) and other intergovernmental and non-governmental partners.

Source: (WMO & GFCS, n.d.[14]), The Global Framework for Climate Services: Value Proposition, https://library.wmo.int/doc_num.php?explnum_id=6275.

Box 4.2. Regional and international weather and climate service initiatives

Enhancing National Climate Services initiative (ENACTS)

ENACTS aims to bring climate knowledge into decision-making processes by improving availability, access to and use of climate information, through the provision of reliable and readily accessible climate high-resolution data to decision makers across Africa. Further, it delivers climate data, targeted information products and training that reflect user needs to facilitate their use of the information in decision-making processes.

Partnership for Resilience and Preparedness (PREP)

PREP is a public-private collaboration that seeks to improve access to data and empower communities and businesses in their efforts to strengthen climate resilience through two components:

- *PREP Partnership*: Brings together stakeholders from the public, private and non-profit sectors, including government agencies, leading technology companies and networks of climate preparedness practitioners.
- *PREPdata*: A map-based, open data online platform that allows users to access and visualise spatial data reflecting past and future climate, as well as the physical and socio-economic landscape for climate adaptation and resilience planning.

Climate for Development in Africa (ClimDev-Africa)

ClimDev-Africa is a joint programme of the African Union Commission, the United Nations Economic Commission for Africa and the African Development Bank. It has a mandate to support Africa's response to climate variability and change by improving the quality and availability of information and analysis to decision makers at the regional level.

Climate Information for Resilient Development in Africa (CIRDA)

CIRDA supports 11 countries in Africa (Benin, Burkina Faso, Liberia, Sierra Leone, Sao Tome and Principe, Ethiopia, The Gambia, Uganda, Tanzania, Malawi and Zambia) to strengthen national climate information systems and to benefit from regional co-ordination. CIRDA further aims to support capacity building, with a particular focus on user populations such as farmers and the private sector as service providers and end users.

West African and Southern African Science Service Centres for Climate Change and Adaptive Land Management (WASCAL) and (SASSCAL)

WASCAL and SASSCAL are research-focused climate service centres designed to strengthen the capacity of ten West African countries and five southern African countries, respectively, to generate and use scientific knowledge products and services for decision making on climate change and adaptive land management. The centres aim to provide information and knowledge at the local, national and regional levels to its member countries. This allows members to cope with the adverse impacts of climate change and devise integrated mid- and long-term options to build up resilient and productive socio-ecological landscapes.

Central Asia Climate Portal (CACIP)

CACIP aims to support stakeholders to access, analyse and visualise data publicly available to support decision-making processes. The information platform provides different types of free climate services, including on soil moisture, temperature, precipitation, historical climate statistics and weather forecasts. It also points to available sources of data from global, regional and local sources, and provides analytical tools and interfaces for the visualisation and interpretation of data and information.

The rest of this section explores how weather and climate services can contribute to strengthened climate resilience, focusing on five priorities for governments and development co-operation to consider:

- Strengthen the institutional capacity of National Meteorological and Hydrological Services (NMHSs)
- Improve observations and modelling capabilities as a basis for strengthened weather and climate services.
- Conduct climate risk assessments to inform decision-making processes for climate resilience.
- Prioritise investments in forecasting and early warning systems and ensure user friendly platforms.
- Facilitate participatory approaches and tailor the data and information to the capacities and constraints of users.

4.1.3. Strengthen the institutional capacity of National Meteorological and Hydrological Services (NMHSs)

NMHSs are in many countries the primary source of weather, water and climate data and information. This work entails the design, operation and maintenance of national observation, monitoring, modelling and forecasting systems. However, it also includes data processing, management, exchange and dissemination of related products (WMO & GFCS, 2016[9]). For NMHSs to contribute to climate resilience, they must have a good understanding of users' needs and capacity to adjust products and services accordingly. This includes both short-term forecasts and seasonal information to farmers, for example. It also includes the ability of users to assess the local implications of forecasts of planetary phenomena such as the El Niño-Southern Oscillation, the North Atlantic Oscillation and the Arctic Oscillation (Snow et al., 2016[15]).

NMHSs are publicly funded entities with a primary focus on generating and sharing weather, water and climate data and information. As such, they are theoretically well-positioned to collaborate with academia, government departments and other stakeholders, including international and civil society organisations (CSOs). Such partnerships can be crucial in enhancing data and information coverage and quality, and in facilitating access to the data in a timely and efficient manner (WMO & GFCS, 2016[9]).

The private sector can also play a role. However, experience from the Philippines has shown that it is not always easy to generate viable business opportunities for weather, water and climate services. For instance, a private-sector initiative called the WeatherPhilippines used to provide short-term weather forecasts for free in the Philippines. However, it has recently closed its operations. The parent company donated its automated weather stations and other weather technology assets to various government agencies, local government units and a CSO (Aboitiz, 2020[16]). There were multiple reasons for the closure, including financial constraints.

Having to compete for state budgets, NMHSs in many developing countries are often relatively poorly resourced. Many have limited human and institutional capacity to support the development of weather and climate services and limited scope for collaboration (Allis et al., 2019[3]). This translates into reduced access for state and non-state actors to data and information, critical for informed decision-making processes. In some countries, NMHSs do not manage support for weather and climate services. Rather, other national ministries or agencies, including for disaster relief, water, transportation, communications, agriculture or finance, fulfil this role (Snow et al., 2016[15]).

Still other countries have centralised platforms such as National Frameworks for Climate Services (NFCS) or National Climate Forums. These provide institutional mechanisms for co-ordinating, facilitating and strengthening collaboration among national institutions and other state and non-state actors in development and use of tailored climate services (WMO & GFCS, 2019[4]). The GFCS monitors progress development of NFCS online (WMO & GFCS, n.d.[17]).

Increased recognition of the importance of weather, water and climate services has brought more development co-operation providers supporting related initiatives (Hansen et al., 2019[5]). This has in some cases resulted in a fragmented approach where NMHSs are under pressure to operate and maintain individual and sometimes overlapping initiatives. They must comply with different approaches to implementation and reporting, leaving little room to strengthen their overall capacity (Snow et al., 2016[15]). Indeed, many NMHSs face human capacity as a constraint; they lack staff with technical skills to maintain equipment and to process the data and information.

Twelve international organisations[1] joined forces in 2019 to co-ordinate their support to weather and climate services in developing countries. The Alliance for Hydromet Development aims to ramp up efforts to strengthen the capacity of developing country NMHSs to produce and deliver high-quality weather forecasts, early warnings and other hydrological and climate services. Members of the Alliance have committed to strengthen collaboration in four areas (WMO, n.d.[18]):

- Improve data quality by strengthening country capacities for sustained operation of observational systems and seek innovative ways to finance developing country observations.
- Strengthen country capacities for science-based mitigation and adaptation planning.
- Strengthen EWSs for improved disaster risk management by developing national multi-hazard EWSs, comprising better risk information, forecasting capabilities, warning dissemination and anticipatory response.
- Boost investments for better effectiveness and sustainability by fostering programmatic approaches that go beyond individual projects.

A range of knowledge products have been developed that can guide efforts to strengthen the institutional capacity, mandate and recognition of National Meteorological and Hydrological Services, some of which are summarised in Table 4.2.

Box 4.3. Learning solutions for the co-development of weather and climate services in Africa

The capacity of many National Meteorological and Hydrological Services (NMHSs) is constrained due to unmet learning needs. The Training Operational Package for Climate Services of the World Meteorological Organization (WMO) aims to contribute to the operational implementation of its educational platform Global Campus. In this way, it encourages multilateral collaboration among Regional Training Centres (RTCs) and other training institutions. To that end, it provides an open platform for sharing training contents, tools and learning technologies open to all providers and users of weather and climate services.

The RTC in Italy, in agreement with WMO, has supported the 17 member states of the Economic Community of West African States[1] since 2016. Together, they strengthen the weather and climate services capacity of their NMHSs. The Training Programme on Climate Change Adaptation and Disaster Risk Reduction in Agriculture (PACC-RRC), funded by the Italian Development Cooperation, was developed to strengthen the capacities of experts in NMHSs, other national technical services, specialised agencies and other public and private institutions. The strategic implementation of PACC-RRC aimed to enhance technical and scientific co-operation among NMHSs. It also sought to promote collaboration on capacity development for providing operational weather and climate services for disaster risk reduction and adaptation to climate change in agriculture and other key sectors.

Note: 1. Benin, Burkina Faso, Cabo Verde, Chad, Côte d'Ivoire, Ghana, Guinea, Guinea-Bissau, Liberia, Mali, Mauritania, Niger, Nigeria, Senegal, Sierra Leone, The Gambia, Togo.

Table 4.2. Strengthen the institutional capacity, mandate and recognition of National Meteorological and Hydrological Services: Guidance and tools

Guidance and tools	Focus	Audience
Step-by-step Guidelines for Establishing a National Framework for Climate Services (NFCSs) (WMO)	This document explains how to develop a functional NFCS that will serve as a key co-ordination mechanism that brings together local, national, regional and global stakeholders for generation and delivery of co-designed and co-produced climate services with and for users.	✓ NMHSs and partner institutions at a national level ✓ Development co-operation supporting the development and implementation of NFCS
Enhancing National Climate Serv ices (ENACTS) (Columbia University)	This initiative delivers climate data, targeted information products and training relevant to the needs of users and decision makers at multiple levels.	✓ Decision makers at local, regional and national levels
Training Operational Package for Climate Services (TOPaCS) (RCT Italy)	This initiative encourages multilateral collaboration among regional training centres and other training institutions and provides an open platform for sharing training contents, tools and learning	✓ Providers and users of weather and climate services

	technologies.	
Checklist for Climate Services Implementation (WMO)	This is a checklist for NMHSs to self-assess progress on climate services implementation and to identify areas where support is needed.	✓ NMHSs and partner institutions at a national level
Guidelines for NMHSs to Contribute to Climate Risk Management (WMO)	This guideline focuses on capacity development for NMHSs to contribute to climate risk management. It provides conceptual principles, examples, checklists and indices to assist in the collation of evidence for different components of climate services.	✓ NMHSs and partner institutions at a national level
Capacity Development for Climate Services: Guidelines for National Meteorological and Hydrological Services (WMO)	These guidelines are intended to provide NMHSs and other climate service providers with up-to-date information on available resources, strategies, procedures and best practices available to help develop their capacities in the provision and use of climate services.	✓ NMHSs and other climate service providers

4.1.4. Improve observations and modelling capabilities as a basis for strengthened weather and climate services

Data and observations, as well as related modelling capabilities, underpin all weather and climate services and related climate science research. Daily, monthly, seasonal or annual data provide essential input for planning processes in areas such as agriculture, water, energy and health. Longer data series inform analysis of the relationship between changes in the climate, the natural environment and society (e.g. migration of species across altitudes and latitudes and public health). This includes data and observations on both the processes and properties of the climate system (see examples in Table 4.3):

- ***Processes***: atmospheric, oceanic, terrestrial
- ***Properties***: physical, chemical and biological properties

Table 4.3. Observations: Processes, properties and variables

Processes	Properties	Variables
Atmospheric	Surface	• Air temperature, wind speed and direction, water vapour, pressure, precipitation, surface radiation budget
	Upper-air	• Temperature, wind speed and direction, water vapour, cloud properties, Earth radiation budget, lightning
	Composition	• Carbon dioxide (CO_2), methane (CH_4), other long-lived greenhouse gases, ozone, aerosol, precursors for aerosol and ozone
Oceanic	Physics	• Temperature (sea surface and sub-surface), salinity (sea surface and sub-surface), currents, surface currents, sea level, sea state, sea ice, ocean surface stress, ocean surface heat flux
	Biogeochemistry	• Inorganic carbon, oxygen, nutrients, transient tracers, nitrous oxide (N_2O), ocean colour
	Biology/ecosystem	• Plankton, marine habitat properties
Terrestrial	Hydrology	• River discharge, groundwater, lakes, soil moisture
	Cryosphere	• Snow, glaciers, ice sheets and ice shelves, permafrost
	Biosphere	• Albedo, land cover, fraction of absorbed photosynthetically active radiation, leaf area index, above-ground biomass, soil carbon, fire, land surface temperature

Source: (WMO, 2016[19]), The Global Observing System for Climate: Implementation Needs, https://library.wmo.int/doc_num.php?explnum_id=3417.

The observation system is globally comprised of more than 10 000 staffed or automatic surface weather stations, 1 000 upper-air stations, 7 000 ships, 100 moored and 1 000 drifting buoys, hundreds of weather radars and 3 000 specially equipped commercial aircrafts, and 30 meteorological and 200 research satellites (WMO, n.d.[20]). Once quality controlled, the observations are made freely available through WMO's Information System (see Box 4.4).

Despite this vast network of observations, coverage varies significantly across countries and continents. This is in part due to inadequate or unreliable investments in many developing countries in the infrastructure and human and technical capacity. However, factors such as inadequate maintenance of the equipment, unreliable energy supply hampering data transmission, conflict, vandalism and regional-scale epidemics also play an important role (Snow et al., 2016[15]).

Digital observations and automated measurement systems can help address data gaps in some contexts. Automatic weather stations can be tailored with a variety of sensors to meet different operational requirements (Snow et al., 2016[15]). Similarly, automatic hydrological observing systems have facilitated a shift from manual readings of staff gauges to automated readings that could increase coverage (Snow et al., 2016[15]). Remote sensing techniques can also address some gaps, such as atmospheric temperature and moisture profiles that inform forecasting. Further, they can shed light on historical trends such as the warming of the Polar regions or high mountain areas. However, certain factors limit the use of remote sensing techniques for many applications. These include uncertain data continuity and continued gaps in the data validation. As a result of these limits, they cannot be relied upon to overcome all data gaps (Guo, Zhang and Zhu, 2015[21]).

Box 4.4. WMO systems and frameworks in support data collection and exchange

The World Meteorological Organization (WMO) Integrated Global Observing System (WIGOS) provides a framework for the integration and sharing of comparable observational data from National Meteorological and Hydrological Services (NMHSs) and other sources through the application of internationally accepted standards and best practices. WIGOS is affiliated with the intergovernmental Group on Earth Observations and includes different component, two of which are summarised below. Other component include the Global Observing System, the Global Ocean Observing System, the WMO Hydrological Observing System:

- ***Global Observing System for Climate (GCOS)*** has specified 54 Essential Climate Variables (ECV): physical, chemical or biological variables or group of variables that contribute to the Earth's climate. The ECV Inventory provides open access to existing and planned data records from space agency- sponsored activities.
- ***Global Basic Observing Network (GBON)*** includes a commitment by WMO members to implement a minimal set of surface-based and upper-air observing stations:
    - ***Systematic Observation Financing Facility*** aims to support countries to generate and exchange basic observational data for weather forecasts and climate services. It will apply the requirements of the GBON to guide investments, using data exchange as a measure of success.

WMO Information System connects all NMHSs and regions for data exchange, management and processing. As such, it serves as a hub for all weather, climate and water data and products. This facilitates exchange between WMO centres and their users.

Global Data-Processing and Forecasting System prepares and makes available to WMO members harmonised meteorological analyses and forecast products. It is organised as a network of global, regional and national centres.

Global Multi-hazard Alert System aggregates official warning information issued by national authorities to serve as a central hub to support the UN humanitarian system, NMHSs and other global users.

For observations to be accessible to weather and climate service providers and users, they must be available in a digital format. This also includes the digitalisation of historical data to fill temporal and spatial gaps. Benefits from such digitalisation or data rescue include the following (WMO, 2016[22]):

- It helps to calibrate different models, including hydrological and climatological models.
- It allows current weather and climate to be better placed within an historical perspective.
- It provides a basis for assessing historical sensitivities of natural and human-made systems to climate variability and change.

Development co-operation plays a role in supporting partner countries in improving weather, water and climate observations. In some cases, it puts processes in place for generating good data and information. In others, it may scale up and maintain data and information processes already in place. Further, development co-operation can support partner countries in making the data accessible to different stakeholders across local, national and regional levels. It is also well-placed to support efforts aimed at strengthening the capacity of different stakeholders to use the data and information available, especially at the local level (OECD, 2020[11]).

A country must complement the availability of data and information by its modelling capabilities to be able to project changes in the climate. When complemented with an understanding of the broader socio-economic variables, modelling can also point to the potential implications of climate change for human and natural systems. The Ghana Space Science and Technology Institute, for example, relies on meteorological data from the Ghana Meteorological Services Agency for providing policy makers with climate data and information. This includes the Institute's involvement in climate scenario development and vulnerability assessment for the country's National Communications (NCs) to the UN Framework Convention on Climate Change (UNFCCC). Ghana's third NC, published in 2015, simulates and downscales data on rainfall and temperature obtained from 22 synoptic stations across the country (Government of Ghana, 2015[23]).

Development of modelling capabilities are resource-intensive and regional climate centres can play an important role in developing and making available to both state and non-state actors this critical data and information. At the global level, the WMO Regional Climate Centres and the NMHSs are supported by the WMO-designated Global Producing Centres for Long-Range Forecasts. One of these centres is the European Centre for Medium-Range Weather Forecasts. For example, it provides global forecasts, climate analysis and datasets that can be tailored to different user needs. These aim to show how the weather is most likely to evolve by producing an ensemble of predictions. This is complemented by the Global Producing Centres for Annual to Decadal Climate Predictions. The most recent update, for example, draws on the expertise of renowned climate scientists and computer models from world leading climate centres to produce actionable information for decision makers around the world (WMO, 2020[24]).

Table 4.4 summarises different guidance and tools that can guide national and international approaches to improve weather, climate and hydrological observations in support of strengthened weather and climate services.

Table 4.4. Improve weather, climate and hydrological observations as a basis for strengthened weather and climate services: Guidance and tools

Guidance and tools	Focus	Audience
World Bank Climate Change Knowledge Portal (World Bank)	This portal provides access to comprehensive data on historical and future climate, vulnerabilities and impacts. The data are available in country, region and watershed views and country profiles provide deeper insights into climate risks and adaptation actions.	✓ Development co-operation ✓ Decision makers across sectors and levels
Guidelines on Climate Observation and Networks and Systems (WMO)	These guidelines provide climatologists with the essential information on observation networks and systems to help ensure	✓ National climatologists and providers of development co-

	that their outputs are adequate for the comprehensive needs of climate services, applications and research.	operation supporting weather and climate observations
Guidelines on Climate Data Rescue (WMO)	This portal includes a range of guidance on how to organise and implement data rescue. It also provides generalised technological solutions.	✓ National Meteorological and Hydrological Services
SERVIR (NASA and USAID)	SERVIR works in partnership with regional organisations to support countries in using information provided by Earth-observing satellites and geospatial technologies for managing climate risks and land use. It empowers decision makers with tools, products and services to act locally on climate-sensitive issues.	✓ National governments ✓ Development co-operation ✓ Non-governmental organisations ✓ Civil society organisations
Copernicus Climate Change Service (C3S) (European Union)	This portal provides information about past, present and future climate in Europe and the rest of the world. It provides free and open access to climate data and tools based on best available science.	✓ Policy makers ✓ Scientists ✓ Media and the public

4.1.5. Conduct climate risk assessments to inform decision-making processes for climate resilience

The past decade has seen a shift in emphasis from assessing the physical nature of weather, water and climate hazards to better understanding the impacts of those hazards on people's lives and livelihoods. With this shift, top-down assessments of the hazards based on observed and modelled climate data have increasingly been complemented with bottom-up approaches that assess the exposure and vulnerability to the hazards. This is consistent with how the Intergovernmental Panel on Climate Change (IPCC) frames climate risks as a function of hazards, exposure and vulnerability (see Figure 4.2). There continues, however, to be a gap in the availability and access to exposure and vulnerability data compared to hazard data, with the former often spread across ministries and levels of government (OECD, 2020[11]). Examples of bottom-up qualitative approaches in understanding and informing climate resilience efforts are summarised in Box 4.5.

Figure 4.2. Risk-based conceptual framework by the Intergovernmental Panel on Climate Change

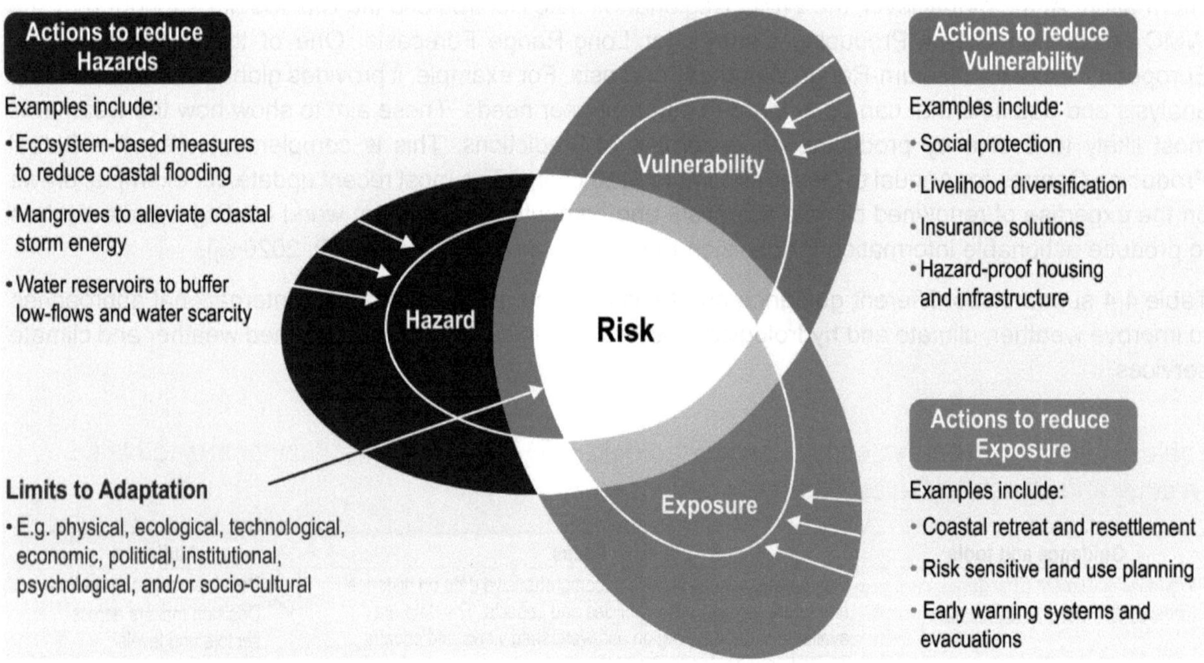

Source: (IPCC, 2019[25]), IPCC Special Report on the Ocean and Cryosphere in a Changing Climate, https://www.ipcc.ch/srocc/

Box 4.5. Bottom-up approaches to climate risk assessments: Lessons from CARIAA

The Collaborative Adaptation Research Initiative in Africa and Asia (CARIAA) supported climate resilience initiatives through research to inform policy and practice. It comprised four multidisciplinary research consortia with partners from the global North and South. The initiative highlighted the role of bottom-up approaches in understanding and informing climate resilience efforts. Such bottom-up approaches seek to locate climate change within a broader set of vulnerabilities and behaviours.

Deltas

Global assessments of climate risks to deltas often focus on biophysical risks from e.g. sea level rise, subsidence and salinisation of coastal waters. Risk management measures strike the balance between hard engineering for protection, working with nature to manage the risks, and addressing the potential risk of loss of coastal areas. Exposure and vulnerability is the outcome of myriads of individual decisions, highlighting the importance of focusing on agency and choice. Semi-structured interviews and focus group discussions with farming communities in the Mahanadi delta in India provided insight into these questions. They showed that spatial patterns of vulnerability are driven by insecure land tenure and uneven access to credit, a common driver of out-migration.

Semi-arid lands

A life history approach was used to understand livelihood responses to climate change in semi-arid regions in Ghana, Kenya, Namibia and India. Characterised by everyday mobility, the initiative examined how this mobility shapes household risk portfolios and response. Mobility is an essential feature of many livelihoods (e.g. pastoralism, farming, nature-based trading); it also provides access to livelihoods (e.g. commuting). Mobility enables people to switch between livelihoods, often in opportunistic ways, addressing both existing risks, but in some cases also creating new ones. Understanding whether people are moving in a positive or negative direction relative to their risk profile can shed light on the type of interventions needed.

Glacier- and snowmelt-dependent river basins

Household surveys in the Gandaki river basin in Nepal considered migration decisions, environmental stressors and adaptation choice. The surveys were complemented by focus group discussions with village development committees and interviews with other stakeholders at local, district and national levels. Such community-level risks assessments elicit information about livelihood contexts, resilience and local hazards through dialogues. By learning about Indigenous capacities, knowledge and practices, local risks and associated response measures can be better understood. The large majority (over 90%) of households reported perceiving changes in the climate (e.g. increased average summer and winter temperatures and decreased rainfall and snowfall). A similar share (over 80%) relied on agriculture for their livelihoods. However, only 35% reported having taken at least one adaptation measure. In most cases, people responded to an immediate risk rather than to effort to strengthen resilience.

Source: (Conway et al., 2019[26]), The need for bottom-up assessments of climate risks and adaptation in climate-sensitive regions, https://doi.org/10.1038/s41558-019-0502-0.

Many guidance and tools have been developed to assess climate-related risks (see some examples in Table 4.6). While the approaches differ, they all provide information on current and projected climate-related risks of societies, economies and ecosystems alongside the dimensions of hazards, vulnerability and exposure (GIZ, EURAC & UNU-EHS, 2018[27]). The assessments help set priorities for additional action on risks. This is followed by a review of the different options, development and implementation of response measures, and monitoring, evaluation and learning.

CoastAdapt, a resource supporting climate change adaptation in coastal Australia, recognises that capacity for such risk assessments will vary across stakeholder groups. Consequently, it has developed a three-tier framework that allows public and private stakeholders to assess the risks depending on the resources and capacity available (see Table 4.5). The first-pass risk screening aims to provide a broad overview of the climate risks to a community or organisation. Stakeholder consultations inform the second-pass risk assessment of exposure and vulnerability of communities or organisations to climate risks. The third-pass risk assessment further reviews priority actions identified through the second-pass assessment (Tonmoy, Rissik and Palutikof, 2019[28]). While developed specifically for the Australian context, it could inspire similar tiered approaches in other country contexts.

Table 4.5. Characteristics and requirements of risk assessment approaches

	First-pass risk assessment	Second-pass risk assessment	Third-pass risk assessment
Objective	Develop a quick high-level understanding of climate change risk in the area to determine whether further research or adaptation planning is required.	Conduct assessment (generally involving expert judgement) to identify specific risks that may become problematic under future climate change.	Understand vulnerability of different systems exposed to climate change-related hazards using more detailed and finer scale data; conduct a detailed risk assessment (quantitative or qualitative) to identify specific risks of different systems.
Data requirement	Nationally available datasets (e.g. projections and/or visualisations of different climate variables). Available localised mapping and information. No costs should be involved.	Nationally available climate change datasets, both observed and projected, together with existing information available from government, studies and/or expert knowledge. Some modest costs may be involved.	Some context-specific data depending on the objective of the assessment, in conjunction with high-resolution climate scenario data and local expert knowledge to understand the scale of the risk. Substantial cost may be involved.
Time and resource requirement	Minimum	Moderate	High
Base knowledge requirement	• minimum expertise required to acquire data • local knowledge required to interpret data • some understanding of climate change and its potential risks	• moderate knowledge to acquire appropriate data • moderate expertise required to interpret data • moderate expertise required to understand the consequences of a specific climate risk	• high expertise required to acquire appropriate data • high expertise to apply data, analyse and interpret results • high expertise required to understand how a given climate risk can translate into different consequences
Engagement requirement	Moderate expertise required for stakeholder identification, communication and liaison.	Moderate expertise required for communication or stakeholder consultation.	High expertise required in stakeholder engagement.
Example outcome	Inundation of coastal areas may be problematic in future.	Due to sea-level rise, there is a high risk that specific coastal areas may get inundated during future storm events.	Specific areas along the coast will be inundated more frequently due to sea-level rise and more intense storms. The infrastructure is not designed to withstand this level of risk, and therefore may require higher maintenance cost.
When it should be used	• Develop a quick and broad understanding of climate change risk. • Identify a need for strategic and ongoing response/commitment. • Identify key localities for attention. • Build awareness of risk	• Develop a more detailed understanding of climate change risks and opportunities. • Identify key risk locations/sectors with follow-up resourcing requirements (e.g. new data).	• Produce detailed impact studies of climate impacts on locations/sectors, with of the uncertainties involved. • Estimate costs of adaptation action and prioritise resource allocation. • Confirm emergency response procedures/requirements.

	among different stakeholders. • Seek social agreement to act on adaptation.	• Develop an adaptation strategy/plan. • Produce targeted climate risk communication materials. • Identify adaptation options and support development of a plan/strategy.	• Develop strategic and economic evaluation of adaptation options. • Develop adaptation action plans for specific issues including supporting detailed design.
Limitations	Based on high-level screening and therefore not suitable for making any final decisions on adaptation actions.	Based primarily on qualitative expert judgement of risk, therefore results are as good as the qualitative judgement of the experts.	Resource- and time-intensive, and so requires expert input.

Source: Adapted from (Tonmoy, Rissik and Palutikof, 2019[28]), A three-tier risk assessment process for climate change adaptation at a local scale, https://doi.org/10.1007/s10584-019-02367-z.

Box 4.6. Climate risk analysis for identifying and weighing adaptation strategies in sub-Saharan Africa (AGRICA)

The AGRICA-project is implemented by the Potsdam Institute for Climate Impact Research (PIK) in co-operation with the Deutsche Gesellschaft für Internationale Zusammenarbeit (GIZ) on behalf of the German Federal Ministry for Economic Cooperation and Development (BMZ). The project provides comprehensive climate risk analyses for selected countries in sub-Saharan Africa, with a focus on the agricultural sector. The analyses are divided into two components:

- **Impact**: This examines the interplay of a changing climate, changing water availability and resulting climate impacts on the agriculture sector, as well as vulnerability.
- **Action**: Based on the impact analysis, this assesses suitable adaptation strategies with the help of biophysical, cost-benefit and socio-economic analyses.

The results of the climate risk analyses provide decision makers in the respective countries with costed adaptation scenarios. These, in turn, can feed into national and sub-national planning processes, such as Nationally Determined Contributions and National Adaptation Plans. Further, the results can guide development co-operation, both in terms of identifying national priorities but also in limiting exposure to climate risks. In-depth climate risk studies have been conducted for Ghana, Ethiopia, Niger and Burkina Faso. A complementary district-level study for Ghana reflects that planning and implementation of adaptation measures often occur at the sub-national level.

PIK, GIZ and KfW on behalf of BMZ are also developing climate risk profiles for 12 African countries: Burkina Faso, Chad, Côte d'Ivoire, Ethiopia, Ghana, Kenya, Mali, Mauritania, Niger, Tanzania, Uganda and Madagascar. The profiles provide an overview of projected climate parameters and related impacts on key sectors until 2080 under different climate change scenarios. They build on state-of-the-art modelling of the latest climate data and make the main findings accessible to non-experts and decision makers.

Source: (PIK, n.d.[29]), AGRICA - Climate Risk Analyses for Identifying and Weighing Adaptation Strategies in sub-Saharan Africa, https://www.pik-potsdam.de/en/institute/departments/climate-resilience/projects/project-pages/agrica/agrica-sv-giz-climate-project.

It can be challenging for decision makers to navigate the wealth of guidance and tools available. Another challenge, especially at the local level, is the lack of data to feed into the assessments. Development co-operation can play a valuable role in supporting partner countries in identifying suitable approaches to their climate risk assessments. In some cases, it can also facilitate peer learning among countries with shared characteristics (e.g. nature of the climate risks, sectors at risk). Further, development co-operation should also make use of national frameworks in the projects and programmes they support when available, to further local capacity. *GIZ* is undertaking a comparative study of more than 100 guidelines or tools, organised according to different categories relevant for application.

Table 4.6. Conduct climate risk assessments to inform decision-making processes for climate resilience: Guidance and tools

Guidance and tools	Focus	Audience
World Bank Climate and Disaster Risk Screening Tools (World Bank)	This portal brings together a suite of climate and disaster risk screening tools developed by the World Bank to help professionals screen climate change and disaster risks during project preparation and sectoral- and national-level planning.	✓ Development co-operation
USAID Climate Risk Screening and Management Tools (USAID)	This portal includes different tools developed to support climate risk screening and management in strategy, project and activity design.	✓ Development co-operation
CRiSTAL (Community-based Risk Screening Tool – Adaptation and Livelihoods) (IISD)	This tool helps users identify and prioritise climate risks that projects at the local or community level might address.	✓ Primarily local or community-level project planners and managers
Disaster and Climate Change Risk Assessment Methodology for IDB Projects: A Technical Reference Document for IDB Project Teams (IaDB)	This methodology aims to provide a technically and operationally robust framework that serves as guidance for assessing disaster and climate change risk in projects grouped into three phases: i) screening and classification; ii) qualitative assessment; and iii) quantitative assessment.	✓ Development co-operation with a focus on infrastructure and potentially broader
Technical Guide on Action-Oriented Comprehensive Risk Assessment and Planning in the context of climate change (forthcoming) (GIZ)	This guide analyses methods and tools for integrated risk assessments that include climate-related extreme weather events and slow onset events, as well as other non-climatic risks that potentially lead to disasters (e.g. pandemics).	✓ National and local authorities e.g. overseeing climate adaptation and disaster risk reduction ✓ National and sub-national policy/decision makers ✓ Non-state actors working across levels of government, with civil society and the private sector
The Vulnerability Sourcebook: Concept and guidelines for standardised vulnerability assessments (GIZ)	This sourcebook provides a standardised approach to vulnerability assessments covering different sectors and topics (e.g. water, agriculture, fisheries, ecosystems), spatial levels (community, sub-national, national) and time horizons. It offers step-by-step guidance for designing and implementing a vulnerability assessment.	✓ Governmental and non-governmental organisations engaged in activities at the intersection of climate change and sustainable development.
Risk Supplement to the Vulnerability Sourcebook (GIZ)	The Risk Supplement provides guidance on how to apply the Vulnerability Sourcebook's approach to the concept of risk as defined in the IPCC 5th Assessment Report.	
Climate Risk Assessment for Ecosystem-based Adaptation: A guidebook for planners and practitioners (GIZ)	The Climate Risk Assessment for Ecosystem-based Adaptation, applies the framework developed in the Vulnerability Sourcebook to the context of ecosystem-based adaptation.	
Climate Finance Impact Tool (FIT) for Adaptation: Guidance on Climate Risk Assessment and Adaptation (JICA)	This tool provides a common concept of climate risk assessment and adaptation to be applied in development projects. This has been done with the goal of considering climate risks in a flexible manner depending on the circumstances of specific projects.	✓ Development co-operation
Capacity for Disaster Reduction Initiative (CADRI) (CADRI Partnership)	This global partnership provides countries with a mechanism to mobilise, through the UN Resident or Humanitarian Co-ordinator, multidisciplinary expertise in disaster risk reduction and climate change adaptation across a wide range of socio-economic sectors to strengthen risk information systems, prioritise risk reduction in national and local plans, and enhance preparedness systems.	✓ Governments
CoastAdapt (Australia)	This portal provides information and guidance focused on climate risks in Australia's coastal regions that can also be relevant to other countries. This includes step-by-step guidance for the three-tier framework presented in Table 4.5.	✓ Governments ✓ Private-sector actors

4.1.6. Prioritise investments in forecasting and early warning systems and ensure user friendly platforms

EWSs can play an important role in mitigating the impact of both extreme and slow onset weather and climate events by empowering individuals and communities to take preventive measures in a timely manner. Estimates suggest that EWSs save lives and assets worth at least ten times their cost, and that a 24-hour warning of a storm or heatwave can reduce damages by 30% (GCA, 2019[30]). Similarly, an upgrade of all hydrometeorological information production and early warning capacity in developing countries could save an average of 23 000 lives annually. Furthermore, it could provide between USD 3-30 billion per year in additional economic benefits related to disaster reduction [Rogers & Tsirkunov, 2013 in (Snow et al., 2016[15])]. Out of the NDCs submitted to the Paris Agreement by Least Developed Countries and Small Island Developing States, almost 90% identified EWSs as a top priority to support adaptation efforts in agriculture and food security, health and water management sectors (WMO, 2020[31]).

EWSs aim to ensure that risks are well understood and can be acted upon by individuals and communities, as well as established emergency services. They must therefore inform broader emergency management systems composed of, for example, health care, firefighters, police, civil protection and the army, which all have distinct and critical roles in disaster response (Hallegatte, Rentschler and Rozenberg, 2020[32]). EWSs focus primarily on weather-related risks over a few days during which specific action by law has to be taken. Longer timescales (months, years or decades) would result in forecasts, outlooks and scenarios. These could all be considered a type of early warning, although with less legal commitment to act. This difference in timescales between weather and climate projections has previously divided the respective research communities. This is gradually changing with growing recognition of the need to look at weather and climate as intimately linked processes on a continuum over time and space.

While modern EWSs combine operational scheduling (e.g. data import and processing) with built-in protocols, less resource-intensive systems can also play an important role in communicating risks and engaging local communities in generating early warning information (UNFCCC, 2020[33]). The International Centre for Integrated Mountain Development has developed a community-based flood early warning system (CBFEWS). It consists of tools and plans managed by local communities that provide near real-time early warnings when rising flood waters are detected (ICIMOD, 2020[34]). Malawi is piloting the CBFEWS approach building on lessons from the Hindu Kush Himalayan region.

Four closely interlinked components must be in place for EWSs to serve their intended purpose (UNDRR, 2017[35]) (see also Figure 4.3):

- disaster risk knowledge based on the systematic collection of data and disaster risk assessments
- detection, monitoring, analysis and forecasting of the hazards and possible consequences
- dissemination and communication, by an official source, of authoritative, timely, accurate and actionable warnings and associated information on likelihood and impact
- preparedness at all levels to respond to the warnings received.

Figure 4.3. Key elements of an early warning system

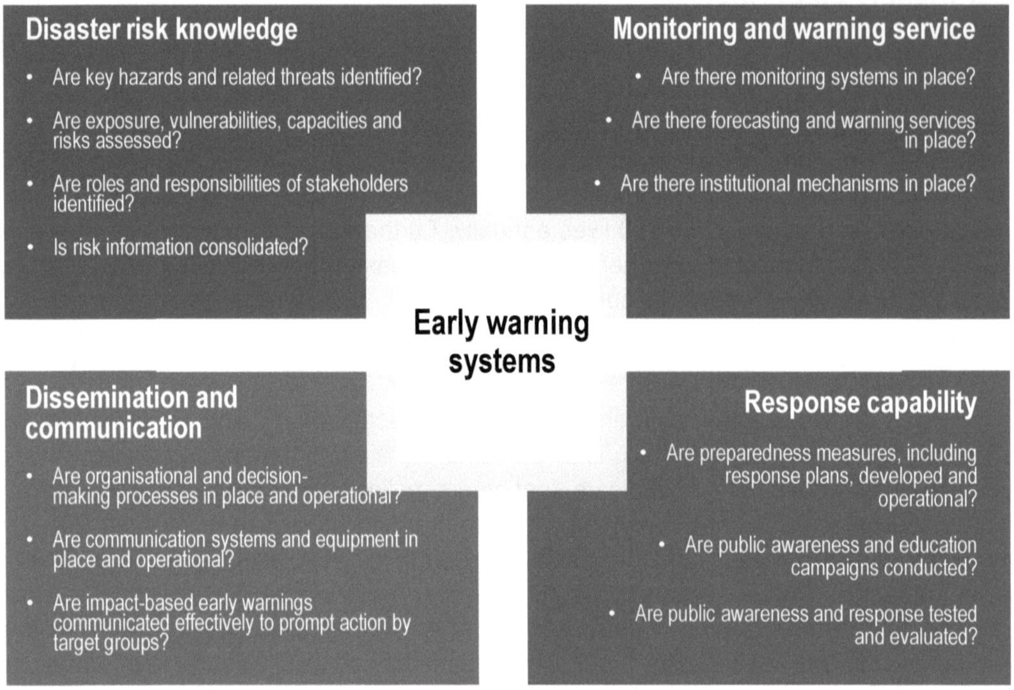

Source: Adjusted from (UNDP, 2019[36]), Five Approaches to Build Functional Early Warning Systems, https://reliefweb.int/report/world/five-approaches-build-functional-early-warning-systems, (WMO, 2018[37]), Multi-hazard Early Warning Systems: A Checklist, https://library.wmo.int/doc_num.php?explnum_id=4463.

Most countries have some form of early warning systems in place. A smaller number of regional and global support mechanisms can play an important role in facilitating exchange of information and collaboration on the management of the risks. However, they rarely have authority to trigger legally binding action (UNDP, 2019[36]). These mechanisms contribute towards the overall capacity of the system but also to the accuracy of warnings. Examples include cross-border collaboration on the management of flood risk in river basins and the management of climate risks across shared terrains or landscapes such as mountainous areas. Independent of the scale, EWSs require careful planning and co-ordination between the diverse set of stakeholders (see Figure 4.3). Effectiveness of the implementation is also subject to the capacity of individual stakeholders, as well as the broader national, regional and international systems. The status of both the individual elements, and the overall capacity of the co-ordination mechanisms or partnerships that operate and maintain them, must be regularly assessed. These assessments should help target investments accordingly.

Box 4.7. Regional and global early warning initiatives

Climate Risk and Early Warning Systems (CREWS)

CREWS, established in 2015, is a collaboration between the World Meteorological Organization, the United Nations Office for Disaster Risk Reduction and the World Bank's Global Facility for Disaster Reduction and Recovery. It is a financial mechanism that aims to save lives and livelihoods through the expansion of early warning systems and services in Least Developed Countries and Small Island Developing States. The initiative is focused on increasing the capabilities of the countries and island states to detect, monitor and forecast severe high-impact weather events. This is complemented by a focus on access to longer-term seasonal predictions and operational early warning and response plans that increase the access of vulnerable people to warnings.

Weather and Climate Information Services for Africa (WISER)

A programme by the UK Foreign, Commonwealth and Development Office (FCDO), split into two components: one Pan-African managed by the African Climate Policy Centre, and a second focused on East Africa and managed by the UK Met Office. The mission of the WISER programme is to make a step change in the quality, accessibility and use of weather and climate information services at all levels of decision making for sustainable development.

Asia Regional Resilience to a Changing Climate (ARRCC)

ARRCC is a four-year programme that started in 2018 managed by the UK Met Office and supported by the World Bank and the UK FCDO. It aims to strengthen weather forecasting systems across Asia, with a focus on Bangladesh, Pakistan, Nepal and Afghanistan. The programme aims to deliver new technologies and innovative approaches to help vulnerable communities use weather warning and forecasts to better prepare for climate-related shocks.

Table 4.7. Prioritise investments in forecasting and early warning systems and ensure user-friendly platforms: Guidance and tools

Guidance and tools	Focus	Audience
Five Approaches to Build Functional Early Warning Systems (UNDP)	The report identifies targeted interventions that can boost the efficiency and effectiveness of early warning systems in five areas: i) institutional and legal capacity development; ii) technology deployment; ii) community outreach and community-based solutions; iv) private sector engagement; and v) international co-operation and data sharing.	✓ Governments officials ✓ Development co-operation ✓ Non-governmental organisations (NGOs) and civil society organisations (CSOs)
Draft Consultation Document on Measuring Early Warning Access and Effectiveness (CREWS)	The document aims to identify a set of metrics to provide guidance on how to measure the effectiveness of, and access to, early warning systems.	✓ Government agencies and officials
Guidelines on Early Warning Systems and Application of Nowcasting and Warning Operations (WMO)	The guidelines focus on the role of National Meteorological and Hydrological Services (NMHSs) in developing early warning systems. This includes forecasting, formatting, presenting and communicating of warnings of severe weather, and the accompanying public education and capacity building of NMHSs.	✓ NMHSs
Multi-hazard Early Warning Systems: A Checklist: Outcome of the First Multi-hazard Early Warning Conference (WMO)	This checklist aims to be a practical, non-technical reference tool to ensure that the major elements of an effective early warning system are in place.	✓ National governments and other entities supporting the development and implementation of early warning systems
Famine Early Warning Systems Network (FEWS NET) (USAID)	FEWS NET aims to provide early warnings and analysis of food insecurity in 36 countries. It provides monthly reports and maps on	✓ National governments ✓ Development co-operation

	current and projected food insecurity with the aim of supporting different stakeholders to respond to humanitarian crises.	✓ NGOs and CSOs
Guidelines on Multi-hazard Impact-based Forecast and Warning Services (WMO)	These guidelines establish a road map that identifies the various milestones from weather forecasts and warnings to multi-hazard impact-based forecast and warning services.	✓ NMHSs
The Future of Forecasts: Impact-Based Forecasting for Early Action (Red Cross Red Crescent & UK Met Office)	This guide outlines the steps and tools needed to develop impact-based forecasting: from understanding risk to producing, issuing and verifying fit for purpose impact-based forecasts and warnings.	✓ NMHSs ✓ Humanitarian assistance ✓ Development co-operation

4.1.7. Facilitate participatory approaches and tailor the data and information to the capacities and constraints of users

Communities dependent on natural resources are particularly vulnerable to the impacts of climate change. Many communities have established traditions of responding to changes in the environment and climate through careful observation and interpretation of meteorological, hydrological and oceanographic phenomena. They also draw on local knowledge, social systems, cultural values and norms in managing the complex ecosystems they depend on (UNESCO, 2017[38]). The role and value of Indigenous knowledge has been widely recognised in areas such as agroforestry, biodiversity conservation, traditional medicine, disaster risk management (Nakashima et al., 2012[39]), and increasingly in the context of climate resilience (IPCC, 2014[40]). For example, women in the Pacific Islands have a wealth of traditional knowledge, including on gardening practices, food preservation and locations of traditional water sources that are valuable when developing activities to support the resilience of local communities to climate change (Mcleod et al., 2018[41]).

Indigenous and local knowledge complement scientific data with detailed information, often at finer spatial scales, on elements of importance to local livelihoods that scientists do not always consider (UNESCO, 2017[38]). Despite their disproportionate exposure to the impacts of climate change, and their deep understanding of the risks and solutions, Indigenous communities have often been excluded from decision-making processes, including on climate change. Due to their distinct social and cultural norms, decisions, policies and actions well-suited for mainstream society may not be appropriate to their circumstances.

Participatory approaches to identify climate risks through the lived experiences of the community can also be effective. They can point to approaches that address those risks and increase acceptance of suggested adaptation measures. Local knowledge can, for example, play an instrumental role in identifying landscape management approaches. Similarly, it can help identify use of nature-based solutions to reduce the risks associated with sea-level rise, including flooding and saltwater intrusion. Where appropriate, this can be complemented by support for technical know-how to adopt mainstream solutions to local contexts, providing room for experimenting, learning and adjusting to local needs (LIFE-AR, 2019[42]). Local knowledge can further offer valuable insights into local social factors such as behaviours and norms that may contribute to and be used to help mitigate risks.

Weather and climate services (including early warnings, forecasts and outlooks) must consider the needs, capacities, constraints and priorities of different users in line with a whole of society approach to be translated into action. They must take particular care to consider the ability of marginalised communities to access the information. In the context of EWSs, the following issues should be considered (UNDP, 2016[43]):

- **Format**: The information must be timely, accurate and accessible by the intended audience. This may entail making the content available in local languages or in non-written format by using universal symbols, basic infographics, maps or different forms of media (radio, television but also social media).
- **Information channels**: Public Service Announcements, television, radio, print media, social media, schools, hospitals and so on can all serve as channels for disseminating the information.

- **Guidance/recommendation**: Complementing information on the risks, the warnings should provide guidance on the response to different threat levels (e.g. yellow, orange or red), and point to where additional information or support is available. The information must also be provided at the right time and at the appropriate spatial scale to inform decision-making processes.
- **Audience**: End users of the information range from farmers, communities, policy makers and the private sector. The type of information required by different stakeholders varies, as do their respective roles in disseminating or responding to the risks, and their capacities to respond to the risks. Local leaders, for example, can play an important role in ensuring that the information reaches affected communities and that appropriate response measures are in place. The private sector can be a user of the information, but in some cases also plays an important role in disseminating it, e.g. telecommunications firms.

Table 4.8. Facilitate participatory approaches and tailor the data and information to the capacities and constraints of users: Guidance and tools

Guidance and tools	Focus	Audience
CRiSTAL (Community-based Risk Screening Tool – Adaptation and Livelihoods) (IISD)	This tool helps users to identify and prioritise climate risks that projects at the local or community level might address.	✓ Primarily local or community-level project planners and manager
Handbook for Community-Led Assessment of Climate-Induced Loss and Damage (ActionAid)	The participatory tools in this handbook aim to support communities to assess and record the economic and non-economic losses and damages they have experienced from climate change.	✓ Local communities ✓ Development co-operation
Participatory Climate Information Services Systems Development Methodology (USAID)	This guide takes practitioners through a five-stage methodology to assess the factors that affect the functioning and efficiency of climate information services programmes, such as social and cultural norms, institutional arrangements and information flows.	✓ Practitioners involved in designing, planning, and implementing activities to improve the quality and inclusive delivery of climate information services

4.2. Awareness and capacity across levels of government

4.2.1. Checklist for action

ACTIONS		ACTOR(S)1
Strengthen individual and organisational capacity to understand and address climate risks		
✓	Strengthen the capacity of universities and other centres of excellence to serve as domestic hubs for climate resilience expertise and to engage effectively in partnerships with established international centres of excellence.	Governments, w/ support from dev-co[2]
✓	Enhance awareness of the climate risks by making scientific understanding of the risks more accessible to the broader public.	Scientific community, international organisations and dev-co
✓	Strengthen the capacity of national and local media to raise awareness and facilitate dialogues on the nature of the climate risks and of approaches to reduce and manage the risks, including residual risks.	International community in close collaboration with local stakeholders
✓	Establish the authority and mandate of the ministry, agency or unit in charge of climate resilience to convene and co-ordinate different stakeholders and to subsequently see agreed priorities through to implementation.	National government unit in charge of climate resilience
✓	Enhance capacity for gender experts, women's organisations and representatives of marginalised groups to support their engagement in the development and implementation of gender-responsive, socially inclusive climate resilience measures.	Governments, w/ support from dev-co
Support piloting of climate resilience approaches with a focus on long-term sustainability		
✓	Continuously learn and respond to emerging risks through pilot initiatives, but complement these with clear exit, and replication strategies, or scale-up plans to be sustainable.	Governments w/ dev-co
✓	Align development co-operation with identified partner country priorities and when possible focus on strengthening country systems.	Dev-co
✓	Strengthen developing co-operation capacity to support partner countries effectively in their climate resilience efforts.	Dev-co

Note 1: Key actors (i.e. governments or development co-operation, or both) that play the primary role in promoting individual actions can greatly vary among countries and sectors. This column nevertheless indicates the likely leader in each of the actions. Some actions are led by governments but in many cases also supported by development co-operation (indicated as "Governments with support from dev-co").
Note 2: Dev-co: providers of development co-operation.
Note 3: Actions in this list are indicative and some may not be relevant to all countries or development co-operation providers.

4.2.2. Rationale

The NDCs submitted by many developing countries highlight potential barriers for the achievement of identified domestic climate targets. Among the capacity constraints identified, 113 NDCs highlight the need for capacity building support. Other types of support identified include mitigation finance (110 NDCs), technology transfer (109) and adaptation finance (79) (Pauw et al., 2020[44]). The identified capacity needs have been grouped into three categories (ECBI, 2018[45]):

- capacity to understand the climate science and the associated impacts to a country, region, sector, livelihoods, and human and societal well-being.
- capacity to formulate and implement domestic climate action.
- capacity to actively contribute to climate negotiations (to analyse, build consensus and articulate national interests) (this falls outside the scope of this guidance and is not covered).

In the Paris Agreement, capacity building in Article 11 is presented as a precondition for enhanced, sustained and co-ordinated climate action. The Article specifies that capacity building must be an iterative process guided by lessons learnt; foster country ownership; and be participatory, cross-cutting, gender-responsive and based on and responsive to country needs at national, sub-national and local levels (UNFCCC, 2015[46]). With the adoption of the Paris Agreement, the Paris Committee on Capacity-building was established to address current and emerging capacity gaps (individual, technical and institutional). It also addresses the associated capacity needs related to the mainstreaming of climate considerations into domestic planning and budgeting (see Box 4.8). Article 12 of the Agreement includes a complementary focus on the importance of enhanced climate change education, training and public awareness, participation and access to information.

Box 4.8. Paris Committee on Capacity-building

The Paris Committee on Capacity-building (PCCB) was established at COP21 to address current and future capacity gaps and needs, and to ensure coherence and co-ordination in capacity-building activities under the Convention. The PCCB fosters collaboration between actors (local, national, regional, global), strengthens networks and partnerships to enhance synergies and promotes knowledge- and experience-sharing. It is also mandated to oversee and co-ordinate the implementation of the Capacity-building Work Plan for 2016-2020, adopted at COP22 that considers nine elements:

- assessing how to increase synergies through co-operation and avoid duplication among existing bodies established under the Convention that implement capacity-building activities, including through collaborating with institutions under and outside the Convention
- identifying capacity gaps and needs and recommending ways to address them
- promoting the development and dissemination of tools and methodologies for the implementation of capacity-building
- fostering global, regional, national and sub-national co-operation
- identifying and collecting good practices, challenges, experiences and lessons learnt from work on capacity-building by bodies established under the Convention
- exploring how developing country Parties can take ownership of building and maintaining capacity over time and space
- identifying opportunities to strengthen capacity at the national, regional and sub-national level
- fostering dialogue, co-ordination, collaboration and coherence among relevant processes and initiatives under the Convention, including through exchanging information on capacity-building activities and strategies of bodies established under the Convention
- providing guidance to the secretariat on the maintenance and further development of the web-based capacity-building portal.

Source: (UNFCCC, n.d.[47]), Paris Committee for Capacity-building, https://unfccc.int/pccb.

Despite the established focus on capacity building in international climate processes, the continued demand for support by developing countries points to the inherent challenge of building sustained and long-term capacity. The urgent need for climate action has in many cases resulted in ad-hoc, short-term and project-based initiatives. These aim to strengthen the capacity of relevant stakeholders, e.g. in the form of workshops often with external expert input (Khan, Mfitumukiza and Huq, 2020[48]). Considerations for sustainable capacity building efforts include the following (Khan et al., 2018[49]; Shakya et al., 2018[50]):

- Understand the different levels at which capacity is needed to take the agenda forward – people, organisations, institutions and society, as well as their interactions (see Table 4.9) (while the importance of all three levels is recognised, discussion on the systematic level is covered in Chapter 3).
- Recognise that capacity needs and the associated support is a dynamic process, given the nature of the challenge and the evolving developments in knowledge and skills.

- Acknowledge that it is a long-term process that requires continuous investment of time and resources (see Table 4.10).
- Ensure that capacity building efforts are an endogenous process, based on ownership, where external support can play an important role in supporting rather than driving it.
- Strengthen institutional functions that identify and prioritise climate risks, and authorise, resource and deliver action on climate resilience.

Table 4.9. Levels of capacity

	Individual	Organisational	Systematic
Focus and objectives	The focus at this level is on individual competencies (understanding of the climate risks and ability to identify climate resilience priorities, develop and implement response measures). Education, training and other measures that can enhance the level of awareness of the risks and response measures can contribute to soft (e.g. building collaborative coalitions, trust and legitimacy) and hard (technical, logistical and managerial skills) competencies.	Organisational capacity refers to organisational structures, functions and systems that enable the capacities of individuals to come together to fulfil the mandate of the organisation effectively and to achieve set climate resilience objectives. This includes both formal organisations such as departments or agencies, private-sector entities, non-governmental organisations and civil society organisations.	Capacity building at systems level refers to the policy, legal, regulatory, economic and social support systems in which individuals and organisations operate. The enabling environment will be determined by international agreements (e.g. the SDGs and the Paris Agreement), national policies, rule of law, accountability, transparency and information flows.
Cross-cutting approaches	• Raise awareness about the need for measures to strengthen climate resilience and the benefits of good practice. • Create platforms for debate and policy dialogue between key stakeholders. • Improve co-ordination procedures on the importance of climate consideration in government policies, among others. • Support pilot projects that test proposed capacity building initiatives. • Award schemes that identify and appreciate good practice.		

Source: Adapted from (OECD, 2012[51]), Greening Development: Enhancing Capacity for Environmental Management and Governance, https://doi.org/10.1787/9789264167896-en.

Table 4.10. Types of capacity

Hard	Semi-hard	Soft
Tangible resources such as infrastructure, finance, buildings, lab facilities, computers, equipment	Technical and functional capacities, such as: • *Individual competencies*: e.g. technical skills and knowledge • *Organisational capacities*: e.g. organisational structures, management systems and procedures, planning, finance, human resources, monitoring, evaluation and learning • *Enabling conditions*: e.g. laws, policies, systems and strategies	Social, relational, intangible and invisible capacities: • *Operational capacities*: e.g. organisational culture and values, leadership, political relationships, implicit knowledge and experience, relational skills (negotiation, teamwork, facilitation) • *Adaptive capacities*: e.g. ability and willingness to self-reflect and learn from experience, analyse and adapt, change readiness and change management, confidence, empowerment

Source: Adapted from (Khan et al., 2018[49]), The Paris Framework for Climate Change Capacity Building, Routledge Advances in Climate Change Research.

Regional or international capacity and co-operation must complement the focus on national institutions (ECBI, 2018[45]). It may not be possible to develop climate modelling capacity in every country. In these cases, developing regional or international models that generate information that can be downscaled to different contexts may be a better approach (ECBI, 2018[45]). A focus on climate resilience further demands a good understanding of local circumstances (climate hazards, exposures and vulnerabilities) and the associated capacities required to respond effectively to the climate risks.

Taking a gender-responsive approach to strengthening climate resilience requires additional capacities within co-ordinating mechanisms (e.g. the National Adaptation Plan process) and among relevant stakeholders. As one important consideration, a gender-responsive approach will require close collaboration between actors with expertise in gender issues and social exclusion. However, they may only have limited knowledge on climate resilience. Similarly, climate experts may have limited understanding of gender and related issues. It is therefore important to consider from the outset their respective capacity needs. This will help ensure a more inclusive process in both the development and implementation of relevant policies, plans and programmes (Dazé and Church, 2019[52]).

There is no one size fits all. Instead, the most appropriate approach will depend on the circumstances and the nature of the climate risks but equally the national and sub-national development objectives and priorities. A diverse set of domestic and international actors can contribute to the capacity building process. They can do this through knowledge and skills development and exchange, as well as through financial resources, recognising this process must continuously be renewed (Khan et al., 2018[49]). With this in mind, and noting that capacity building is a cross-cutting issue that directly or indirectly is highlighted in most of the mechanisms (Chapter 3) and enablers (Chapter 4) covered by this Guidance, the rest of this section focuses on two priorities for governments and development co-operation:

- Strengthen individual and organisational capacity to understand and address climate risks.
- Support piloting of climate resilience approaches with a focus on long-term sustainability.

4.2.3. Strengthen individual and organisational capacity to understand and address climate risks

Relevant stakeholders need the capacity to access and use the information available to fully understand the nature of the risks as it relates to their respective roles, funding or investment decisions and so on. This allows them to translate the growing awareness of a changing climate into measures that strengthen resilience. While scientific understanding at the global level has seen impressive progress as documented by the work of the IPCC, the analysis is often too technical for the broader public. Efforts to bridge this gap include the creation of partnerships between science and policy. UNFCCC climate negotiations, for example, facilitate collaboration between negotiators and IPCC authors (UNFCCC, n.d.[53]). IPCC authors are also encouraged to explore ways of communicating research findings effectively to the wider public (Corner, Shaw and Clarke, 2018[54]). Two examples of other initiatives that aim to enhance the accessibility of climate science, data and information include:

- The NASA Earth Exchange Global Daily Downscaled Projections (NEX-GDDP) provides an online tool for scientists and local decision makers to help examine the impacts of climate change at local to regional levels at the spatial scale of individual towns, cities and watersheds (NASA, n.d.[55]).
- The Consultative Group on International Agricultural Research (CGIAR), a global research partnership for better food security, works to bridge academic research in climate-smart agriculture. CGIAR's co-operation includes a farmer-led experimentation model that supports local solutions (Kristjanson and Jost, 2014[56]).

Universities or other centres of excellence also play an important role in raising awareness of climate risks. They do this through the generation of scientific information, as well as development of individual and organisational capacities through academic programmes (Khan, Mfitumukiza and Huq, 2020[48]). The capacity of universities, in developing countries, however, is often limited by human and financial resources. For example, they may be unable to fund research, buy technical equipment or gain access to global knowledge databases.

Climate resilience initiatives rely on a good understanding of local climate risks. Such risks include the hazards, exposures and vulnerabilities of people and assets in a given area. This makes universities a potentially strong partner for development co-operation, especially if they have a long-term commitment to strengthen capacity (see Box 4.9). Examples of partnership include engagements with established centres of excellence through international research collaborations; student and teacher exchanges; and access to peer-reviewed knowledge (Khan et al., 2018[49]). In addition, trainings or seminars on climate resilience could be made available to other educational institutions. These could target both students and interested alumni and professionals. Other stakeholders such as NGOs, CSOs and in some cases the private sector can play similar or complementary roles.

Box 4.9. The role of universities in strengthening climate resilience capacity: Examples from Guatemala or the Philippines

In the Philippines, academia and research institutes contribute significantly to the climate resilience capacity of local government units (LGUs), communities and businesses. For instance, the Resilience Institute of the University of Philippines (UP), established in 2016, conducts research on climate change and disaster risk reduction. This includes research and extension services provided through the UP Nationwide Operational Assessment of Hazards Center in support of climate adaptation and mitigation as well as disaster risk reduction efforts. The Resilience Institute also trains LGUs on the development of Local Climate Change Action Plans and Comprehensive Land Use Plans, both of which LGUs are legally required to develop. The UP's Institute of Small-Scale Industries, which combines academic expertise in small business development and disaster risk reduction, collaborates with the Philippine Disaster Resilience Foundation. Together, they organise lectures and workshops on business continuity management for micro-, small- and medium-sized enterprises in case of disasters.

In Guatemala, the Universidad del Valle de Guatemala collaborates with large companies in the sugar, coffee and palm industries. Together, they support smaller businesses (e.g. their suppliers and business partners) in strengthening climate resilience throughout the value chain. The Guatemalan Sugar Association created the Institute for Climate Change, a research body that collaborates with the Universidad del Valle de Guatemala as well. The Institute provides businesses in the sugar industry, and beyond, with climate- and weather-related data and trainings to support decision-making processes. This partly complements the work of the country's National Institute for Seismology, Vulcanology, Meteorology and Hydrology.

Source: (Casado-Asensio, Shin and Kato, forthcoming[57]), Private-sector Engagement in Strengthening Climate Resilience, OECD Publishing.

Media communication (e.g. television, radio, newspapers and the Internet) also plays an important role in raising awareness of, and facilitating a dialogue on, the nature and impacts of climate change (Schäfer, 2015[58]). Lack of basic knowledge on climate change is at the same time one of the largest perceived barriers to climate action (Depoux et al., 2017[59]). This suggests that in addition to raising awareness, the media can play a role in presenting possible solutions – not an easy task given how climate risks and associated responses are context-specific.

The international climate community recognises this challenge. To that end, it holds workshops for journalists in the margins of the UNFCCC climate negotiations. It also develops handbooks to strengthen the capacity of journalists to become effective messengers of climate risks and solutions. UNESCO, for example, has developed tools for journalists based in Africa (UNESCO, 2013[60]), and in Asia and the Pacific (UNESCO, 2018[61]). Media communication must be inclusive in the presentation of the risks and possible approaches. It should include different dissemination channels to ensure that alerts and risk information reach all segments of society.

At the organisational level, governments need the capacity to understand the risks. In addition, a ministry or agency in charge of climate change needs the authority and mandate to convene different stakeholders to inform climate resilience planning and budgeting. Subsequently, these stakeholders should see agreed priorities through to implementation. This mandate will also be determined in part by the nature of the climate risks in a given country, and by the priority assigned to climate action at the highest political level (OECD, 2020[11]).

Key ministries such as the Prime Minister's Office, the Ministry of Finance and other central ministries and agencies play a key role to match allocation of roles and responsibilities with commensurate resources. For their part, local governments implement most of the policies. Independent statutory bodies, such as the Climate Change Committee in the United Kingdom, also play an important role in supporting and holding governments to account for their action on climate change. Strong political leadership can be instrumental in convening stakeholders. However, meaningful engagement resulting in ownership of agreed objectives and commitment to deliver them is not automatic. Focus must therefore be on jointly developing capacities to co-ordinate, prioritise and implement climate resilience objectives (El-Taliawi and Van Der Wal, 2019[62]).

Box 4.10. Role of national co-ordination on climate resilience: Example from Ghana

The National Development Planning Commission in Ghana plays a central co-ordinating role in the formulation of the country's long-term development strategy. The Commission also provides local authorities with guidance and technical support to ensure that local development plans are aligned with national priorities. With Ghana's adoption of the Paris Agreement, this includes guidance on the integration of the objectives of Ghana's Nationally Determined Contribution (NDC) into sectoral and local development plans by sub-national assemblies. The guidance is complemented by a checklist to support local assemblies in integrating Ghana's NDC objectives into their development plans. The checklist specifies that climate actions must be addressed in an integrated manner through the local assemblies' policy planning and implementation. On adaptation, it identifies priority actions across six sectors with the overarching objective to "increase climate resilience and decrease vulnerability for enhanced sustainable development".

Source: (OECD, 2020[11]), Common Ground Between the Paris Agreement and the Sendai Framework: Climate Change Adaptation and Disaster Risk Reduction, https://dx.doi.org/10.1787/3edc8d09-en.

Local governments have a critical responsibility in putting in place enabling environments for climate resilience planning and implementation. This is especially the case in countries with decentralised governance structures (see Box 4.10). In some countries, other stakeholders such as CSOs and the private sector also play an important role in strengthening climate resilience. Shared platforms that facilitate collaboration across levels of government, academia and the private sector can help identify and understand capacity-building gaps and needs.

Development co-operation plays an important role in facilitating access to available tools and guidance, and in sharing lessons learnt on different climate resilience approaches. Approaches are also being developed and jointly piloted to exchange lessons learnt, demonstrating the value of strong co-operation across stakeholder groups. The One UN Climate Change Learning is an online platform that supports countries in achieving climate action by providing learning resources offered by the UN system (UN CC:e-Learn, n.d.[63]). Examples include short tutorials on climate information and services and their application in decision-making processes, and the role of adaptation appraisal and prioritisation and tools available.

Table 4.11 summarises different guidance and tools that can guide national and international approaches to strengthen individual and organisational capacity to understand and address climate risks.

Box 4.11. Further areas of capacity development

Additional areas of capacity development for climate resilience highlighted in other sections of this guidance are briefly summarised below with further discussion provided in the respective sections:

- Organise trainings for both gender and climate focal points in government ministries and agencies, focusing on the assessment of climate risks and vulnerabilities, and the capacities needed to ensure that assessments consider exposures or vulnerabilities that may be differentiated by gender (see section 3.1 on governance).
- Training and awareness can help commercial banks and other financial institutions adjust their practices by creating financial products specifically targeting the needs of sectors vulnerable to climate risks. Examples include loans for climate-smart agriculture and the development and dissemination of insurance products (see section 3.3 on finance).
- Capacity building is also needed to develop the ability of relevant government bodies. They must be able to assess the ability of the country's technology to address climate risks and to identify appropriate technologies and help create or expand markets for such technologies (see section 4.3 on technology).

Table 4.11. Strengthen individual and organisational capacity to understand and address climate risks: Guidance and tools

Guidance and tools	Focus	Audience
Communicating Climate Change: A Practitioner's Guide – Insights from Africa, Asia and Latin America (UNFCC)	This guide shares tips for communicating climate change effectively. It is intended for communications practitioners and other champions of climate action working in developing countries.	✓ Government, business, civil society or academia
Climate.gov – Science & Information for a Climate-smart Nation (NOAA)	A platform that promotes public understanding of climate science and climate-related events through videos, stories, images and data visualisations.	✓ Different stakeholders contributing to climate resilience policy and action
One UN Climate Change Learning Partnership (UN CC:Learn) (UN)	The online platform that brings together climate change learning resources and services offered by the UN system with a focus on general climate literacy and applied skills development.	✓ Officials responsible for climate resilience planning ✓ Development co-operation
Greening Development: Enhancing Capacity for Environmental Management and Governance (OECD)	This guidance outlines steps to be considered when building capacity for greening national development planning, national budgetary processes and key economic sector strategies. The guidance is intended to support developing countries in their efforts to move to a greener development path, and to assist development co-operation and environment agencies in their efforts to support that process.	✓ Development co-operation ✓ Environment agencies

4.2.4. Support piloting of climate resilience approaches with a focus on long-term sustainability

For developing countries with limited human and technical capacity, development co-operation can play a valuable role in supporting efforts to build technical capacity, facilitate learning and exchange across different communities of expertise, and support developing country representatives in the international climate process (OECD, 2020[11]; OECD, 2012[51]). As one component of this process, development co-operation can support piloting of new climate resilience initiatives. Experience from Ghana, Peru and the Philippines highlights the role of development co-operation in supporting partner countries. For example, it piloted risk financing instruments such as the Philippine City Disaster Insurance Pool and created contingent credit lines in Peru (OECD, 2020[11]). Such pilots provide valuable opportunities for relevant stakeholders to build capacity and identify examples of good practice. However, experience shows they must include clear exit, replication or scale-up plans to be sustainable. Further, it is important to align development co-operation with identified partner country priorities and to focus on strengthening country systems when possible. Recommendations include the following (OECD, 2012[51]):

- Align capacity building measures with the climate resilience priorities of the partner country to ensure country ownership, oversight and management of the support.
- Collaborate across domestic agencies to exploit their comparative advantages.
- Strive to harmonise approaches among development support providers to ensure effective programme delivery, facilitate exchange of information and avoid duplicated efforts.
- Build in clear exit strategies so those doing the capacity building are no longer needed by the time they leave.

Emerging climate resilience initiatives piloted by development co-operation are diverse and relevant to every aspect of climate resilience. Illustrative examples include the following:

- ***Nature-based solution (NbS)***: NbS focus on protecting, sustainably managing and restoring natural capital to maintain or enhance ecosystem services to address a variety of social, environmental and economic challenges (OECD, 2020[64]). With evidence emerging of the value and multiple benefits of such approaches, different countries are piloting the role of NbS for climate action (University of Oxford, n.d.[65]; UNEP, 2019[66]).
- ***Forecast-based financing***: An initiative that complements early warning with early action by enabling access to humanitarian funding based on in-depth forecast information and risk analysis. By using innovative technologies, data and weather forecasts in a global network, the goal is to anticipate disasters, limit their impact and reduce human suffering and losses. The approach has been pioneered by the International Federation of the Red Cross and Red Crecent Societies, the World Food Programme, the Food and Agricultural Organization of the United Nations, START Network and others with funding from different bilateral providers of development co-operation (see also Box 3.17).

Development co-operation also supports investment in local capacities. The French Development Agency and the Asian Development Bank, for instance, have supported the decentralisation reform policy in the Philippines. This aims to empower local government units and help them improve institutional and technical capacity to reduce the level of disaster risk (AFD, n.d.[67]). The World Bank and the Green Climate Fund have supported the Greater Accra Climate Resilient and Integrated Development project. Complementing a focus on infrastructure investments, the project aims to strengthen the capacity of the city of Accra to plan, co-ordinate, monitor and evaluate climate-smart urban development planning; facilitate access to climate risk information; and improve co-ordination between different stakeholders (World Bank, 2018[68]).

Development co-operation providers themselves also need capacity to enhance their ability to support partner countries effectively. Like partner countries, they are faced with the challenge of having to address multiple priorities simultaneously, including environment, gender and health. Their mandates will often be influenced by political priorities domestically, but also by technological possibilities, both of which evolve over time (OECD, 2019[69]). To integrate these different priorities effectively, the mainstreaming strategies of development co-operation providers need to account for their own capacity building needs and the importance of continuous staff development (see Box 4.12 for the approach by the Swedish International Development Cooperation Agency).

Box 4.12. Good practice in continual staff training

The Swedish International Development Cooperation Agency (Sida) makes significant efforts to train all staff in handling environment and climate issues. This includes training sessions at the embassies in partner countries and in the operational departments at headquarters, mostly with support and participation from Sida's Environment and Climate Helpdesk. The scope of the training has evolved from being focused on the "What and why" of integration to "How?" The training is said to have shaped a common understanding among staff in Sida departments, units and embassies of the diverse and context-specific challenges in relation to environment, including climate change. Further, the training is considered most effective when it focuses on specific themes, including links with other cross-cutting issues and notably gender, and when it includes partners.

Source: (OECD, 2019[69]), Greening Development Co-operation: Lessons from the OECD Development Assistance Committee, https://doi.org/10.1787/62cc4634-en.

Table 4.12. Support piloting of climate resilience approaches with a focus on long-term sustainability: Guidance and tools

Guidance and tools	Focus	Audience
Greening Development: Enhancing Capacity for Environmental Management and Governance (OECD)	This guidance outlines steps to be considered when building capacity for greening national development planning, national budgetary processes and key economic sector strategies.	✓ Development co-operation ✓ Environment agencies
Greening Development Co-operation: Lessons from the OECD Development Co-operation Assistance (OECD)	This report examines critical areas for mainstreaming the environment, lessons that can also inform climate change mainstreaming.	✓ Development co-operation

4.3. Technologies

4.3.1. Checklist for action

ACTIONS	ACTOR(S)[1]
Understand technology needs and contexts of potential users	
✓ Assess technology needs through consultation with target sectors and a broad range of stakeholders (e.g. government entities, technology-related firms, academia, development agencies and civil society organisations [CSOs] working on climate change and broader socio-economic development).	Governments with support from dev-co2
✓ Ensure that assessment of technologies considers not only their costs and performance, but also local climatic, environmental and socio-economic contexts of their potential users, including gender-disaggregated needs for technologies.	Governments and dev-co
✓ Ensure technologies "Do No Significant Harm" to other objectives on environmental sustainability.	Governments and dev-co
Invest in institutional arrangements and networks to facilitate development and dissemination of technologies	
✓ Establish or strengthen an inclusive approach to facilitate development, adoption and dissemination of technologies for climate resilience, which also connects (e.g.) government entities, technology suppliers and maintenance firms, academia, development agencies and CSOs working on climate change and broader socio-economic development.	Governments with support from dev-co
✓ Empower private-sector actors and national and local research institutions as part of the inclusive network to facilitate country- or locally-led development and dissemination of technologies for climate resilience.	Governments with support from dev-co
✓ Harness knowledge and understanding of Indigenous peoples and women of local context to maximise the effectiveness of adopted technologies for climate resilience.	Governments and dev-co
✓ Collaborate with public and private financial institutions to explore options for affordable financial solutions to support development and piloting of innovative technologies in support of climate resilience.	Governments and dev-co
Strengthen supply- and demand-side policies to promote technology development and dissemination	
✓ Develop and implement enabling policies that encourage or incentivise public- and private-sector actors to increase their efforts for development and commercialisation of technologies.	Governments with support from dev-co
✓ Secure sufficient funding to policy and fiscal support for research, development and demonstration of technologies for climate resilience, and shield the funding from fluctuations.	Governments and dev-co
✓ Facilitate market creation and expansion for the technologies so that the private sector recognises the business potential of such markets.	Governments with support from dev-co
✓ Remove disincentives for the uptake of the technologies (e.g. addressing insufficient enforcement of building codes and land-use regulations, rationalising agriculture subsidies, etc.).	Governments with support from dev-co

Note 1: Key actors (i.e. governments or development co-operation, or both) that play the primary role in promoting individual actions can greatly vary among countries and sectors. This column nevertheless indicates the likely leader in each of the actions. Some actions are led by governments but in many cases also supported by development co-operation (indicated as "Governments with support from dev-co").
Note 2: Dev-co: providers of development co-operation.
Note 3: Actions in this list are indicative and some may not be relevant to all countries or development co-operation providers.

4.3.2. Rationale

Technologies are a crucial enabler for strengthening the resilience of human or natural systems to climate change. Achieving the goals of the Paris Agreement requires accelerated and strengthened development and dissemination of technologies in support of climate mitigation and adaptation. They must be cost-efficient and consider potential environmental and social implications (TEC, 2017[70]; UNFCCC, 2015[46]). Such technologies should also be selected and deployed in accordance with countries' needs, priorities and capacities (Haselip, Narkeviciute and Rogat Castillo, 2015[71]).

Technologies that support climate resilience can take different forms. They range from hardware (equipment and products, such as irrigation systems, early warning systems and sea walls) to software (processes, knowledge and skills required to use the hardware) (UNFCCC, 2006[72]; UNFCCC, 2014[73]). Many activities also combine hardware and software: for instance, an early warning system combines measuring devices with knowledge and skills that enable action in response to hazards. Understanding the difference between these technology types can be useful for exploring their synergies and complementarities, which can guide efforts by governments and development co-operation providers to identify the most effective combination of technologies for a given issue (Ajayi, Fatunbi and Akinbamijo, 2018[74]).

While this section primarily focuses on these hard and soft technologies, some literature suggests that technologies go beyond them, and include organisational technologies or "orgware". These would encompass, for example, ownership and institutional arrangements for adoption and diffusion of hardware and software (Ajayi, Fatunbi and Akinbamijo, 2018[74]; Nygaard and Hansen, 2015[75]; Christiansen, Olhoff and Trærup, 2011[76]). Box 4.13 uses early warning systems (see section 4.1 for further discussion) to illustrate the difference between the three types of technology.

Box 4.13. Different technology types for climate resilience: An example of early warning systems

Early warning systems include the three technology components (hardware, software and orgware). The hardware component includes the sensor equipment, telecommunication systems, computer programmes and calculation models needed to collect, transmit, filter and analyse the data. The software component includes the knowledge and expertise to handle these datasets and control systems, as well as the combination of analytical processes. The orgware component comprises the institutional arrangement and decision support systems, enabling effective collaboration between different actors and organisations to respond to emerging threats.

Source: (Nygaard and Hansen, 2015[75]), Overcoming Barriers to the Transfer and Diffusion of Climate Technologies, Second Edition, https://tech-action.unepdtu.org/publications/overcoming-barriers-to-the-transfer-and-diffusion-of-climate-technologies-second-edition.

Approaches to strengthen climate resilience may employ various hard and soft technologies. These address current and future vulnerabilities to climate hazards that may be compounded by other environmental and socio-economic variables (ADB, 2014[77]). Exploring, assessing and selecting technologies that meet the need for managing a particular climate risk is a challenge in itself. A UNFCCC survey has revealed that assessing technology needs, identifying appropriate technologies for those needs and adjusting them to local conditions are among the highest priorities for countries' capacity development in addressing climate risks (TEC, 2018[78]).

While this section does not explain individual technologies, Table 4.13 provides a non-exhaustive list to illustrate technologies that have been applied to sectors vulnerable to the impacts of climate change.

Table 4.13. Examples of technologies for climate resilience by sector

Sector	Examples of technologies for climate resilience
Agriculture	Systematic observation and forecasting, early warning systems, drought-resistant crops, crop management processes, land management systems, equipment for improved water use (including rainwater harvesting), leakage reduction, hydroponic farming, building shelter-belts and wind-breaks to improve the resilience of rangelands, spatially separated plots for cropping and grazing, salt-resistant crops
Water resources and hydrology	Water transfer, water recycling and conservation, water harvesting, increased reservoir capacity, desalination, erection of protection dams against avalanches and increased debris flows from permafrost thawing, use of Global Positioning Systems technology
Coastal zones	Sea walls, tidal barriers, detached breakwaters, revetment, wetland restoration or creation, beach nourishment, artificial reef, Indigenous options (such as walls of wood, stone or coconut leaf), mangrove afforestation, improved drainage systems, desalination systems
Health	Vector control, vaccination, impregnated bed nets, greater care with water storage, using appropriate clothing, using storm shelters, health education, distribution of bottled water, operation of an information line to answer heat-related questions, training for medical staff, disease monitoring and prevention and treatment, health alert information

Infrastructure	Passive cooling (for more efficient indoor temperature control), storm-resistant housing, flood-secure housing, physical barriers to protect from flooding, minimal paved surfaces and planting of trees to moderate urban heat island effects
Transportation	Warm-mix asphalt, engineered cementitious composite, active motion damping systems, intelligent transportation systems
Disaster risk reduction and management	Artificial lowering of glacial lakes, remote sensing technologies (e.g. Light Detection and Ranging), monitoring systems, early warning systems, emergency shelters, social media in disaster response

Source: Authors' elaboration based on (ADB, 2014[77]), Technologies to Support Climate Change Adaptation in Developing Asia, https://www.adb.org/publications/technologies-support-climate-change-adaptation-developing-asia, (Nygaard and Hansen, 2015[75]), Overcoming Barriers to the Transfer and Diffusion of Climate Technologies, Second Edition, https://tech-action.unepdtu.org/publications/overcoming-barriers-to-the-transfer-and-diffusion-of-climate-technologies-second-edition/, (TEC, 2020[79]), Policy Brief: Technologies for Averting, Minimizing and Addressing Loss and Damage in Coastal Zones, https://unfccc.int/ttclear/misc_/StaticFiles/gnwoerk_static/2020_coastalzones/cfecc85aaa8d43d38cd0f6ceae2b61e4/2bb696550804403fa08df8a924922c2e.pdf.

This section uses the term "technology development and dissemination" to represent the different steps to develop and disseminate technology to strengthen climate resilience. The steps include research and development (R&D), pilot and demonstration, transfer (within or across countries), adoption and diffusion (Figure 4.4). International technology transfer is also an important means to address gaps in the availability of technologies supporting climate resilience (Dechezlepretre et al., 2020[80]). This is relevant especially to developing countries where domestic R&D capacity remains weak (Article 10, (UNFCCC, 2015[46]; Dechezlepretre et al., 2020[80]). In some cases, however, technologies that could support climate resilience are difficult to import. This could be due to several issues, including a lack of domestic capacity or market, or insufficient climate or trade policies to encourage import of such technologies (Hallegatte, Rentschler and Rozenberg, 2020[32]).

Countries need policy frameworks and governance that support development and dissemination of relevant technologies, between countries and within a country (Olawuyi, 2018[81]). Such arrangements may include support for clean technology entrepreneurship, mechanisms that facilitate stakeholders' access to information about technologies for climate resilience, legal protection for innovation, trainings to strengthen domestic capacities to deploy and maintain the technologies, and more effective planning and implementation of climate and environmental regulations (Olawuyi, 2018[81]).

While innovations and cross-border transfer of newly invented modern technologies are important, technologies for climate resilience often already exist in many developing countries (Biagini et al., 2014[82]). Examples in the context of agriculture include small-scale irrigation, crop management practices, use of the more climate-resilient crops, improved crop rotation and intercropping (Nygaard and Hansen, 2015[75]; Adebayo et al., 2011[83]; Parajuli, 2017[84]).

Figure 4.4. A stylised process of technology development and dissemination

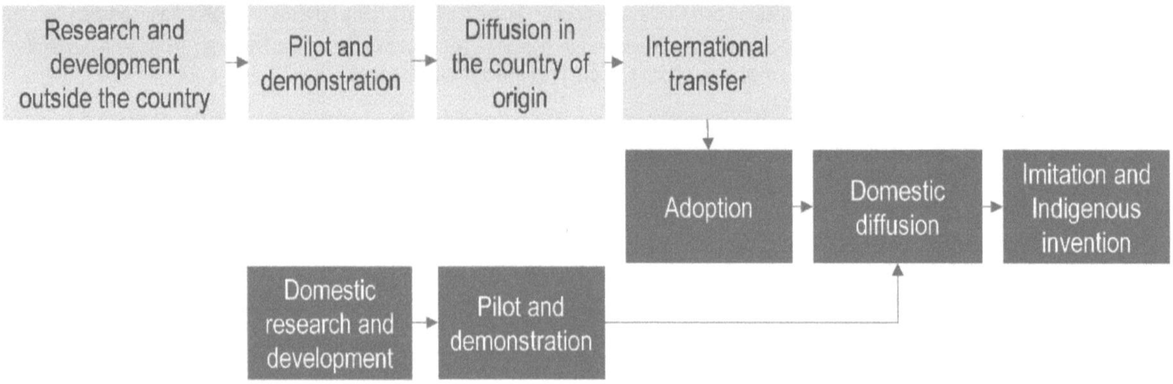

Source: Authors' elaboration based on (Pagato et al., 2020[85]), Technology Transfer and Innovation for Low-Carbon Development, http://documents.worldbank.org/curated/en/138681585111567659/Technology-Transfer-and-Innovation-for-Low-Carbon-Development.

Effective technology development and dissemination requires several key components. The characteristics of the technologies must match the needs of users and their socio-economic and environmental contexts (Biagini et al., 2014[82]; ADB, 2014[77]). There has been a long history of failed attempts of technology dissemination, due partly to a lack of understanding of user needs and circumstances (Ockwell and Byrne, 2016[86]; Forsyth, 2005[87]). In some cases, intended users had not fully understood the benefits of new technologies. In others, technologies had proven inappropriate for specific socio-economic contexts and consequently been abandoned. In still others, project proponents failed to assess the availabilities of local resources needed for operating the technology (Ockwell and Byrne, 2016[86]; Forsyth, 2005[87]) (see also Box 4.14).

The capabilities of domestic institutions and their networks also determine the ability of a country to develop, demonstrate, absorb, deploy and maintain technologies (TEC, 2018[78]). Enhanced domestic capacities can also promote demand-driven approaches to development and dissemination of technologies in support of climate resilience, while facilitating learning across different contexts and countries (Olawuyi, 2018[81]; Ockwell and Byrne, 2016[86]). The broader policy environment also affects the ease of developing and disseminating new or improved technologies that support climate resilience (Biagini et al., 2014[82]; Olawuyi, 2018[81]). Against these contexts, this section focuses on the following issues:

- Understand technology needs and contexts.
- Invest in institutional arrangements and networks to facilitate development and dissemination of technologies.
- Strengthen supply- and demand-side policies to promote technology development and dissemination.

Box 4.14. Economic and non-economic barriers to dissemination of technologies

Various factors may affect dissemination of a technology to different contexts, including socio-economic contexts of the targeted country or users. Even when a technology in support of climate resilience has been developed, tested and proven effective in a given context, it may still face barriers for dissemination to other contexts. These barriers may be economic, financial (e.g. low financial viability, high cost of capital) or market-related (e.g. poor market infrastructure, market control by incumbents) (Boldt et al., 2012[88]). These challenges can be linked to policy, legal and regulatory issues (e.g. insufficient legal frameworks and policy incentives), organisational capacities (e.g. lack of professional institutions or service providers, limited institutional capacity of users) and human skills (e.g. inadequate training, lack of skilled personnel) (Boldt et al., 2012[88]).

Analysis from Armenia shows some barriers to the dissemination of land amelioration technologies and low-volume drip irrigation for newly planted orchards. Such barriers included limited technical capacities in melioration of rocky soils within the country, insufficient information on economic potential of unused lands, weak legislative incentives, and limited scientific and consulting activities on these technologies in the country (Government of the Republic of Armenia, 2017[89]). These challenges are not necessarily linked with the maturity of such land amelioration and drip irrigation technologies.

In The Gambia, barriers to the uptake of certain climate-resilient aquaculture technologies include inadequate number of trained experts, lack of efficient fish seed production methods, lack of experience in using efficient feed production technologies and a low level of awareness among the public about benefits of the aquaculture industry (Badji et al., 2016[90]).

4.3.3. Understand technology needs and contexts of potential users

Approaches to climate resilience are highly context-specific. This is also reflected in the demand for technology in support of these approaches. A technology that works well in one country may not be appropriate or cost-efficient in another due to different economic and non-economic barriers as highlighted in Box 4.14 (TEC, 2014[91]; Haselip, Narkeviciute and Rogat Castillo, 2015[71]). Determining the technological options available for climate resilience first requires clear understanding of the needs of target sectors and stakeholders for specific actions to which technologies can be applied. Climate risk assessments will point to the most vulnerable sectors and populations. Complementary action plans can include a review of suitable technologies available to manage the risks.

Needs for and access to technologies that support climate resilience can also differ between women and men. For instance, in some low- and middle-income countries, women are 10% less likely than men to own a mobile phone and 23% less likely to use the mobile Internet, due to, for instance, affordability, literacy and digital skills (Rowntree, 2019[92]). Both women and men need to benefit from available technologies in support of climate resilience. A systematic gender analysis (see Chapter 3.1) can help governments and development co-operation better understand gender-differentiated needs for technologies and opportunities to access them (De Groot, 2018[93]).

Technology needs of vulnerable sectors or populations should be assessed in consultation with different stakeholders to understand the local climatic, environmental and socio-economic contexts that may affect the uptake of certain technologies (Boldt et al., 2012[88]) (see also Box 4.15). Technology Needs Assessment (TNA), established in the context of the UNFCCC, provides a framework to guide a country-driven, participatory process to identify, select and implement climate mitigation and adaptation technologies. TNAs also focus on barriers to technology adoption and diffusion, and solutions to overcome them (Nygaard and Hansen, 2015[75]). The overall goal is identifying technology options to support low-carbon and climate-resilient pathways. In this context, Table 4.14 proposes several steps for a TNA. As of

June 2020, UNEP DTU Partnership had published about 120 TNA reports on its website (UNEP DTU Partnership, n.d.[94]).

Table 4.14. Key steps of a Technology Needs Assessment

Key step	Example of action
1. Organise the assessment	• Decide the structure of the team to conduct the Technology Needs Assessment (TNA). • Organise stakeholder involvement. • Develop a work plan.
2. Understand development priorities	• Understand the country's development priorities and related targets. • Discuss implications of climate change for the priorities. • Cluster development priorities.
3. Prioritise sectors	• Assess sectors based on priorities for climate action, based on their vulnerabilities and development objectives. • Shortlist prioritised sectors.
4. Assess and prioritise technologies	• Identify a long list of technologies. • Assess the technologies by multi-criteria analysis. • Identify priority technologies needed by the priority sector(s).
5. Construct a national strategy and action plan	• Clarify objectives and establish key milestones. • Identify measures to develop capacities and enabling policies. • Compile a national strategy and action plan for technology development and dissemination.

Source: Adapted from (UNDP, 2010[95]), Handbook for Conducting Technology Needs Assessment for Climate Change, https://www.undp.org/content/undp/en/home/librarypage/environment-energy/low_emission_climateresilientdevelopment/technology_needsassessmenthandbook.html.

Box 4.15. Ensuring that technologies match local needs: An example from Ethiopia

Ensuring that technologies are appropriate for local needs and context is critical to the success of technology development and dissemination. There have been practices whereby climate-related projects have taken a range of approaches to ensure appropriateness in their technology selection process. For instance, in a project in Ethiopia supported by the Global Environment Facility, the project team presented committees of local leaders with possible technologies to identify those that would meet the needs of the villages. The local leaders participated in the presentation in part to ensure that technologies were clearly aligned with the needs of farmers in the region (Biagini et al., 2014[82]).

There can be multiple criteria against which technologies in support of climate resilience can be assessed. While not exhaustive, Table 4.15 different criteria for assessing the effectiveness of a technology in addressing climate vulnerabilities of different sectors or populations. ADB (2014[77]), for instance, scores different technologies based on some of these criteria. A technology is scored "most desirable" if it is deemed highly effective to reduce vulnerabilities within a given cost, among other positive factors. It is scored "intermediate" for moderate ratings on those criteria. Finally, it is scored "less desirable" if it has a low cost-effectiveness performance or few co-benefits, or if its ratings based on the other criteria are relatively low.

Another key consideration in assessing technologies for climate resilience is to ensure the chosen technologies "do no significant harm" (DNSH) to other environmental objectives. These objectives include climate change mitigation, protection of healthy ecosystems, sustainable use and protection of water and marine resources, transition to a circular economy, waste prevention and recycling, and pollution prevention and control. The Technical Annex to the EU Technical Expert Group's final report on the EU Taxonomy provides useful descriptions of the DNSH criteria for various measures for climate change adaptation (and mitigation). These aim to specify the minimum DNSH requirements to be met (EU TEG, 2020[96]).

Table 4.15. Examples of criteria for assessment of technology needs

Criteria	Description and examples
Effectiveness (in building climate resilience)	Expected degree at which a technology in question reduces vulnerability or increases resilience based on agreed indicators *(e.g. percentage of households at reduced drought risk due to a water-efficient irrigation system)*
Co-benefits	Other benefits besides reducing vulnerability or increasing resilience to climate change *(e.g. increasing ecosystem services, reducing pollution, creating jobs, improving local health care systems)*
Economic benefits	Expected benefit from investment in the technology *(e.g. avoided economic losses, increased revenues)*
Costs	Initial and operational costs as well as "indirect" costs *(e.g. the negative consequences of using the technology, such as ecosystem destruction, job loss)*
Geophysical factors	Suitable geophysical characteristics of locations to which the technology may be applied
Social, cultural and behavioural factors	Consumer preferences and social norms, biases, traditions, preference for status quo *(e.g. continued use of existing crop types despite an alternative with greater adaptability to climate change)*
Barriers to implementation	Technical, political and cultural challenges to implementation of the technology *(e.g. a specialised set of skills needed, insufficient market maturity or infrastructure to operationalise the technology in question)*
Scalability and replicability	Potential for the technology to be further scaled up or replicated within the country after its pilot phase
Financing opportunity	Attractiveness for public/private providers of finance, and possibility of co-financing or public-private partnerships *(e.g. technological maturity of technologies, which can reduce uncertainty for financial institutions)*
Market conditions	Existence of markets where the technology can be sold, local suppliers of auxiliary goods and services, level playing field with competing technologies, market control by industry incumbents
Legal and regulatory frameworks	Legal frameworks, vested interest in the sector in question, conflicts of interest, political instability, bureaucracy, rent-seeking behaviour, etc.
Do no significant harm requirements	Criteria to prevent the technology from causing significant harm to other environmental and social objectives *(e.g. sandbags put along banks to reduce coastal erosion may negatively affect nearby marine ecosystems or recreational values of beaches)*

Source: Authors' elaboration based on (ADB, 2014[77]), Technologies to Support Climate Change Adaptation in Developing Asia, https://www.adb.org/publications/technologies-support-climate-change-adaptation-developing-asia, (Ajayi, Fatunbi and Akinbamijo, 2018[74]), Strategies for Scaling Agricultural Technologies in Africa, https://research4agrinnovation.org/wp-content/uploads/2018/02/Scalingstrategies_Africa.pdf, (Nygaard and Hansen, 2015[75]), Overcoming Barriers to the Transfer and Diffusion of Climate Technologies, Second Edition, https://tech-action.unepdtu.org/publications/overcoming-barriers-to-the-transfer-and-diffusion-of-climate-technologies-second-edition/, (EU TEG, 2020[96]), Technical Annex to the TEG Final Report on the EU Taxonomy, https://ec.europa.eu/knowledge4policy/publication/sustainable-finance-teg-final-report-eu-taxonomy_en.

A range of knowledge products supports assessments of technology needs through stakeholder participation, economic and non-economic characteristics of technologies, selection of multiple criteria for such assessments and DNSH requirements (Table 4.16).

Table 4.16. Understand technology needs and contexts: Guidance and tools

Guidance and tools	Focus	Audience
Handbook for Conducting Technology Needs Assessment for Climate Change (UNDP)	This handbook aims to help countries make informed choices in their technology through Technology Needs Assessments (TNAs). It offers approaches to identify, evaluate and prioritise mitigation and adaptation technologies.	✓ Developing country government
TNA Step by Step: A Guidebook for Countries conducting a Technology Needs Assessment and Action Plan (UNEP DTU Partnership)	This guidebook outlines the different steps for preparing TNAs and Technology Action Plans (TAPs).	✓ Developing country government (TNA Team and consultants)
Guidance for a Gender-responsive Technology Needs Assessment (UNEP DTU Partnership)	The guidebook introduces the key aspects of gender-responsive TNAs for climate adaptation and mitigation. It also presents a practical approach to integrate these aspects across the different steps in a TNA process.	✓ Developing country governments and development co-operation
Technical Annex to the TEG Final Report on the EU Taxonomy (EU TEG)	This document outlines, among others, 68 activities on climate change adaptation and their technical descriptions, including criteria for "Do No Significant Harm" to other environmental objectives.	✓ While focusing on EU countries, the reference may inspire other countries as well
Climate Change Adaptation Technologies for Water (UNEP-DHI)	This document provides practitioners with a guide to adaptation technologies for increased resilience of the water sector.	✓ Developing country governments and development co-operation
Assessing and Selecting Adaptation Options (in Urban Adaptation Support Tool by Climate-ADAPT)	This online tool offers technical guidance and related material on selection of options, including an assessment framework for adaptation options and multi-criteria analysis.	✓ Developing country governments, especially at the sub-national level
Technologies to Support Climate Change Adaptation in Developing Asia (ADB)	This showcases a number of technologies that can be used to address the impact of climate change and provides an overview of various criteria against which technology needs can be assessed.	✓ Developing country governments and development co-operation
Guidance of Multi Criteria Analysis on Determining Technologies for Climate Change Adaptation (UNEP DTU Partnership)	This guidance provides support on how to facilitate discussions for prioritising adaptation technologies and for supporting stakeholders in identifying appropriate criteria for this analysis.	✓ Developing country governments and development co-operation

4.3.4. Invest in institutional arrangements and networks to facilitate development and dissemination of technologies

Effective development and dissemination of technologies for climate resilience also depends on capacities of key technology-related institutions within a country and networks among them (World Bank, 2010[97]; TEC, 2015[98]). A combination of individuals, institutions and their networks can support the process of developing and disseminating technologies for climate resilience. This could occur, for instance, through facilitating the exchange of knowledge and collaboration between firms, universities and research institutes (TEC, 2015[98]).

Identifying and partnering with appropriate suppliers of technologies and providers of complementary maintenance services may also determine the effectiveness and dissemination potentials of technologies (Biagini et al., 2014[82]). As one approach, governments can work with the private sector to establish an industrial cluster that comprises a group of companies, suppliers, service providers and associated research institutions (Nallari and Griffith, 2013[99]). A climate-resilient, circulatory water system for fisheries in Armenia provides an example of such an approach. The absence of suppliers to provide equipment, consulting and support to the fisheries was believed to have increased initial costs and perceived technological risks. The development of networks between suppliers of technologies, including importers and local producers, and providers of consulting and maintenance services, is important for the effective and reliable operation of such systems for Armenian fisher folks. (Government of the Republic of Armenia, 2017[89]).

Capabilities required for institutions that may develop or disseminate technologies for climate resilience within a country are diverse. They include those related to basic and applied research, development, demonstration, commercialisation and diffusion. Scientific research capacities are particularly important for the initial research phase. Meanwhile, the technology development and dissemination phases are more likely to require institutions to build engineering- and design-related capacities, as well as marketing skills. Commercialisation and large-scale diffusion require a greater degree of manufacturing capacities in refining the business models (TEC, 2015[98]; Sagar, 2010[100]).

Capacities of domestic institutions (e.g. research institutes, government agencies, companies) in understanding, selecting and adopting existing technologies, as well as developing new ones, are a crucial building block for effective technology developing and dissemination. The Technology Executive Committee of the UNFCCC stresses the importance of combining domestic research institutes, government agencies and companies, referring to the approach as a "national system of innovation". A UNFCCC study suggests the following general strategies for governments and development co-operation to enhance the capacities of domestic institutions, recognising they need to be tailored to individual countries (TEC, 2018[78]):

- **Provide tailored, multi-level training**: Climate-related technologies require many types of competencies, including that of risk assessors, technicians, legal advisers, funders and policy makers. Capacity building activities should target appropriate groups from the local to the national levels.
- **Enhance capacities of national co-ordination bodies**: Those bodies can play a major role in enhancing domestic capacities and local technologies. They may need support to develop their own capacity to assess technology needs, identify appropriate technologies and understand the demands and implications of processes such as TNAs and the preparation of TAPs, and other relevant policy documents.
- **Monitor progress using appropriate indicators**: Countries may monitor and evaluate their progress in the development and enhancement of endogenous capacities. For this, they need indicators to measure progress. These consider each country's needs and conditions, as well as the need for common indicators that may enhance transparency and comparability.
- **Share knowledge widely**: Regular communications among stakeholders about relevant issues and best practices on enhancement of domestic capacities can help those involved with planning and reporting of activities.

Inclusive networks of governments, firms, academia, research institutes, development agencies and providers of finance are also key. They can develop, adopt and disseminate climate-related technologies based on their expertise, knowledge, views and needs (TEC, 2017[70]). Such inclusive networks may also facilitate the incorporation of Indigenous knowledge into development and dissemination of technologies. Such technologies are likely to be better suited to local environmental contexts and traditional practices on climate risk management, as well as the socio-economic and cultural circumstances (TEC, 2017[70]). Inclusive networks can also contribute effectively to the continuous development of local institutions, technical staff and their expertise required to develop, adopt and use technologies (TEC, 2017[70]). Key considerations for building an inclusive network that can support countries in developing and disseminating technologies for climate resilience, include the following [see (TEC, 2018[78]; TEC, 2014[91]; Ajayi, Fatunbi and Akinbamijo, 2018[74]) for further information]:

- **Support and engage private-sector actors, as well as national and local research institutions** as part of the inclusive network to facilitate country- and locally-led development and piloting of new technologies for climate resilience.
- **Involve the users of the technology** (e.g. communities, local businesses and households) at an early stage of establishing an inclusive network and in maintaining it.
- **Support local governments** to promote and co-ordinate efforts to disseminate small-scale or community-led technologies, or contribute to strengthening the enabling environments for local adoption and dissemination of new or existing technologies.

- **Harness local and Indigenous people's knowledge and understanding** of the local context and needs.
- **Facilitate stakeholder discussions on the technical feasibility and cultural acceptability** of technological options to determine their scalability and replicability, and whether the technology may cause culturally sensitive issues (education, health, family planning).
- **Collaborate with public and private finance institutions** to explore options of de-risking or making financial solutions for the development and piloting of innovative technologies affordable.

Table 4.17. Invest in institutional arrangements and networks to facilitate development and dissemination of technologies: Guidance and tools

Guidance and tools	Focus	Audience
Strengthening National Systems of Innovation to Enhance Action on Climate Change (TEC)	One section of this document called Possible Actions provides a summary of proposed actions for the Technology Mechanism of the UNFCCC in promoting innovation for climate change. This list nevertheless could also be useful for development co-operation providers to identify their potential involvement.	✓ Development co-operation
Climate Innovation Centres: A New Way to Foster Climate Technologies in the Developing World? (infoDev/World Bank)	This document aims to provide policy recommendations on developing and deploying technologies to mitigate greenhouse gas emissions and adapt to climate change. It also provides key capacity requirements for institutions and examples of climate innovation centres from all over the world.	✓ Governments and development co-operation
Agricultural Innovation Systems: An Investment Sourcebook (WB)	While this sourcebook focuses on innovation in the agriculture sector, it provides a variety of insights relevant to other sectors. These include actions to help identify, design and implement the investments, approaches and interventions to promote innovations. It also includes a module on co-ordination and collective action for agricultural innovation.	✓ Governments and development co-operation

4.3.5. Strengthen supply- and demand-side policies to promote technology development and dissemination

Public policies strongly affect the rate and direction of the development and dissemination of technologies in developing countries. They also affect the capacities of technology-related institutions and networks as described in the previous sub-section (USAID, 2014[101]; Ajayi, Fatunbi and Akinbamijo, 2018[74]; de Coninck and Sagar, 2014[102]). A clear signal on climate-related policies can therefore create a demand for certain technologies in support of climate resilience. This, in turn, can incentivise private-sector actors to invest in the development and dissemination of such technologies (TEC, 2016[103]). Clear policy signals also increase the awareness and interest of potential users of those technologies. Such policies include international agreements, long-term development visions, various policies on science and technology, environmental laws and regulations, fiscal policies, administrative procedures, among others (Ajayi, Fatunbi and Akinbamijo, 2018[74]). They provide economic and regulatory incentives, determine allocation of public funding and form institutional arrangements for technology development and dissemination. Enabling policy frameworks target the supply-side (push) or demand-side (pull) aspect of development and dissemination of technologies (Nygaard and Hansen, 2015[75]). Table 4.18 summarises examples of such policy frameworks.

Table 4.18. Examples of enabling policies for development and dissemination of technologies for climate resilience

Supply-side policies	Demand-side policies
Grants, loans and equity finance for research, development and dissemination	Direct subsidies to decrease market prices of technologies
Subsidised professional and technological training and qualification	Public procurement of goods and services in support of climate resilience
Support for scientific forums and workshops	Technology and performance standards, including building codes
Support for entrepreneurship	Labelling programmes
Support and award for early-stage accelerators and incubators	Public information campaigns and awareness raising
Development of high-tech clusters	

Source: Authors based on (Pagato et al., 2020[85]), Technology Transfer and Innovation for Low-Carbon Development, http://documents.worldbank.org/curated/en/138681585111567659/Technology-Transfer-and-Innovation-for-Low-Carbon-Development, (TEC, 2017[70]),
https://unfccc.int/ttclear/misc_/StaticFiles/gnwoerk_static/brief10/8c3ce94c20144fd5a8b0c06fefff6633/57440a5fa1244fd8b8cd13eb4413b4f6.pdf.

On the supply side, governments play a key role in developing and implementing enabling policies that encourage or incentivise public and private actors to increase their efforts to develop new technologies and make them commercially viable (TEC, 2017[70]). Examples include government grants and concessional loans to support technology-related research and demonstration, as well as technical assistance to facilitate innovations. Such assistance might entail provision of technical trainings, support of research institutions and formation of high-tech clusters. Policies to improve the quality of higher education systems are also key given their role as centres of excellence at the heart of national processes for technology development and dissemination (see also section 0). Government support in the form of loans and other financial services (e.g. with preferential interest rates) can also support dissemination and upscaling of proven technologies.

Such public policy interventions can be especially important in developing countries where public actors often do R&D. As a country develops, the private sector tends to replace the public sector as the main vehicle for R&D (OECD, 2019[104]). However, in most developing countries, government funding for R&D tends to be limited, which often compromises the quantity and quality of research outputs (USAID, 2014[101]). Government funding for research is also vulnerable to budget cuts when faced with competing development priorities with more immediate impacts. It is therefore important to secure sufficient public funding for research, development and demonstration of technologies for climate resilience but also to shield it from fluctuations (Johnstone, Haščič and Kalamova, 2011[105]).

Development co-operation can play an important role in funding research initiatives. It can facilitate cross-border knowledge transfers, provide technical trainings and demonstrations, and provide finance or co-finance to scale-up application of technologies (OECD, 2019[104]). In so doing, support by development co-operation can, for instance, share the cost of public investments and facilitate economies of scale (OECD, 2019[104]). The Renewable Energy and Adapting to Climate Technologies Window in Africa programme supported by the European Union, for example, provides risk capital to businesses with potentially transformative solutions for low-cost climate-resilient technologies. These include irrigation and water efficiency measures, as well as ones that contribute to climate mitigation (AECF, 2018[106]).

The awareness among businesses and households of the need for action on climate resilience is increasing. However, it does not always translate into demand for technological solutions on the markets (Dechezlepretre et al., 2020[80]). To address such demand-side challenges, governments can improve the enabling environments that facilitate market creation and expansion. In this way, the private sector can recognise the business potential of such markets (Dechezlepretre et al., 2020[80]; Nygaard and Hansen, 2015[75]). Examples include the planning and implementation of policies, regulations and standards that create favourable market conditions for technologies for climate resilience (e.g. public procurement of technologies in support of climate resilience). Another approach is removal of disincentives for the uptake of such technologies. Examples include agriculture subsidies, insufficient enforcement of building codes and land-use regulations (OECD, 2017[107]; OECD, 2020[11]).

Table 4.19. Strengthen supply- and demand-side policies: Guidance and tools

Guidance and tools	Focus	Audience
Overcoming Barriers to the Transfer and Diffusion of Climate Technologies (UNEP DTU Partnership)	This document provides operational guidance on how to assess the barriers to identified technologies in the countries, and on how to address and overcome these barriers through different types of measures.	✓ Developing country government (e.g. TNA teams and consultants)
Innovation Policy for Green Technologies: Guide for Policymakers in the Transition Economies of Europe and Central Asia (UNECE)	This guide consists of several modules, including one that introduces key concepts to help readers gain a broad understanding of national innovation systems and policies in innovation activity and describes main innovation policies.	✓ Governments (primarily in transition economies of Europe & Central Asia)
Agricultural Technologies for Climate Change in Developing Countries: Policy Options for Innovation and Technology Diffusion (Lybbert and Sumner)	While focusing on agriculture sector, this document provides policy priorities for innovation and dissemination of climate-related technologies, including those on market integration and public research support and capacity.	✓ Governments and development co-operation
Enhancing Financing for the Research, Development and Demonstration of Climate Technologies (UNFCCC)	This document provides, among others, definitions of key concepts related to finance for research, development and demonstration, and some recommendations on action to enhance finance for research, development and dissemination.	✓ Governments and development co-operation

References

Aboitiz (2020), "Aboitiz donates weather technology assets to government", 30 June, Aboitz, Taguig City, Phillipines, https://aboitiz.com/aboitiz-donates-weather-technology-assets-to-government/ (accessed on 15 February 2021). [16]

ADB (2014), *Technologies to Support Climate Change Adaptation in Developing Asia*, Asian Development Bank, Mandaluyong City, Philippines, https://www.adb.org/publications/technologies-support-climate-change-adaptation-developing-asia. [77]

Adebayo, K. et al. (2011), "Emerging and Indigenous technology for climate change adaptation in Southwest Nigeria", *Research Paper*, No. 10, African Technology Policy Studies Network, Nairobi, https://media.africaportal.org/documents/rps10.pdf. [83]

AECF (2018), "Renewable Energy and Adaptation to Climate Change (REACT)", webpage, http://www.aecfafrica.org (accessed on 14 January 2021). [106]

AFD (n.d.), "Supporting the Decentralization Policy and Improving Natural Risk Management in the Philippines", webpage, http://www.afd.fr/en/supporting-decentralization-policy-and-improving-natural-risk-management-philippines (accessed on 21 October 2020). [67]

Ajayi, M., A. Fatunbi and O. Akinbamijo (2018), *Strategies for Scaling Agricultural Technologies in Africa*, Forum for Agricultural Research in Africa, Accra, https://research4agrinnovation.org/wp-content/uploads/2018/02/Scalingstrategies_Africa.pdf (accessed on 15 February 2021). [74]

Allis, E. et al. (2019), "The future of climate services", *WMO Bulletin*, Vol. 68/1, https://public.wmo.int/en/resources/bulletin/future-of-climate-services. [3]

Badji, L. et al. (2016), *Technology Needs Assessment Phase II: Barrier Analysis Report II*, Republic of The Gambia, https://unfccc.int/ttclear/misc_/StaticFiles/gnwoerk_static/TNA_key_doc/ea2fbadbe0a84140b86e491f766ee5b3/b8367caa3554415da062240edec67dfc.pdf (accessed on 15 February 2021). [90]

Biagini, B. et al. (2014), "Technology transfer for adaptation", *Nature Climate Change*, Vol. 4/9, pp. 828-834, https://doi.org/10.1038/nclimate2305. [82]

Boldt, J. et al. (2012), *Overcoming Barriers to the Transfer and Diffusion of Climate Technologies*, UNEP Risø Centre on Energy, Climate and Sustainable Development, Risø DTU National Laboratory for Sustainable Energy, https://orbit.dtu.dk/en/publications/overcoming-barriers-to-the-transfer-and-diffusion-of-climate-tech-2. [88]

Butler, J. et al. (2015), "Integrating top-down and bottom-up adaptation planning to build adaptive capacity: A structured learning approach", *Coastal Management*, Vol. 43/4, pp. 346-364, http://dx.doi.org/10.1080/08920753.2015.1046802. [7]

Casado-Asensio, J., H. Shin and T. Kato (forthcoming), *Private-sector Engagement in Strengthening Climate Resilience*, OECD Publishing, Paris. [57]

Christiansen, L., A. Olhoff and S. Trærup (eds.) (2011), *Technologies for Adaptation: Perspectives and Practical Experiences*, UNEP Risø Centre, Roskilde, https://wedocs.unep.org/bitstream/handle/20.500.11822/8114/-Technologies%20for%20Adaptation%20Perspectives%20and%20Practical%20Experiences-20111146.pdf?sequence=3&isAllowed=y. [76]

Conway, D. et al. (2019), "The need for bottom-up assessments of climate risks and adaptation in climate-sensitive regions", *Nature Climate Change*, Vol. 9/7, pp. 503-511, http://dx.doi.org/10.1038/s41558-019-0502-0. [26]

Corner, A., C. Shaw and J. Clarke (2018), *Principles for Effective Communication and Public Engagement on Climate Change: A Handbook for IPCC Authors*, Climate Outreach, Oxford, https://www.ipcc.ch/site/assets/uploads/2017/08/Climate-Outreach-IPCC-communications-handbook.pdf (accessed on 10 February 2021). [54]

Dazé, A. and C. Church (2019), *Toolkit for a Gender-Responsive Process to Formulate and Implement National Adaptation Plans (NAPs): Supplement to the UNFCCC Technical Guidelines for the NAP Process*, International Institute for Sustainable Development, Winnipeg, https://napglobalnetwork.org/resource/toolkit-for-gender-responsive-national-adaptation-plans/. [52]

de Coninck, H. and A. Sagar (2014), "Making sense of policy for climate technology development and transfer", *Climate Policy*, Vol. 15/1, pp. 1-11, http://dx.doi.org/DOI: 10.1080/14693062.2014.953909. [102]

De Groot, J. (2018), *Guidance for a Gender-responsive Technology Needs Assessment*, UNEP DTU Partnership, Copenhagen, https://tech-action.unepdtu.org/wp-content/uploads/sites/2/2019/07/web-tna-gender-guidebook-01.pdf (accessed on 8 January 2021). [93]

Dechezlepretre, A. et al. (2020), *Invention and Global Diffusion of Technologies for Climate Change Adaptation: A Patent Analysis*, World Bank, Washington, DC, https://elibrary.worldbank.org/doi/abs/10.1596/33883. [80]

Depoux, A. et al. (2017), "Communicating climate change and health in the media", *Public Health Reviews*, Vol. 38/1, http://dx.doi.org/10.1186/s40985-016-0044-1. [59]

ECBI (2018), *Pocket Guide for Capacity Building for Climate Action: 2018 Edition*, European Capacity Building Initiative, Oxford, https://ecbi.org/sites/default/files/FINAL-Capacity-Building_0.pdf. [45]

El-Taliawi, O. and Z. Van Der Wal (2019), "Developing administrative capacity: An agenda for research and practice", *Policy Design and Practice*, Vol. 2/3, pp. 243-257, http://dx.doi.org/10.1080/25741292.2019.1595916. [62]

EU TEG (2020), *Technical Annex to the TEG Final Report on the EU Taxonomy*, Technical Expert Group on Sustainable Finance, Brussels, https://ec.europa.eu/knowledge4policy/publication/sustainable-finance-teg-final-report-eu-taxonomy_en (accessed on 15 February 2021). [96]

Forsyth, T. (2005), "Enhancing climate technology transfer through greater public–private cooperation: Lessons from Thailand and the Philippines", *Natural Resources Forum*, Vol. 29/2, pp. 165-176, https://doi.org/10.1111/j.1477-8947.2005.00125.x. [87]

GCA (2019), *Adapt Now: A Global Call for Leadership on Climate Resilience*, Global Commission on Adaptation, Washington, DC, https://cdn.gca.org/assets/2019-09/GlobalCommission_Report_FINAL.pdf. [30]

GIZ, EURAC & UNU-EHS (2018), *Climate Risk Assessment for Ecosystem-based Adaptation – A Guidebook for Planners and Practitioners*, GIZ, Bonn. [27]

Government of Ghana (2015), *Ghana's Third National Communication Report*, Government of Ghana, https://unfccc.int/resource/docs/natc/ghanc3.pdf. [23]

Government of the Republic of Armenia (2017), *Technology Needs Assessment for Climate Change Adaptation: Barrier Analysis and Enabling Framework Report*, The Ministry of Nature Protection, Government of the Republic of Armenia, Yerevan, https://unfccc.int/ttclear/misc_/StaticFiles/gnwoerk_static/TNA_key_doc/67eb2f922aea47d6ba2c53f0a673844f/5eedfa9366934a928177577e0668a48b.pdf. [89]

Guo, H., L. Zhang and L. Zhu (2015), "Earth observation big data for climate change research", *Advances in Climate Change Research*, Vol. 6/2, pp. 108-117, http://dx.doi.org/10.1016/j.accre.2015.09.007. [21]

Hallegatte, S., J. Rentschler and J. Rozenberg (2020), *The Adaptation Principles A Guide for Designing Strategies for Climate Change Adaptation and Resilience*, World Bank, Washington, DC, http://hdl.handle.net/10986/34780. [32]

Hansen, J. et al. (2019), *Scaling Climate Services to Enable Effective Adaptation Action*, Global Centre on Adaptation, Rotterdam and Washington, DC, https://www.cgiar.org/research/publication/scaling-climate-services-to-enable-effective-adaptation-action/. [5]

Haselip, J., R. Narkeviciute and J. Rogat Castillo (2015), *A Step-by-Step Guide for Countries Conducting a Technology Needs Assessment*, UNEP DTU Partnership, Copenhagen, https://orbit.dtu.dk/en/publications/a-step-by-step-guide-for-countries-conducting-a-technology-needs-. [71]

Hewitt, C. et al. (2020), "Making society climate resilient: International progress under the Global Framework for Climate Services", *Bulletin of the American Meteorological Society*, Vol. 101/2, pp. E237–E252, http://dx.doi.org/10.1175/BAMS-D-18-0211.1. [10]

ICIMOD (2020), "Reaching the most vulnerable: Community-based flood early warning system (CBFEWS)", (flyer), International Centre for Integrated Mountain Development, Kathmandu, https://lib.icimod.org/record/34899. [34]

IPCC (2019), "Summary for policymakers", in *IPCC Special Report on the Ocean and Cryosphere in a Changing Climate*, Intergovernmental Panel on Climate Change, Geneva, https://www.ipcc.ch/srocc/ (accessed on 23 January 2020). [25]

IPCC (2018), *Global Warming of 1.5 °C*, Intergovernmental Panel on Climate Change, Geneva, http://www.ipcc.ch/pdf/special-reports/sr15/sr15_draft.pdf. [13]

IPCC (2014), *Climate Change 2014: Synthesis Report. Contribution of Working Groups I, II and III to the Fifth Assessment Report of the Intergovernmental Panel on Climate Change*, Pachauri, R.K. and L.A. Meyer (eds.), Intergovernmental Panel on Climate Change, Geneva, https://www.ipcc.ch/report/ar5/syr/. [40]

Johnstone, N., I. Haščič and M. Kalamova (2011), "Environmental Policy Design Characteristics and Innovation", in *Invention and Transfer of Environmental Technologies*, OECD Publishing, Paris, https://dx.doi.org/10.1787/9789264115620-3-en. [105]

Khan, M., D. Mfitumukiza and S. Huq (2020), "Capacity building for implementation of nationally determined contributions under the Paris Agreement", *Climate and Policy*, Vol. 20/4, pp. 499-510, http://dx.doi.org/10.1080/14693062.2019.1675577. [48]

Khan, M. et al. (2018), *The Paris Framework for Climate Change Capacity Building*, Routledge Advances in Climate Change Research. [49]

Kristjanson, P. and C. Jost (2014), *Tackling Innovation in Climate Change Research*, presentation at ICRAF Research Seminar, Nairobi, 20 May, https://www.slideshare.net/cgiarclimate/tackling-innovation-in-climate-change-research-presentation-by-chris-jost-and-patti-kristjanson-ccafs. [56]

Kull, D., C. Graessle and B. Aryan (2016), "Strengthening national hydrometeorological services through cascading forecasting: Investing for sustainability and impact across global, regional, and national centers", *Policy Research Working Paper*, No. 7609, World Bank, Washington, DC, https://openknowledge.worldbank.org/handle/10986/24151. [12]

LIFE-AR (2019), *Delivering our Climate-resilient Future: Lessons from a Global Evidence Review*, LDC Initiative for Effective Adaptation and Resilience, http://www.ldc-climate.org/wp-content/uploads/2019/09/web_LDCevidencereview.pdf. [42]

Luther, J. et al. (2019), "Contributing to building a weather-ready, resilient and sustainable society", *WMO Bulletin*, Vol. 68/1, https://public.wmo.int/en/resources/bulletin/contributing-building-weather-ready-resilient-and-sustainable-society. [1]

Mcleod, E. et al. (2018), "Raising the voices of Pacific Island women to inform climate adaptation policies", *Marine Policy*, Vol. 93, pp. 178-185, http://dx.doi.org/10.1016/j.marpol.2018.03.011. [41]

Nakashima, D. et al. (2012), *Weathering Uncertainty: Traditional Knowledge for Climate Change Assessment and Adaptation*, United Nations Educational, Scientific and Cultural Organization, Paris, http://www.unesco.org/new/en/media-services/single-view/news/weathering_uncertainty_traditional_knowledge_for_climate_ch/. [39]

Nallari, R. and B. Griffith (2013), *Clusters of Competitiveness*, World Bank, Washington, DC, http://dx.doi.org/10.1596/978-1-4648-0049-8. [99]

NASA (n.d.), *NASA Earth Exchange Global Daily Dowlscaled Projections (NEX-GDDP)*, (database), https://www.nccs.nasa.gov/services/data-collections/land-based-products/nex-gddp#:~:text=The%20NASA%20Earth%20Exchange%20Global,of%20the%20four%20greenhouse%20gas (accessed on 25 November 2020). [55]

Nygaard, I. and U. Hansen (2015), *Overcoming Barriers to the Transfer and Diffusion of Climate Technologies, Second Edition*, UNEP DTU Partnership, Copenhagen, https://tech-action.unepdtu.org/publications/overcoming-barriers-to-the-transfer-and-diffusion-of-climate-technologies-second-edition/. [75]

Ockwell, D. and R. Byrne (2016), "Improving technology transfer through national systems of innovation: Climate relevant innovation-system builders (CRIBs)", *Climate Policy*, Vol. 167/7, pp. 836-854, https://doi.org/10.1080/14693062.2015.1052958. [86]

OECD (2020), *Common Ground Between the Paris Agreement and the Sendai Framework: Climate Change Adaptation and Disaster Risk Reduction*, OECD Publishing, Paris, https://dx.doi.org/10.1787/3edc8d09-en. [11]

OECD (2020), "Nature-based solutions for adapting to water-related climate risks", *OECD Environment Policy Papers*, No. 21, OECD Publishing, Paris, https://dx.doi.org/10.1787/2257873d-en. [64]

OECD (2019), "Connecting ODA and STI for inclusive development: Measurement challenges from a DAC perspective", 2 July, Development Assistance Committee, OECD, Paris, http://www.oecd.org/officialdocuments/publicdisplaydocumentpdf/?cote=DCD/DAC(2019)38&docLanguage=En. [104]

OECD (2019), *Greening Development Co-operation: Lessons from the OECD Development Assistance Committee*, The Development Dimension, OECD Publishing, Paris, http://dx.doi.org/10.1787/62cc4634-en. [69]

OECD (2017), *Investing in Climate, Investing in Growth*, OECD Publishing, Paris, https://dx.doi.org/10.1787/9789264273528-en. [107]

OECD (2012), *Greening Development: Enhancing Capacity for Environmental Management and Governance*, OECD Publishing, Paris, http://dx.doi.org/10.1787/9789264167896-en. [51]

Olawuyi, D. (2018), "From technology transfer to technology absorption: Addressing climate technology gaps in Africa", *Journal of Energy & Natural Resources Law*, Vol. 36/1, pp. 61-84, https://doi.org/10.1080/02646811.2017.1379667. [81]

Pagato, M. et al. (2020), *Technology Transfer and Innovation for Low-Carbon Development*, World Bank, Washington, DC, http://documents.worldbank.org/curated/en/138681585111567659/Technology-Transfer-and-Innovation-for-Low-Carbon-Development. [85]

Parajuli, D. (2017), "Coping strategies to climate change through Indigenous technology knowledge in agriculture", *International Journal of Agricultural Science and Research*, Vol. 7/5, pp. 143-162, https://doi.org/10.24247/ijasroct201721. [84]

Pauw, W. et al. (2020), "Conditional nationally determined contributions in the Paris Agreement: Foothold for equity or Achilles heel?", *Climate Policy*, Vol. 20/4, pp. 468-484, http://dx.doi.org/10.1080/14693062.2019.1635874. [44]

PIK (n.d.), "AGRICA - Climate Risk Analyses for Identifying and Weighing Adaptation Strategies in sub-Saharan Africa", webpage, https://www.pik-potsdam.de/en/institute/departments/climate-resilience/projects/project-pages/agrica/agrica-sv-giz-climate-project (accessed on 25 September 2020). [29]

Rowntree, O. (2019), *The Mobile Gender Gap Report 2019*, Groupe Speciale Mobile Association, London, https://www.gsma.com/mobilefordevelopment/wp-content/uploads/2019/03/GSMA-Connected-Women-The-Mobile-Gender-Gap-Report-2019. [92]

Sagar, A. (2010), *Climate Innovation Centres: A New Way to Foster Climate Technologies in the Developing World?*, United Nations Industrial Development Organization and Department for International Development (Government of United Kingdom), https://www.unclearn.org/sites/default/files/inventory/unido02.pdf. [100]

Schäfer, M. (2015), "Climate change and the media", in James, D. (ed.), *International Encyclopedia of the Social & Behavioral Sciences*, http://dx.doi.org/10.1016/B978-0-08-097086-8.91079-1. [58]

Shakya, C. et al. (2018), "Building institutional capacity for enhancing resilience to climate change: An operational framework and insights from practice", *Learning Paper*, Oxford Policy Management and International Institute for Environment and Development, London, http://www.acclimatise.uk.com/wp-content/uploads/2018/02/GIP01916-OPM-Strengthening-institutions-Proof4-web.pdf. [50]

Snow, J. et al. (2016), *A New Vision for Weather and Climate Services in Africa*, United Nations Development Programme, Nairobi, https://www.adaptation-undp.org/resources/communications-products/new-vision-weather-and-climate-services-africa. [15]

Street, R. et al. (2019), "How could climate services support disaster risk reduction in the 21st century", *International Journal of Disaster Risk Reduction*, Vol. 24/March, pp. 28-33, http://dx.doi.org/10.1016/j.ijdrr.2018.12.001. [8]

TEC (2020), *Policy Brief: Technologies for Averting, Minimizing and Addressing Loss and Damage in Coastal Zones*, United Nations Framework Convention on Climate Change, Geneva, https://unfccc.int/ttclear/misc_/StaticFiles/gnwoerk_static/2020_coastalzones/cfecc85aaa8d43d38cd0f6ceae2b61e4/2bb696550804403fa08df8a924922c2e.pdf. [79]

TEC (2018), *Developing and Enhancing Endogenous Capacities and Technologies: Technology Stakeholders' Perspectives*, Technology Executive Committee, United Nations Framework Convention on Climate Change, Geneva, https://unfccc.int/ttclear/misc_/StaticFiles/gnwoerk_static/endogenous_index/783d7125afec404da1bef315fe3be600/861a47c1627244deabca4b12e949ebfa.pdf. [78]

TEC (2017), "Technological innovation for the Paris Agreement", *TEC Brief*, No. 10, Technology Executive Committee, United Nations Framework Convention on Climate Change, Geneva, https://unfccc.int/ttclear/misc_/StaticFiles/gnwoerk_static/brief10/8c3ce94c20144fd5a8b0c06fefff6633/57440a5fa1244fd8b8cd13eb4413b4f6.pdf. [70]

TEC (2016), "Enhancing financing for the research, development and demonstration of climate technologies", *Working Paper*, Technology Executive Committee, United Nations Framework Convention on Climate Change, Geneva, https://www.ctc-n.org/sites/d8uat.ctc-n.org/files/resources/tec-_enhancing_financing_for_rdd_of_climate_technologies.pdf. [103]

TEC (2015), "Strengthening national systems of innovation to enhance action on climate change", *TEC Brief*, No. 7, Technology Executive Committee, United Nations Framework Convention on Climate Change, Geneva, https://unfccc.int/ttclear/misc_/StaticFiles/gnwoerk_static/TEC_documents/5be1bf880cc34d52a4315206d54a711b/60d1580f741a4bc783da5a00cf64a879.pdf. [98]

TEC (2014), "Technologies for adaptation in the agriculture sector", *TEC Brief*, No. 4, Technology Executive Committee, United Nations Framework Convention on Climate Change, Geneva, https://unfccc.int/ttclear/misc_/StaticFiles/gnwoerk_static/TEC_column_L/544babb207e344b88bdd9fec11e6337f/bcc4dc66c35340a08fce34f057e0a1ed.pdf. [91]

Tonmoy, F., D. Rissik and J. Palutikof (2019), "A three-tier risk assessment process for climate change adaptation at a local scale", *Climatic Change*, Vol. 153, pp. 539-557, http://dx.doi.org/10.1007/s10584-019-02367-z. [28]

UN CC:e-Learn (n.d.), "Think, Talk, Act Climate", webpage, https://unccelearn.org/course/ (accessed on 20 October 2020). [63]

UNDP (2019), *Five Approaches to Build Functional Early Warning Systems*, United Nations Development Programme, New York, https://reliefweb.int/report/world/five-approaches-build-functional-early-warning-systems. [36]

UNDP (2016), *Climate Information & Early Warning Systems Communications Toolkit: UNDP Programme on Climate Information for Resilient Development in Africa*, United Nations Development Programme, New York, https://www.undp.org/content/undp/en/home/librarypage/climate-and-disaster-resilience-/climate-information-and-early-warning-systems-communications-too.html. [43]

UNDP (2010), *Handbook for Conducting Technology Needs Assessment for Climate Change*, United Nations Development Programme, New York, https://www.undp.org/content/undp/en/home/librarypage/environment-energy/low_emission_climateresilientdevelopment/technology_needsassessmenthandbook.html. [95]

UNDRR (2017), "Report of the open-ended intergovernmental expert", *General Assembly, Seventy-first session, Agenda item 19(c), A/71/644*, United Nations, New York, https://www.undrr.org/terminology. [35]

UNEP (2019), "NBS Contributions Platform", webpage, https://www.unenvironment.org/fr/node/25257 (accessed on 12 February 2020). [66]

UNEP DTU Partnership (n.d.), *Technology Needs Assessment (TNA)*, (database), https://tech-action.unepdtu.org/tna-database/ (accessed on 1 July 2020). [94]

UNESCO (2018), *Getting the Message Across: Reporting on Climate Change and Sustainable Development in Asia and the Pacific: A Handbook for Journalists*, United Nations Educational, Scientific and Cultural Organization, Paris. [61]

UNESCO (2017), *Local Knowledge, Global Goals*, United Nations Educational, Cultural and Scientific Organization, Paris, http://www.unesco.org/new/fileadmin/MULTIMEDIA/HQ/SC/pdf/ILK_ex_publication_E.pdf. [38]

UNESCO (2013), *Climate Change in Africa: A Guidebook for Journalists*, United Nations Educational, Scientific and Cultural Organization, Paris. [60]

UNFCCC (2020), *Policy Brief: Technologies for Averting, Minimizing and Addressing Loss and Damage in Coastal Zones*, United Nations Framework Convention on Climate Change, Bonn, https://unfccc.int/ttclear/misc_/StaticFiles/gnwoerk_static/2020_coastalzones/cfecc85aaa8d43d38cd0f6ceae2b61e4/2bb696550804403fa08df8a924922c2e.pdf. [33]

UNFCCC (2015), *Paris Agreement*, United Nations Framework Convention on Climate Change, Bonn. [46]

UNFCCC (2014), *Background Paper on Technologies for Adaptation*, United Nations Framework Convention on Climate Change, Bonn, https://unfccc.int/ttclear/misc_/StaticFiles/gnwoerk_static/events_workshops_adaptationtechs/f1b531ab99084107950d65c2c2de1d6d/d02425f42d614aa99c40fe39758b3ded.pdf. [73]

UNFCCC (2006), *Technologies for Adaptation to Climate Change*, United Nations Framework Convention on Climate Change, Bonn, https://unfccc.int/resource/docs/publications/tech_for_adaptation_06.pdf. [72]

UNFCCC (n.d.), "Cooperation with IPCC", webpage, https://cop23.unfccc.int/topics/science/workstreams/cooperation-with-the-ipcc (accessed on 22 September 2020). [53]

UNFCCC (n.d.), "Paris Committee for Capacity-building", webpage, https://unfccc.int/pccb (accessed on 25 November 2020). [47]

University of Oxford (n.d.), *Nature-based Solutions Evidence Tool*, website, https://www.naturebasedsolutionsevidence.info/evidence-tool/ (accessed on 12 February 2020). [65]

USAID (2014), "Building an enabling environment for agricultural technology commercialization: Bridging the gap between Innovation and uptake", *Policy Brief*, No. 5, United States Agency for International Development, Washington, DC, https://www.agrilinks.org/sites/default/files/resource/files/USAID-EAT%20Policy%20Brief%20Scaling%20Ag%20Tech.pdf. [101]

Weaver, C. et al. (2017), "Reframing climate change assessments around risk: Recommendations for the US National Climate Assessment", *Environmental Research Letters*, Vol. 12/9, http://dx.doi.org/10.1088/1748-9326/aa846a. [6]

WMO (2020), *2020 State of Climate Service: Risk Information and Early Warning Systems*, World Meteorological Organization, Geneva, https://library.wmo.int/index.php?lvl=notice_display&id=21777#.YCmtXGhKg2y. [31]

WMO (2020), "New climate predictions assess global temperatures in coming five years", 8 July, News Release, World Meteorological Organization, Geneva, https://public.wmo.int/en/media/press-release/new-climate-predictions-assess-global-temperatures-coming-five-years. [24]

WMO (2018), *Multi-hazard Early Warning Systems: A Checklist*, Outcome of the first Multi-hazard Early Warning Conference 22 to 23 May 2017 – Cancún, Mexico, World Meteorological Organization, Geneva, https://library.wmo.int/doc_num.php?explnum_id=4463. [37]

WMO (2016), *Guidelines on Best Practices for Climate Data Rescue*, World Meteorological Organization, Geneva, https://library.wmo.int/doc_num.php?explnum_id=3318. [22]

WMO (2016), *The Global Observing System for Climate: Implementation Needs*, World Meteorological Organization, Geneva, https://library.wmo.int/doc_num.php?explnum_id=3417. [19]

WMO (n.d.), "Alliance for Hydromet Development", webpage, https://public.wmo.int/en/our-mandate/how-we-do-it/partnerships/wmo-office-of-development-partnerships (accessed on 4 May 2020). [18]

WMO (n.d.), *Climate Knowledge for Action: A Global Framework for Climate Services - Empowering the Most Vulnerable. Frequently Asked Questions*, World Meteorological Organization, Geneva, https://gfcs.wmo.int//sites/default/files/FAQ/HLT/HLT_FAQ_en.pdf. [2]

WMO (n.d.), "Observations", webpage, https://public.wmo.int/en/our-mandate/what-we-do/observations (accessed on 25 October 2020). [20]

WMO & GFCS (2019), *2019 State of Climate Services*, World Meteorological Organization, Geneva, https://library.wmo.int/doc_num.php?explnum_id=10089. [4]

WMO & GFCS (2016), *Climate Services for Supporting Climate Change Adaptation: Supplement to the Technical Guidelines for the National Adaptation Plan Process*, World Meteorological Organization, Geneva, https://library.wmo.int/doc_num.php?explnum_id=7936. [9]

WMO & GFCS (n.d.), "Current Status of the Implementation of National Frameworks for Climate Services (NFCS)", webpage, https://gfcs.wmo.int/NFCS_status (accessed on 25 October 2020). [17]

WMO & GFCS (n.d.), *The Global Framework for Climate Services: Value Proposition*, World Meteorological Organization, Geneva, https://library.wmo.int/doc_num.php?explnum_id=6275. [14]

World Bank (2018), *Concept Note: Greater Accra Climate Resilient and Integrated Development Project*, World Bank, Washington, DC, https://www.greenclimate.fund/document/greater-accra-climate-resilient-and-integrated-development-project. [68]

World Bank (2010), *Climate Innovation Centres: A new way to foster climate technologies in the developing world? An infoDev publication in collaboration with UNIDO and DFID prepared by Ambuj Sagar and Bloomberg New Energy Finance*, World Bank, Washington DC, https://www.uncclearn.org/wp-content/uploads/library/unido02.pdf. [97]

Notes

[1] The founding members are the Adaptation Fund, African Development Bank, Asian Development Bank, European Bank for Reconstruction and Development, Global Environment Facility, Green Climate Fund, Islamic Development Bank, United Nations Development Programme, United Nations Environment Programme, World Bank, World Food Programme and World Meteorological Organization, with the Alliance being open to other international providers of support for hydromet capacity.

Printed by Libri Plureos GmbH in Hamburg,
Germany